FORGOTTEN CONVERSATIONS
WITH FAMOUS WRITERS

the Lost Saranac
Interviews

JOE DAVID BELLAMY & CONNIE BELLAMY

WRITER'S DIGEST BOOKS
Cincinnati, Ohio
www.writersdigest.com

11 10 09 08 07   5 4 3 2 1

Distributed in Canada by Fraser Direct, 100 Armstrong Avenue, George-town, ON, Canada L7G 5S4, Tel: (905) 877-4411. Distributed in the U.K. and Europe by David & Charles, Brunel House, Newton Abbot, Devon, TQ12 4PU, England, Tel: (+44) 1626 323200, Fax: (+44) 1626 323319, E-mail: postmaster@davidandcharles.co.uk. Distributed in Australia by Capricorn Link, P.O. Box 704, Windsor, NSW 2756 Australia, Tel: (02) 4577-3555.

Visit our Web site at www.writersdigest.com for information on more re-sources for writers. To receive a free weekly e-mail newsletter delivering tips and updates about writing and about Writer's Digest products, register directly at our Web site at http://newsletters.fwpublications.com.

Library of Congress Cataloging-in-Publication Data

The lost Saranac interviews : forgotten conversations with famous writ-ers / edited by Joe David Bellamy & Connie Bellamy. -- 1st ed.
    p. cm.
 ISBN-13: 978-1-58297-481-1 (alk. paper)
 ISBN-10: 1-58297-481-0 (alk. paper)
  1. Authors, American--20th century--Interviews. 2. Authors, Eng-lish--20th century--Interviews. 3. Authorship. I. Bellamy, Joe David. II. Bellamy, Connie.
 PS129.L67 2007
 810.9'005--dc22   2007011311

Edited by Lauren Mosko
Designed by Grace Ring
Production coordinated by Mark Griffin

Dedication

For Elizabeth Inness-Brown

And in memory of our fallen comrades:
Mary Taylor Garrity,
Michael Benedikt, Asa Baber, John Hawkes,
Seymour Lawrence, Robie Macauley,
Ted Stratford, and Ted Weiss

Acknowledgments

Connie Bellamy wishes to thank Virginia Wesleyan College, and particularly President Billy Greer and Deans Steve Mansfield and Joyce Howell, for ongoing support and a sabbatical leave that allowed her to complete some of the work presented here.

Joe David Bellamy wishes to thank President Frank Piskor, as well as Jim Van Ness and Bob Clark, then of St. Lawrence University, for their early support of the conference, Judy Gibson for her contributions, and Dean Tom Coburn of St. Lawrence University (now president of Naropa University) for initial approval of an archival project that led to this book.

Both authors wish to thank Jane Friedman, editorial director of Writer's Digest Books, editors Amy Schell and Lauren Mosko, and designer Grace Ring of Writer's Digest Books, and, of course, the many students and writers who attended the *Fiction International*/St. Lawrence University Writers' Conference during those years and helped to make it such a memorable experience. Among them, special thanks to Beth Anton Dooley, Karen Alpha, John Clogston, Lael Bellamy, G.E. Murray, Robie Macauley, and Gail Godwin.

Joe David Bellamy and Connie Bellamy
at Saranac, 1978.

Joe David Bellamy is a member of the National Book Critics Circle and the author of fourteen books, including *Literary Luxuries*, a collection of essays; *Atomic Love*, a collection of stories; and the novel *Suzi Sinzinnati*.

Connie Bellamy is the Batten Professor of English and director of the American Studies Program at Virginia Wesleyan College.

TABLE of CONTENTS

INTRODUCTION

"Next morn, we swept with oars the Saranac with skies of benediction ..."

—Ralph Waldo Emerson

Among the early campers in the Saranac region was a group of ten distinguished Cambridge intellectuals, which included Ralph Waldo Emerson, James Russell Lowell, and Louis Agassiz, who founded what they called a "Philosophers' Camp" there in 1858. Longfellow had been invited, but he declined to join the group when he heard that Emerson was bringing a gun. They were attracted to the Adirondacks because of the great natural beauty and wildness of the place, and because the lakes and forest encouraged contemplation.

< Saranac, 1973.

David Madden confided to the assembled dinner crowd of writers and students the first year at the *Fiction International*/St. Lawrence University Writers' Conference at Saranac Lake that he had been so affected by the beauty of one of the small, deserted islands out in the middle of the mist on the lake that morning that he had rowed all the way out there, had taken off all his clothes, and had stormed about through the rough forest and rocky wastes like a wild man. A few eyebrows went up, but those of us who had been there even a day—and had walked through the woods, inhaling the balsam, and had seen the eerie way the sunlight fell through the enormous branches of virgin trees four and five and six feet thick—*understood.*

In spite of our disappointment that our headliner Erica Jong failed to show up that year—because, she told me tearfully over the phone, she was simply too afraid to climb aboard the airplane—there was, from the beginning, something special and magical about the place and what happened there. Over the six years of the conference, nearly everyone associated with Saranac noticed and commented about its uniqueness and felt its mysterious power.

Gail Godwin said she thought it had to do with "the spirit of the place (the landscape) combined with the intensities of the various people." Saranac veteran Robie Macauley said, "Saranac is like a week in the country in the company of friends carrying on an informal, continuous, frequently brilliant conversation about the creation of literature .... And that Saranac conversation is very hard to leave at the end of the week. All year long, I have letters, snapshots, short story manuscripts, telephone calls from writers I first met there. They have a feeling of community and stimulation that is just astounding .... St. Lawrence has added something new and original to American literary life and the teaching of writing."

It all started the year following my Bread Loaf experience, 1974, when, full of youthful hubris and ignorance, I decided to start my own writers' conference, modeled after the famous Bread Loaf Writers' Conference but with certain strategic "improvements" I hoped to make. With a smaller conference and the advantage of a lovely and intimate lakefront conference center called "Canaras" owned by St. Lawrence University at Upper Saranac Lake in upstate New York, I thought it might be possible to bring students and faculty together without some of the rigid status distinctions that had sometimes gotten in the way of interactions at Bread Loaf. I wanted the ambience to be cordial and upbeat, an atmosphere that would convey the message:

$\mathcal{T}$HOSE OF US WHO HAD BEEN THERE EVEN A DAY—AND HAD WALKED THROUGH THE WOODS, INHALING THE BALSAM—UNDERSTOOD.

"You can do this, too—if you work at it," rather than the usual: "No matter what you do, you can never walk among gods like these, except at a place like this."

Whatever secret chemistry existed, it came about, as far as I could tell, from luring people to the middle of an almost pristine wilderness to talk about literary and spiritual matters, just as Emerson had done in almost the same location a century earlier. We were attracting some of the best literary talent in North America to do it—in case anybody noticed—and, increasingly, people *did* notice. An additional reason for the radiance of Saranac and the fondness participants felt for their experience there was the fact that—outside of New York and Boston and a few other cultural meccas—there are so few literary crossroads in this country that any coming together of talent and energy and the right people with the time to get to know one another would have been valued.

Our philosophy was to try to bring the right people together, to create what we perceived to be the appropriate mood, and to let the fireworks begin. And what resulted was almost always interesting: whether it was education, new books written or discovered, jobs offered, marriages, friendship, love—all the basic human transactions (though we assiduously avoided murder and—very much on purpose—we discouraged opportunities for hatred, greed, or envy). In general, we encouraged people. We showed them that writers are human and that they can be kind and generous to one another. With instantaneous good results, we pushed onward in spite of the black flies, and in spite of the often unpredictable and erratic weather in the Adirondacks in June.

Our second year, it rained continuously for six days running, and everyone huddled in front of the flagstone fireplaces and drank Cutty Sark and talked and talked, and all the readings that year—in the main lodge surrounded by the heads of moose and elk, and the full-feathered bodies of mounted owls and loons—were full of rainy-day emotions. Clark Blaise won the St. Lawrence Award for Fiction and read from *Tribal Justice*. Bharati Mukherjee introduced us to India, and Asa Baber, to *The Land of a Million Elephants*. On the last two days of the conference, the sun came out like a beacon, and I remember Diane Wakoski doing deep knee-bends for the longest time and Michael Benedikt sitting quietly at a rattan table in front of the Jackson Lodge boathouse in the sunshine, writing poetry in his bathing trunks.

In 1976, the weather was fine. John Hawkes talked with great eloquence about "aesthetic bliss" and argued against the autobiographical impulse in fiction, and Gail Godwin defended autobiography as the *sine qua non* and the *ne plus ultra*. Russell Banks won the St. Lawrence

Michael Benedikt at Saranac, 1975.

Award for Fiction for *Searching for Survivors*, and Jim Tate and Robie Macauley gave the funniest readings ever heard in the Northeast.

In 1977, three major women writers were among the faculty at Saranac: Joyce Carol Oates, Gail Godwin, and Ann Beattie. Oates did not travel much in those days and, so far as I know, had never before served as a faculty member at a writers' conference. Luckily, my friend Gail Godwin was her friend too and helped me in persuading her to come to Saranac, and what a coup it was to have landed her!

In those days, and for many years before, I admired Joyce Carol Oates—though I had never met her—with a degree of passion, commitment, and wild and reckless enthusiasm that could only be described as a literary crush. To my mind, she was a celebrity roughly equivalent in stature to Marilyn Monroe, the Virgin Mary, Joan Baez, and the goddess Athena all rolled into one, far beyond mere mortal queens, movie stars, or presidents. I had written to her, I had published her work, I had taught her work, I was one of the few people who had read everything in print that she had written, and I had imagined meeting her, and had actually dreamed about it on several occasions as a version of divine communion. So far, I had met two others who had actually seen

Oates in the flesh, and one had described her as "tiny" and the other had described her as "tall and imposing." Somehow these conflicting descriptions had fed my imagination and made Oates seem even more ethereal. And now I was actually going to have the opportunity to meet her firsthand.

Oates was reputed to be shy and emotional and unpredictable, and so I was quite concerned that she be made to feel comfortable. I was willing to go to whatever lengths might be required. I assigned her the best room at the conference center and had it specially cleaned, and I rearranged the furniture and placed a bouquet of wildflowers on the dresser. The conference schedule had worked out in such a way that Oates would not be arriving until the second day of the conference at a late afternoon hour when I would be teaching, so I had alerted my assistants to be on the lookout for her and her husband, who were driving down from Windsor, Ontario, and I had told them to escort Oates and her husband to her room as soon as they arrived, and I would catch up with them later.

That day as my class was ending, one of my assistants ran up with a stricken look on her face and said that Oates had arrived all right, but that things had gone badly and now she was talking about leaving. Apparently the trip had been longer and more arduous than expected, and she was very tired, and then when they had taken her to her room to rest, she had stumbled into a room filled up with noisy people and flailing bottles! An hour or so earlier, a bunch of students had seen this lovely empty room and had decided to have a party in there. So what Oates had seen when they opened the door for her was a bacchanalia-in-progress, and she had reeled back across the threshold with her limp wrist across her forehead as if this was simply more than anyone should be asked to endure after so long a journey, and she was now sitting dejectedly with her solicitous husband in the otherwise empty dining hall trying to decide what to do next.

I hurried along the path beside the lake and through the forest on my way to the dining hall and went in, and there they were. Oates was staring down into a plate of cold mashed potatoes and congealing gravy that the cook had rustled up quickly in hopes of cheering her up and staving off starvation, and Oates had not touched one bite of it; and her husband, Ray, was sitting by her side with a look of grave concern and consternation on his face.

I sat down and introduced myself and apologized for the misunderstanding regarding her room. The students would be terribly embarrassed, I said, when they found out what difficulties they had caused by their rampant partying. I told her we would have the room cleared out and cleaned up instantaneously. She said she thought perhaps it would just be better if she got back in the car and went home. I said, "Oh no, please don't do that. We can work this out." We were so glad to have her here, I said, and we would do whatever was necessary to make her comfortable. All she had to do was whistle. She said that if she was going to be able to stay, she would have to have a room with quite a bit more privacy. I said I knew of just the room, and if she would like to come along with me now, I would show it to her.

We walked along the lake front and through the lush forest, and we stopped off at Jackson Cottage, where Gail Godwin was staying, and Joyce and Gail embraced; and Gail immediately began to regale Joyce with rhapsodies about Saranac, and Joyce began to relax. Within five minutes, she was having such a good time, she didn't want to leave, so Ray and I walked on down to the room I had in mind at the far end of the camp facing into the deep woods. Ray looked it over and pronounced it suitable, and so it was settled.

After a good night's sleep, Joyce assumed her teaching duties the next day, and the students who had been lucky enough to gain admission to her workshop progressed quickly from awe and amazement to admiration and rapport and cordiality.

I realized that the person who had described her as "tiny" must have meant "slender," and the person who had described her as "tall and imposing" must have been talking about her mind and her teaching abilities, as well as her physique. That week, Gail, Ted and Renee Weiss, and I went searching through the woods for a "lost" lake—and found it—and Joyce met Ted and Renee. Soon after that, she was offered a job at Princeton, where Ted was a senior member of the creative writing faculty, and Joyce and Ray left western Ontario, and she has been a fixture at Princeton ever since.

Ann Beattie was not yet famous in 1977, not so famous as Joyce and Gail, at least. She had written for *The New Yorker*, and she had published two books— a novel, *Distortions*, and a collection of stories, *Chilly Scenes of Winter*—on the same day, her publisher's idea for a splashy debut, which indeed it was. Her picture in *Newsweek* had made her seem childlike, even "tiny," so I was a bit surprised when she turned out to be tall, long-legged, flamboyant, and buxom, with the longest set of real fingernails I had ever seen on a living human being, though I had seen pictures of the Genghis Khan, who had

even longer ones. That year Ann wore black T-shirts and tight jeans that quietly scandalized several of the more sedate, middle-aged women in attendance. In general, Ann was so unselfconscious and young and full of herself that she inspired great cattiness. One evening at our get-acquainted cocktail party, one of the middle-aged women stalked up to Ann and without batting an eyelash said pointedly, "I hear you published two books on the same day. Who did you sleep with?" Ann looked at her in horror and disbelief and, without saying a word, spun around and walked straight out of the room.

That night, for her reading, Ann read the short story "Shifting," which is a story about an alienated young woman who takes driving lessons from a teenage boy. The next day, Ann consented to be interviewed for the local college radio station by one of my undergraduate students—call him John.

John was one of the shyest kids I had ever seen. As a freshman, his face would turn beet-red whenever he was called upon in class, and he had a minor but quite noticeable stutter. At some point during his sophomore year, this gentle and shy fellow had the bright idea that he would pursue a career as a radio personality, and he began the project of transforming himself into the sort of person who can talk about any subject with glibness, frankness, and dispassion, and who can manipulate a microphone. He experimented on me for one of his early interviews, and he had one of those hand-held mikes that had to be shoveled under the nose of whoever was speaking whenever they opened their mouths and then returned to the mouth of the inquisitor. John was remarkably inept. Before we were finished, John's face was so red I was worried about his health, and I was certainly worried about his choice of career—it seemed so completely out of character.

At any rate, after her interview with John, Ann and I happened to have lunch, and Ann told me in elaborate detail, complete with hand-held mike gestures, about her interview with John, which had climaxed with John asking her, "Ms. Beattie, can you reveal to me now, somewhat more clearly perhaps, exactly why you slept with the boy in the story." John turned dangerously red in the face at that point, and, after stifling her laughter, Ann had given him a stern little lecture about how first-person narrators in fiction are not necessarily the same as the author.

Some writers would have been offended, I'm sure, but Ann thought it was a great joke, and she turned it instantly into a comical anecdote. She was especially pleased when I told her what a triumph of machismo it must have been for John,

ignorant though he was, to have asked her such a question. And I'm happy to be able to report that—against all odds—John went on to quite a successful career in the media. Ann, of course, went on to become Ann Beattie.

Later that same week, Ann gave a talk during which she revealed the "secret" of how she managed to break into print in *The New Yorker*. Early on in one of the rejection letters she had received from *New Yorker* editor Roger Angell, he had conveyed the information that he was quite certain her work would eventually be acceptable for *The New Yorker*. His advice was to keep working and to keep sending him new work, and he predicted that by the time she submitted her twentieth story, she would be ready.

For some reason, Ann found this enormously encouraging. She worked and worked; she submitted each new story to Roger Angell, one after the other; and each new story was returned with a kind note and a rejection until she finally submitted the twentieth story. The twentieth story was accepted! She didn't know whether she had simply gotten better or whether she had worn him down.

One of the "fellows" in the audience that day was an unpublished fiction writer who was extremely impressed with Ann's story because she had been corresponding with Roger Angell lately, too, and he had

fiction international

St. Lawrence University Writers' Conference

June 14 - 21, 1978

On Saranac Lake in the Adirondacks

ANNIE DILLARD won the Pulitzer Prize in 1975 for Pilgrim at Tinker Creek, her first book of prose. Her second prose work, **Holy the Firm**, was published last year by Harper and Row. Her poetry has appeared widely in such magazines as **The Atlantic, The American Scholar,** and **Field**; and in her collection, **Tickets for a Prayer Wheel**, published by the University of Missouri Press and, in paperback, by Bantam. Her essays have appeared in magazines ranging from **The Living Wilderness** to **Cosmopolitan** and **Sports Illustrated**; her fiction, in **The Antioch Review, Chicago Review,** and **TriQuarterly**. A native of Pittsburgh, she is a Phi Beta Kappa graduate of Hollins College. Currently, she is a contributing editor and columnist for **Harper's** magazine and Scholar-in-Residence at Western Washington University.

MARGARET ATWOOD is well-known as a novelist, poet, and critic. The first of her seven books of poetry, **The Circle Game**, received the Governor General's Award; her thematic study of Canadian literature, **Survival**, is already a classic in criticism; and her three novels, **The Edible Woman, Surfacing,** and **Lady Oracle**, have received wide popularity and enthusiastic critical attention. Her first collection of short fiction, **Dancing Girls**, is the recipient of the St. Lawrence Award for Fiction for 1977. Her stories and articles have appeared in Canadian and American magazines such as **Chatelaine, Ms, Harper's, Ontario Review,** and **Saturday Night**.

ROBIE MACAULEY, currently Senior Editor at Houghton Mifflin, was formerly editor of the distinguished literary quarterly, **The Kenyon Review**, and former Fiction Editor of **Playboy**. His long awaited new novel is forthcoming soon from Alfred A. Knopf. His other work includes **The Disguises of Love**, a novel, and **The End of Pity**, a story collection, as well as **Technique in Fiction**, a study of the craft of fiction widely used for college writing courses. His stories have appeared in magazines such as **Esquire, Playboy,** and **Cosmopolitan**; and his reviews and articles, in **Vogue, Saturday Review, The New Republic,** and **The New York Times Book Review**. He has been a fiction judge for the National Book Awards and a recipient of Fulbright, Rockefeller, and Guggenheim fellowships.

ROSELLEN BROWN is the author of the novel **The Autobiography of My Mother**; a collection of stories, **Street Games**; and poetry collections, **Cora Fry** and **Some Deaths in the Delta**, the latter of which was a National Council on the Arts selection. Her new novel is forthcoming from Alfred A. Knopf later this year. Her poems and stories have appeared in **The Atlantic, Poetry, New American Review, Hudson Review, TriQuarterly, fiction international,** and elsewhere; and her stories have been frequently anthologized in the **O. Henry Prize Stories** and **Best American Short Stories** collections. She has been a recipient of Howard Foundation, National Endowment for the Arts, and Guggenheim fellowships and has been a fellow of the Radcliffe Institute. She has taught at Goddard and Bread Loaf and is teaching currently in the writing program at Boston University.

ROBLEY WILSON, JR., editor of **The North American Review**, has published two widely admired story collections, **The Pleasures of Manhood** (University of Illinois Press) and **Living Alone** (fiction international); and his stories have appeared in **Antaeus, Esquire,** and **fiction international** and in several anthologies, including **All Our Secrets Are the Same** and **SuperFiction**. His poetry has been published in **The New Yorker, The Atlantic, Poetry,** and many others, and in his collections, **Returning to the Body** and **All That Lovemaking**. He is also co-editor of **Three Stances of Modern Fiction**. A graduate of Bowdoin and the Iowa Writers Workshop, he has taught at Beloit and Valparaiso and is presently Professor of English at the University of Northern Iowa.

JOE DAVID BELLAMY is publisher and editor of **fiction international**. His books include **The New Fiction; SuperFiction, or the American Story Transformed;** and the forthcoming **Apocalypse: Dominant Contemporary Forms;** and the forthcoming **American Poetry Now: Interviews with Contemporary Poets** (University of Illinois Press). His fiction, poetry, criticism, and reviews have been published in: **Saturday Review, The New York Times Book Review, Partisan Review, Playboy, Paris Review,** and elsewhere; and his literary interviews have appeared in such magazines as **The Atlantic Monthly, Chicago Review,** and **New American Review**. Mr. Bellamy teaches writing and literature at St. Lawrence University and is Director of the Conference.

General Information

The St. Lawrence University Writers' Conference is designed for aspiring writing students and those seriously interested in writing as a career — for students of literature interested in how writers practice their art — and for free-lance writers seeking to sharpen their skills and gain insights about the current publishing situation. Instruction will include professional training in the art and craft of writing as well as practical attention to editorial needs of fiction, poetry, and nonfiction markets, and guidance toward producing marketable manuscripts.

The conference will include these features:

- Daily workshops in the novel, the short story, poetry, and the magazine article.
- Lectures and panel discussions of: Recent Poetry; Writing a First Novel; Magazines: Big and Small, Popular and Literary; The New Fiction; and other topics.
- Eminently qualified staff of widely published writers and editors.
- Close personal contact between students and staff in an informal setting.
- Individual manuscript conferences.
- Unusual range of recreational opportunities.
- A lovely natural lake-and-forest site and relaxed atmosphere.

teahouse; a boathouse; a reading lounge and library; a recreation hall; well-equipped meeting rooms; and numerous comfortable residential cottages — many combining architectural features of the Swiss chalet and the Adirondack log cabin. Meals are served in Loysen Hall, a modern, air-conditioned facility.

For leisure hours, there are two excellent, crescent-shaped swimming beaches of firm sand. A variety of watercraft is available: motorboats, both inboard and outboard; sailboats; rowboats; a paddle wheel; and canoes. A nature trail winds through several acres of wild forest south of the main lodge. There is a tennis court on the tract, and the 18-hole Saranac Inn Golf Course is within a five-minute drive.

Upper Saranac Lake itself is eight miles long, about two miles wide at either end and reaches depths of 100 feet or more. It is an excellent lake for sailing and one of the best Adirondack waters for lake trout. Accessible islands offer opportunity for picnicking, exploration, or solitude.

The Adirondack Park is the largest of all state or national parks in the Continental United States. This enormous patchwork of mountains, wild forest, and lakes is the most authentic wilderness left east of the Mississippi.

Registration: Individuals wishing to attend the St. Lawrence University Writers' Conference should complete the Registration Form (or a facsimile) and return it with a $50 deposit to: **fictional international**, St. Lawrence University, Canton, New York 13617. The deposit will be applied to the tuition cost. Balance of tuition and fees will be collected at registration.

Register early. Conference size is limited. Students will be notified of acceptance on receipt of application and deposit. Deposit will be returned in

I thought the conference was superb. We all came back with stories waiting to be written and the creative energy to carry them through. At Saranac, I had the feeling that each staff member was still excited about writing, still expected to produce greater work, still expected to discover something new to do with language, with the material of living. The entire staff was excellent. The setting was beautiful and the accommodations first-rate. Good food! How does Coach run such a smooth ship? It was a great week.

—Pamela S., Winnetka, IL

Joe Bellamy's Fiction International Writers' Conference is one of the best run of any series of writers' conferences or meetings I have ever been so fortunate as to participate in. They are obviously carefully thought out, coordinated with remarkable grace and consideration, and leave this particular instructor with the feeling afterwards that everything has been done to make students and teachers comfortable. The phrase "the joy of learning" (and teaching) is perhaps overused, but it has come alive at Saranac Lake. It is a truly inspiring writers' conference.

—Michael Benedikt

From left: Jayne Anne Phillips, Elizabeth Cox, and Carolyn Forché, 1979.

Joyce Carol Oates and Joe David Bellamy
at Saranac, 1977.

been rejecting her work with a series of
kind notes. She said at dinner that night
that she didn't know if she could write
twenty stories in her lifetime, but if that's
what it took, she would certainly try to
do it—because she wanted to be in *The
New Yorker* more than almost anything.
In fact, this particular writer, after many
rejections, eventually had her twentieth
submission accepted by *The New Yorker*,
and quite a few since. Her name is Bobbie
Ann Mason.

Other students and fellows who first
attended Saranac as unpublished or slightly published writers and who later published work of some note include: Dianne
Benedict, Elizabeth Cox, Ursula Hegi,

Elizabeth Inness-Brown, Jayne Anne
Phillips, Pamela Painter, C.E. Poverman, Jean Thompson, Tess Gallagher,
and Kelly Cherry—not a bad record for
six years of meetings.

In 1978, about two weeks before
the conference was to begin, I received
a phone call from someone who said he
was Seymour Lawrence. Of course, I recognized his name immediately—he was
a legend as a publisher. If he was who he
said he was, then I was talking to *the* Seymour Lawrence of Seymour Lawrence/
Delacorte, but I had never spoken to him
before, and it was a little difficult to imagine what he might want with me.

Saranac, for me, was one of those idylls. Even in the midst of it, I knew it was. I think it had to do with the spirit of the place (the landscape), combined with the intensities of the various people. God, I love to talk about writing, especially in lovely surroundings.

—Gail Godwin

Joe David Bellamy in Canaras Lodge at the *Fiction International*/St. Lawrence University Writers' Conference.

A great pleasure of the conference was the approach-ability of the faculty. They didn't clique together. They talked to us, read our stuff, ate with us, even came to our parties. We got, therefore, a whole gamut of relationships, which were professionally exhilarating and personally delightful. Where else would a writer like Gail Godwin seek out a student's room, sit cross-legged on the bed, and talk writing and LIFE for a fascinating hour?

—Sylvia A., Canton, NY

He said he had recently received my conference flyer in the mail and he had, of course, followed the progress of *Fiction International* for several years, and he just wondered if I would mind too awfully much if he stopped by the conference for a few days. I could hardly believe my ears. "I wouldn't mind at all, Mr. Lawrence," I said. "In fact, we would love to have you. The only problem is it's so late in the game, I'm afraid I've committed all of my budget, so I won't be able to pay you anything."

"Oh, for heaven's sake," Seymour Lawrence said. "I just want to come up for the fun of it. I don't expect you to pay me anything. I'm rich!"

"Wonderful," I said. "Say, how would you like to be part of a panel discussion on—oh ... the future of publishing ... or something like that?"

"Oh, I think I could manage that," he said. "By the way, everyone calls me Sam."

"Okay."

"Is Margaret Atwood still on your program?"

I confirmed that she was.

"Good—I'd like to meet her while I'm there."

I assured him that if he came to Saranac, I would personally introduce him to Margaret Atwood, and I kept my promise.

It is my theory that Sam's primary reason for wanting to come to Saranac in the first place was to try to recruit Margaret Atwood for his list, which at that time, except for Tillie Olsen, showed a notable absence of significant women writers. With Sam's nose for literary talent, he recognized that Atwood was a major writer, and I think he wanted to sign her up for his team, or at least to find out firsthand if she was available.

Atwood had just finished *Lady Oracle*, and she had decided that nothing was going to stop her from starting her next novel (which eventually became *Life Before Man*) during the week of the conference. We made elaborate arrangements, in advance, so that she could accomplish this. Her schedule was arranged so that she would have every afternoon free to write, and I agreed to provide expert child-care assistance for her two-year-old daughter, Jess, in the form of a young woman who needed scholarship assistance in order to attend the conference.

Margaret Atwood was unfailingly polite to everyone, and she performed all of her teaching duties with care. But perhaps because of the hunkering-down-to-start-a-new-book mood she was in, or simply because of a clash of temperaments, she appeared to be not the least bit impressed that Sam Lawrence had come all the way from Boston into the wilds of the Adirondack Park to meet her. She wanted peace and quiet in order to think

NEVER BEFORE IN HUMAN HISTORY HAS SO MUCH LITERARY TALENT BEEN SO EMBARRASSED IN ONE BOWLING ALLEY.

and write, and every time Sam came around and wanted to talk, it was like someone had turned the radio up to a station playing loud, offensive music. Sam was so jolly, goofy, gregarious, and down to earth that everyone loved him, but Atwood fled in apparent horror whenever he entered the room, as if he was some annoying buffoon ready to twist her arm to sell her more life insurance.

Another visitor that year was Jayne Anne Phillips, whom I had invited as a fellowship participant. Jayne Anne had been sending me stories that were knock-outs, and I was determined to get her together with Sam, if I could, because I knew she was looking for a publisher. Jayne Anne wore nothing that year but diaphanous white dresses with little filigrees of embroidery along the bodice, and she resembled a particularly lovely angel. Jayne Anne was so sweet and hip and beautiful, it was difficult to believe she was a literary genius, but I already knew that she was.

One night, on a lark, a big group of us from the conference got together and we all went down to the village of Saranac Lake to go bowling. Annie, Sam, Rosellen Brown, and Jayne Anne were all there. Sam had never gone bowling before in his life, so every time his turn came, he rolled a gutter ball. Not that any of us was that great, but Sam was by far the worst, and the harder he tried, the more humiliated he became. We kept saying things like, "Never before in human history has so much literary talent been so embarrassed in one bowling alley," to make Sam feel better.

Finally, on our way home in the car, with everyone in a totally exhausted state, I told Sam quietly that I thought it was probably destiny that had brought him to that bowling alley on this particular night to be so completely humiliated because it had actually been his golden opportunity to get to know his next great literary discovery, Jayne Anne Phillips.

"Jayne Anne is good?" he said, with an astonished look on his face.

"Jayne Anne is very good," I said.

"I'll ask her to send me something."

"You definitely should. If you don't publish her, I will," I said. "But something tells me you can do a better job."

The next time I walked into Brentano's on Fifth Avenue in New York, my visit happened to coincide with the pub date of Jayne Anne Phillips's *Black Tickets* from Seymour Lawrence/Delacorte. Just inside the glass doors was a monumental column of Jayne Anne's lavender-covered volumes that measured six feet across and reached floor to ceiling. There was also a review and an interview with Jayne Anne in *Newsweek*—this kind of exposure for a first book of literary short stories from a previously unknown author! Well, she wasn't unknown for long. Staring up at that gigantic column of books, I thought, *Is Sam Lawrence a great publisher or what?* Sam knew how to get the job done.

Far across the glassy surface of Upper Saranac Lake from the Canaras Center was the wreckage of a once great hotel, the Saranac Inn, whose remaining walls and chimneys caused it to resemble a

Jayne Anne Phillips and Elizabeth Inness-Brown (SLU 1976) at Saranac, 1979.

magnificent white palace in the distance. Guests at the Writers' Conference often gazed across to the distant shore and inquired about it. It was only close up that one could see it was a derelict structure, its roof destroyed in many places with birds flying in and out, its once graceful parquet buckling, and its spacious rooms and corridors haunted by ghosts from the balls and banquets and romances and quiet tea-time talks of an earlier time. In the silence of the mountains, it was easy to imagine that one could almost hear the clinking of the china. America does not have many authentic ruins, but this was one; over the years of the conference, our writers and students visited the place because there was something ineffable there that was unspeakably sad, and that pressed upon the heart.

On a bright June afternoon in 1978, several of us were standing out on the sundeck above the water at Canaras. Annie Dillard glanced across the lake and suddenly said, "Look! It's on fire!" We all stared off in the direction she was pointing and could see that the beautiful white hull of the hotel was bright with orange flames. "Oh, my God," someone yelled. "What a sight."

Ted Stratford, the camp director, ran down to the boathouse and leaped into his speedboat, and Annie and Jayne Anne Phillips and Rob Wilson, I think, leaped in behind him, and we all went streaking out across the lake straight toward the fiery hotel. When we got close, we could see it was hopeless. An enormous wall of heat kept us at a distance, bobbing and listing in the boat, while embers floated down around us and hissed on the water. Even if the fire department could have gotten to such a remote location quickly, I suppose there wasn't much there of real practical value worth saving. But it felt as if history itself was being destroyed in front of our eyes.

The fire was an electrifying spectacle, more exciting than I could have imagined. We sat there watching it burn and collapse, hypnotized by its beauty and strangeness, until the sun started to set and the air began to grow darker and the burning hotel warmed us against the chill approach of evening. *What does this mean?* I kept thinking. *Does it mean anything?* It seemed so full of dramatic import that it should surely be the climax of something, or perhaps the end.

Well, it was nearly the end of the Writers' Conference. We went on one more year, a year that gave us E.L. Doctorow reading from his novel *Loon Lake*, and Carolyn Forché reading her poems from El Salvador, and Dan Halpern lecturing on "The Rhetoric and Pursuit of Suffering." Bill Kittredge and Jayne Anne Phillips were co-winners of the

St. Lawrence Award for Fiction. Whitley Streiber attended as a modest student hoping to work with E.L. Doctorow, and, so far as I know, had not yet encountered either vampires or extraterrestrials. Carolyn Forché didn't sleep for six straight days, so far as I could tell, and, like a gypsy, she hung her sexy underwear out on bushes to dry, and she insulted the dean's wife, and she led a secret invasion party on a sneak attack of the kitchen facilities at 3 A.M. one night and made off with a chocolate cake and the next day's dessert for the whole camp.

One of the best writers' conferences in the history of the Republic ended in 1980 because a new director of summer sessions was appointed who wanted to usurp our time slot at Saranac in order to organize a wonderful new conference devoted to "mid-level academic administrators." It was decreed that we would have to hold our writers' conference on campus instead of at the Canaras Conference Center at Saranac Lake, where we had always held it previously. I was opposed to this change though, without any apparent choice, I was willing to consider it, and I even accompanied the new director of summer sessions on a fact-finding tour of the dormitories, which we would now have to utilize if we were to continue.

I was having a hard time imagining where John Updike might be willing to sleep. I had been trying for years to persuade Updike to attend, and I thought this might be the year he would finally say yes. One triple on the top floor of one of the dorms seemed as if it might be possible, but when I asked the new director of summer sessions if some of the extra furniture could be removed for the duration of the conference—I thought it might seem a little strange to Updike to be staying in a room with three beds, three dressers, and three desks—the director flew into a rage. No, it would not be possible to move any furniture! Who did these people think they were, anyway? John Updike, whoever the hell he was, would just have to rough it!

The papers, files, photographs, letters, and tapes from the Writers' Conference went into several cardboard boxes, and the boxes were stored in my third-floor attic next to the chimney. There, over the next twenty years, the boxes accumulated a fine coating of dust. They survived snow and ice storms, winds that blew out the attic window, a chimney fire, the construction of a new chimney from the basement up, several erratic tenants who did not take good care of the house, and a move with all my belongings to a different state.

They were "lost" in the following sense: I knew the boxes were there if I

Bobbie Ann Mason (center) at Saranac, 1979.

thought about it, though I would not have been able to describe the contents, and I hardly ever thought about it. I had spent the decade of the seventies engaged in far too many activities that began to seem by 1980 to be a distraction from my true purpose or intention in life, which was to try to write real books of my own. In short order, I was to divest myself of the Writers' Conference, of *Fiction International* magazine and press and the St. Lawrence Award for Fiction associated with *Fiction International*, and of my habit of frequent book reviewing. I had already produced one interview book (*The New Fiction*, Illinois, 1974), and I was swamped by a

deluge of poetry interviews I was reading in preparation for a second interview book (*American Poetry Observed*, Illinois, 1984). I didn't have time for any more interviews! In some dim corner of my brain, I had had the forethought to record the Saranac performances in the first place, but I did not pause to consider their historical significance until I rediscovered the boxes and listened to the tapes some twenty years later.

The interviews recorded on the tapes in these lost boxes were from the public presentations made by the writers and panelists during the *Fiction International/* St. Lawrence University Writers' Conference at Saranac Lake, mostly from the years 1976 through 1979, and they capture the spirit and much of the content of all the many conversations that took place during those weeks and years. The tapes were made, in every instance, before a live audience, and members of the audience often took part in the interviews by asking some of the best questions. (In cases where we recognize the identity of the speaker, we have used his or her name in our transcriptions from the tapes. Otherwise, we have simply listed the questioner as "Question." My apologies to anyone who may feel neglected because of my faulty ear or memory—or because of the condition of the tapes. The celluloid was not always perfect, and the crackling of the fire in the hearth at Saranac sometimes obscured the timbre of the voices.)

These interviews may serve as a time capsule, I suppose, though many of the writerly concerns that were discussed at Saranac are still very much the same now as they were then. In that sense, these conversations are still relevant and interesting. More importantly, the interviews reveal in provocative detail exactly what was on the minds of several of our leading writers during that stage of their lives and careers, information we may never have had quite so clearly except for the coincidence that, on a particular day on the banks of Upper Saranac Lake in the heart of the Adirondacks in upstate New York, a tape recorder was turned on when writers spoke to one another. Their thoughts and words were preserved. For a while, these voices were lost, but now they are found again.

—Joe David Bellamy

interview with

MARGARET ATWOOD

Margaret Atwood is the author of more than thirty books, including fiction, poetry, and essays. Her works include the best-selling novels *Alias Grace*, *The Robber Bride*, *Surfacing*, *The Handmaid's Tale*, and *The Blind Assassin*, which was a winner of the Booker Prize, and the story collections *Wilderness Tips* and *Good Bones and Simple Murders*, among others.

This interview was conducted in June 1978 at Saranac Lake in the Adirondacks, where Atwood received the St. Lawrence Award for Fiction for her first collection of stories, *Dancing Girls*.

< Margaret Atwood.

Margaret Atwood: I was on the plane recently going up to Vancouver, and I was sitting beside a man who ran an independent business. The business logo was Jonathan Livingston Seagull,[1] and it was a management consultant firm; and his job was to go around and teach people in business how to get on better with each other, as far as I could gather. I'm always interested in people's jobs because it's potential material.

At the end, when the plane was about to land, he pulled one of his management consultant things on me. He said, "In three words, how would you describe yourself?" I said, "I never describe myself in three words." And he said, "Well, just have a try." And I said, "Well, I'm a writer, I'm a mother, and I'm 38." And he said, "Those aren't adjectives." [Laughter.] He wanted adjectives. Nevertheless, I thought that they really summed it up. But he didn't buy that. He thought for a while and he said that I was "intelligent, sensitive, and—um, um, um"—and finally he said "aggressive." I said, "Once upon a time, that would have bothered me, but it doesn't anymore." I said, "I would say 'ruthless.'"

I write fiction and poetry and nonfiction, and I've been an editor with a small publishing company, as well as many other things. So you can really ask anything, and if I can't answer it, I will intelligently, sensitively, and aggressively tell you that I can't answer it. Otherwise, I will answer it.

Question: In writing poetry and fiction, in particular, do you find that you have different parts of your mind motivating you into those genres, or do they seem to come from the same source? What do you have to say about the differences between poetry and fiction, from your point of view?

Atwood: From my point of view, they come from quite different sources, but it often causes a problem on paper in the reviewing of my books because, especially with the fiction, they like to say this book is a novel—"This book is a poet's novel"—whereas if I weren't a poet, they wouldn't say that. I think it's possibly true about one of my prose books but not about the other two. However, it sometimes gets said about the other ones as well—because people can't resist it, you know. It also gives people an easy out. If they are reviewing a novel, they can say, "It's time she got back to writing poetry," or if they are reviewing poetry, they can say, "Why doesn't she write an-

---

1 *Jonathan Livingston Seagull* is the title of a best-selling book by Richard Bach published in 1970. Many reviewers thought it simplistic or maudlin, but readers flocked to its message, a parable about the importance of seeking a higher purpose in life.

I'M NOT ONE OF THOSE PEOPLE WHO CAN SAY, "I'M GOING TO SPEND FIVE HOURS A DAY WRITING POETRY." I JUST CAN'T DO IT—IT'S JUST NEVER WORKED FOR ME.

other novel?" So it's difficult in that way, but it's not difficult for me because I've always written both. If I felt that one or the other could do the things that the other one could, then I wouldn't write both. I would just write one.

For me, the difference is that fiction has to be *willed*. That is, although you can have the conception for a book which comes from somewhere beyond your will, in order to actually write it down, all 250 pages or 350 pages, you have to be disciplined and you have to work. Otherwise, it just never gets done. It may be a beautiful book in potential, but it's not there. Whereas poetry—I'm not one of those people who can say, "I'm going to spend five hours a day writing poetry." I just can't do it—it's just never worked for me. If I do do that, what comes out is something like a piano exercise, which there is some value in, but not as a way of life.

Question: What is a "poet's novel"?

Atwood: I'm not sure. I think when they say "poet's novel," they're talking about a certain use of language. But I think lots of writers, James Joyce, just to take an example, use language in a very condensed way. He also wrote poetry, but nobody ever says, "This is a poet's novel" about Joyce's work—because he's not primarily known as a poet. I don't think they usually say that about Thomas Hardy because he came to poetry later in life. He had made enough money on his novels so that he could afford it. Because, let's face it, unless we play the guitar or are Rod McKuen,[2] it's not really possible to support yourself on poetry. I think it was possible in the age of Tennyson, when there was a huge mass market for poetry. But it's not possible right now for most people, including myself, to do that. (That was a digression.)

---

2 Rod McKuen (1933-), author of *Listen to the Warm* and *Come to Me in Silence*, among others, was an immensely popular poet in the late sixties and early seventies, though he was often scorned by the critics and other poets as overly sentimental.

I think they're talking about the way language is used. But I'm not sure because I never say that about anybody. I think a novel should be judged as a piece of prose fiction, and, in a way, I think sometimes they are either making excuses or making a derogatory comment.

Question: Could it be that they are criticizing it for not appealing to the mass market?

Atwood: It depends on who's using it and how they're using it. But I think that it probably does imply that. In other words, I think that they are probably saying, "This isn't *Jaws*" or "This is 'Airy Fairy'" or something like that. I don't know what it means. It's a term I never use so you can't really ask me to define it, and I always object to it when anybody uses it about me.

Question: How do you defend yourself?

Atwood: I don't defend myself—because I long ago learned that people who do that like nothing better, especially magazines that publish attacks on you, like nothing better than for you to write a letter in reply because then they think, *Oh, we have a literary controversy and we will sell more copies.* So, I don't. I think everything balances itself out sooner or later.

Question: When you are working on a novel, how far evolved is it before you

actually start writing it? Do you have it all planned out?

Atwood: No, I'm not one of those lucky people. Some people are able to plan everything in advance, and then they write pages and they write each page until that page is perfect, the way they want it— because they know what's coming next. I'm almost the opposite extreme. I'll start something with only a couple of scenes in mind or maybe a couple of characters, and then I write away at it, and I usually write it through about three or four times—at least.

Question: That one scene, you mean?

Atwood: No, the whole book. I start at the beginning and I kind of write as quickly as I can through to the end to find out what happens. Then usually what happens is not what I had intended at the beginning, so then I have to go back to the beginning and look at that. So, I'm one of those people who do it like a kind of ski run; and if I get stopped in the middle, then I have to go back to the beginning and start again. I can't just pick it up later.

Question: How much of a change is there? Do the main characters change very much during that revision process?

Atwood: I can only talk about novels I've written, rather than ones that I might write or will write. With *Edible Woman*, it didn't change too much because I wrote it in a fairly condensed space of time. With *Surfacing*, I made the notes for it in 1965, the original notes. I didn't write it until 1970.

Question: How extensive were the notes?

Atwood: About three pages.

Question: Three pages?

Atwood: Yes. But from those notes, I knew that I was some time going to write the book. I didn't have the space to write it, and also I started another one in between that didn't work out. I wrote 250 pages of it, and it wasn't working for the following reason: There were eight characters, and each character was going to have one section in each of five larger sections, making a total of forty sections. I'd written through two of those larger sections, i.e., each character had two chapters or things, and *nothing had happened yet*. I mean, no events had taken place because I had spent all that time introducing the characters, and I thought, *This novel is going to be a thousand pages long, and it's going to be four hundred pages anyway before I can get any action happening* and *I'm doing this wrong*. This was the one time I tried to plan it! I even had filing cards. It was a terrible failure. So I threw it out. Then I wrote *Surfacing*.

Margaret Atwood receiving the St. Lawrence Award for Fiction at the conference in 1978. Making the presentation is Joe David Bellamy, publisher and editor of *Fiction International* magazine and press.

Question: You spun *Surfacing* out from three pages?

Atwood: I started with the three pages, but everything had changed in those five years except two things: the two scenes that I had started with, namely, the scene where they approach the light for the first time and the scene where the mother changes into a bird. But the central character, for instance, had been about forty-five when I started the book, and that changed, and the people with her changed. There were three other people with her, but they were different. They were different—one was her sister. So, yes, everything changed except those kinds of key points ….

Question: What sorts of things had you been working on during those five years?

Atwood: Well, let's see. You always have to postulate, "One does something to earn a living." You know, if you haven't gotten to the point where you can coast on things, and from about 1961, I was alternating between doing something to make money and saving some of that money and then taking time to write. And 1964 or '65, I was teaching in the lowliest slot on the totem pole at the University of British Columbia. I was teaching Composition and From Chaucer to Eliot—for second-year engineers

or whatever—and I saved up half that money. The Canadian teaching year ends in April. So I had from April until the end of September, when I knew I was going back to graduate school, to write, and that's when I wrote *Edible Woman*.

Then I went back to graduate school for two years, using partly that money that had been saved up, but I always found it sort of easy to write when I was at graduate school, and I wrote a lot of poetry. It was hard to write fiction. So, I wrote two books of poetry. I wrote *The Animals in That Country* and *The Journals of Susanna Moodie*. I needed to get another job because I had run out of money, and I taught for a year at St. George Williams University in Montreal. I lost about twenty pounds because I was teaching in the daytime and at night, and revising *Edible Woman,* which by that time was going to be published, and writing poetry. Everybody said what nice cheekbones I had.

It was a very high-energy year coupled with the fact that you never knew whether to speak French or English to people on the street because if you chose the wrong one, they would hit you with an umbrella. So I had that one year. Then I had two years. I was in Edmonton because I was married to somebody who was teaching there, and I had one year on account of a Canada Council grant and I wrote another book of poetry. And the second year I wrote another book of poetry. I was supposed to be writing my thesis, and, in fact, I did get about three-quarters of it written. But then I also got a film offer, and I started writing a film script. Then I took the money I had saved up from those years and went to England. Then I wrote *Surfacing*. The novel of 250 pages that I had to throw out, I wrote in the summer of 1967 before I went to Montreal. But, as I say, it didn't work.

Question: Did you ever throw it away?

Atwood: No. I never throw anything away. I'm a pack rat. I saved it, and I managed to get one sentence out of it that I was able to use for something else. [Chuckles.] One summer, one sentence. Yes.

Question: Do you support yourself from your publishing job?

Atwood: No, I am supporting myself on my writing. As for the publishing job, publishing in Canada is quite a different thing from publishing in the States. Publishing in Canada is sort of like small press publishing in the States; that is, very few people make any money on it. It's government subsidized—even the biggest publishers get some kind of government grant. Nobody gets rich on it. It's a labor of love, and because of that, a lot of blood gets spilled. I think it's because there are no financial rewards and few rewards of

any other kind that a lot of emotion gets concentrated into things that hopefully wouldn't happen elsewhere.

I don't know what publishing is like in the States because I've never been at it, but the small press publishing in Canada—there's always a trail of bodies. You look at any one of those publishers—there are five bodies that have been discarded on the way because people have strong disagreements about what they are going to publish, how they are going to publish it, and where the meager amounts of money should go, etc. So it was never anything I made money out of.

Anyway, when I needed to make money, I either taught at the university or acted as a cashier or something like that … camp counselor. I was hired as a cashier because I couldn't work a cash register. This is true. They had a cashier who was stealing them blind, they suspected, but she was so adept with the cash register that they couldn't find out. So she was going on holiday. I didn't know this until later. They hired me because they knew that I was completely naive, and I could hardly even make the drawer open. But I certainly wouldn't be smart enough to figure out in two weeks how to pull what she was pulling. And they found out that their receipts were increased by about $90 a day—with the same number of people in the

A POEM STARTS WITH SOME WORDS THAT ARE NOT VISUALIZED BUT ARE HEARD, WHEREAS A NOVEL USUALLY STARTS WITH SOMETHING I SEE.

coffee house. So that's why I was a cashier. Never been one again. It was horrible.

Question: In writing a novel, have you ever started out with several characters and believed that they were going to do something important together, but not known what it was?

Atwood: Yes. I usually start with not only a potential character but also a couple of scenes, which tend to be visual—whereas when I'm starting a poem, it tends to be aural. A poem usually starts with some words that are not visualized but are heard, whereas a novel for me usually starts with something I see. Other people have told me that they are the exact opposite. So I don't think there's any universal truth in that—it's just the way I work.

Question: Would you ever start a novel from just hearing a phrase?

Atwood: I would start a poem from hearing a phrase. I do a lot of eavesdropping. And a lot of that gets into my fiction. But

it's not usually the thing that starts it off; it's not the motivating force.

Question: Could you discuss the difference between film writing and straight fiction writing?

Atwood: The main difference for me is: A film is not a writer's medium. A film is a director's medium, and the person who really makes the film is the person who cuts the film. That, to me, is where the real art comes in. You can make a good movie out of a terrible amount of footage, or you can at least save something. But it's the director and cutter who do it. So, when you are hired to do a film script, you just give up right away any notions of autonomy. You just know that you are a hired gun. You're there to give a skeleton. You are there to work with other people, and if you can't work with other people, you should just forget it. If you can't get on with the director or producer or whoever you have to work with, you can quit right then. And you should know that what you write may be changed, totally changed between the first time you write it and the time it gets shot. It may be totally changed between the time it gets shot and the time it appears because the cutter may rearrange the whole thing.

So, you are doing the best you can with a very limited and technical medium. It can be great fun in a sort of perverse way. But it's not at all the same as writing fiction or poetry, which is your own. When you write a piece of fiction or a poem, you put your name on it. You are the person who has made that, and you have to stand behind it one hundred percent. When you are doing a film, you are working for somebody else. Although you are doing your best, you can't say that it's yours because it isn't. It's only partly yours.

Question: Do many people submit screenplays to the industry, or are they generally commissioned?

Atwood: They are generally commissioned. But it's possible to do one, as they say, "on spec," and some people actually do quite well that way. But generally, you are approached by a producer who says, "Will you write this? We will pay you that." Then you meet with them and discuss their concept and your concept, and if the two are too far apart, then you don't take the job. If there's some feeling that you may agree on what you're doing, then it's possible.

But the other thing to remember about the film world is that everybody in it is crazy. The writers are the least crazy. The producers are the most crazy because they are gamblers. It's a gamblers' mentality. The directors are medium crazy. The directors are crazy in the same way that novelists are crazy. But producers are crazy in a completely different way. You have to be prepared to deal with that.

You also have to be prepared to deal with the fact that it is a pressure-cooker situation. You are often together with people for days on end, working day and night, taking a lot of Vitamin B pills, and that's the thing. You become very close with these people, and then you may never see them again. So it's a very funny kind of thing. It's not at all like being a novelist. Novelists go off by themselves in a room somewhere, and I think, temperamentally, I am better equipped for that. I always enjoyed it in a kind of masochistic way.

Question: At this time, what component or aspect of your fiction do you consider the most experimental?

Atwood: At *this* time—I just started a novel a week ago. I thought I was going to start it either while I was here or just after I left here, but, in fact, I started it before. Of course, everything you start you think is going to be quite different from anything you've ever done. I think previously what I was doing was playing with certain conventions and rearranging them. I think that right at the moment, I'm playing with voices. I'm playing with the voice—which means that I am a lot closer to playing with language. I was doing a certain amount of that in *Surfacing*. In other words, the language there is very elliptical. It makes a lot of jumps. But I think *Lady Oracle*, for instance, is a novel that plays almost entirely with conventions rather than with the voice.

Question: Do you know of Toney? He's a British writer. He talks about something called "foreground," in which the surface texture of language in fiction has a show of its own going on.

Atwood: It does—yes.

Question: It seems to be what you were just saying. There are those writers who concentrate just on event and narrative and plot in a kind of conventional way—that kind of sequencing—and there are those others like Nabokov who write in a way that language is the main show, the main intent.

Atwood: I agree with that partly, although I would disagree in that if the characters and events in the book aren't interesting, then it doesn't matter how splendid your language is. I think it then becomes an indulgence, a kind of embroidery. I think it can get very baroque and narcissistic. Nabokov is very good. He's a very good writer. But when other people take that up and sort of play with that, they can just produce reams of highly ornamented rhetoric, and after about the tenth page, you just think, *Why am I reading this?* It's very beautifully embroidered, but then what?

Question: You are wary of doing that?

Atwood: I'm wary of taking it to an extreme because I think that's all you get—you get embroidery. Embroidery is very nice—if it's an embroidery *of* something, or if there is more going on than the beauty of the little stitches.

Question: When you write poetry, which is usually more lyrical than prose, do you feel the freedom to embroider?

Atwood: Well, there again, I don't think I ever do ... I'm not an embroiderer. I think I'm too damned puritanical to be totally an embroiderer. I think you would have to be a decadent, eighteenth-century writer in order to really go all the way with embroidery. It seems to me that even in *Tristram Shandy*, which is the sort of ultimate in baroque embroidery, the author's always titillating you by dangling little pieces of plot in front of you, and then you say, "Then what?

Then what?" And you turn the page and he's done something else entirely. But that wouldn't work unless you were able to be hooked that way. If you were just embroidering, it becomes … well, who would it become?

Question: Are there any technical considerations that could possibly help when writing fiction if the exposition seems too long? How much is enough? How much is too much? I feel I always have a tendency to write too many scenes or write things down in too many parts to get things moving the way they should be. Do you have any problems with that?

Atwood: Well, let me say that when I am rewriting, I almost always cut. I almost always cut rather than add, which means that I think the difficulty for me is that I say too much and then I have to take out some of it. So in a very, very simple way, that's one piece of advice. But another one about writing prose is simply: Sentences are of certain kinds, and if you use one kind of sentence too much, it develops a very monotonous rhythm. But how do you vary the rhythm and make it mean something? All of these things bear thinking about. I'm probably concerned with exactly the same kinds of things that everybody else who writes prose is, although we might have different names for it.

I have to say, also, that I'm almost entirely without theory, so that, in a way, it's quite hard for me to talk about what I'm doing or what I'm writing. If I were French, I would be able to give you a beautiful exposition of my theory.

Question: But since these things happen during your revisions, you are not really thinking about them while you're actually writing?

Atwood: What I'm thinking about while I'm writing is how to get from one page to the next.

Question: Plus what the character is thinking?

Atwood: My own problem in writing happens to be that I'd rather do almost anything else, so that I am easily distracted. I have that old homework syndrome where you went into your room, you sharpened the pencils, you made yourself a cup of Ovaltine, you looked out the window, you looked at the clock, you said, "I can get this done before tomorrow; therefore, why worry? I'll read a book." I will postpone endlessly. I find that I have to isolate myself, but even when I've done that there is a certain amount of pacing.

So, the main problem is to keep myself in the chair, you know. I'll write a page and I'll think, *Okay, now I deserve a reward. I can get up.* Then I say, "That's

From left: Bharati Mukherjee, C.E. Poverman, and Asa Baber at Saranac, 1975.

fatal. If you get up, you're not going to sit down again." So, there's a lot of wrestling with the angel of that kind. "Will you do it? Won't you do it?"

Question: You say you write first drafts as fast as you can?

Atwood: As fast as I can—because if I stop, I'm doomed.

Question: What happens if you just finish four or five pages and you look at it and you realize it's off?

Atwood: I don't look at it! I don't look at it. [Laughter.] It's fatal to look at it. I *know* it's crap, okay? I know the first time through that it's crap, and you just have to have faith that you can get through to the end and then fix it up.

Question: How fast is fast?

Atwood: Four pages a day. Four or five a day.

Question: That includes revisions?

Atwood: No. Oh, no, I don't revise until I'm finished. As I said before, I don't look at it because if you look behind you, you're lost. You know about Orpheus and Eurydice. Don't look back.

Question: How do you know where you were? How do you keep up with where you are?

Atwood: That's in my head. I know that …. I don't have to look.

Question: At that rate, how long would it take you to write the first draft?

Atwood: Okay, *Surfacing* took me about six months.

Question: Working every day?

Atwood: Well, you know after what I just told you, you know that isn't true. Otherwise it would only take me three months. So you have to allow for a certain amount of interruption. Sometimes you have to go get the groceries, and sometimes your friends come around, and sometimes you can't stand it anymore, and sometimes you get sick—and all those things take time. *Edible Woman*—I think it was maybe four months because I had a lot of uninterrupted time then. My time is more constricted now. It is more constrained.

Lady Oracle, on the other hand, took me about three years because I got interrupted in the middle. I had to go back to the beginning, and I rewrote it about five times. It was a long haul. It's a longer book, and there are a lot more people in it, and it covers a longer time span. There were all kinds of other problems with it—

the voice had to be a normal-sounding voice, a normal-sounding voice relating impossible events, which is different from having an abnormal voice relating normal events. That's easier, in fact. That's easier. It's easier to write tragedy than comedy, in my experience.

Question: Have you found some ways to control your own self-critical tendencies so you can go on, so you won't be paralyzed?

Atwood: As I've said, I don't look at it until I've finished. Or I don't look at it in detail. I may look at it from time to time, but I don't look at it with that self-critical eye. I think that very critical look comes at about the second draft for me.

Question: At what point will you seek someone else's advice?

Atwood: When I either feel I've gone as far as I can with it, or when I believe it's finished. Now, it rarely is quite finished, and I've rarely gone quite as far as I can with it, which is why I show it to somebody else. But I'm lucky in that I have one or two people who have been friends of mine for a long time who are very good at that. And these people—and one in particular—are very, very helpful.

Question: Is that also when you get stuck?

Atwood: When I get stuck, that's my problem. It might help to talk it over with someone, but it doesn't help me because I'm not that sort of person. I know that it does help a lot of other people, so it might work for you.

Question: What is your approach to teaching writing? Do you encourage students to use the same approaches to writing that you use? How do you know when to encourage students, in general?

Atwood: Okay. I begin with the assumption that you can't turn anybody into a writer who isn't one already. You can teach them to read, but you can't teach them to be a writer. My second assumption is: You can never tell who is a writer and who isn't. Only time will tell that. So, I go on the assumption that if they *are* a writer they *are* one, and if they *aren't* one, they *aren't* one—but that I don't know. So, I assume they *are* one.

Now, I've taught writing two ways. I've taught it in a very open way in which they bring in the material and everybody reads it and then they say, "It works" or "It doesn't work"—that whole number. And I've taught it in a very structured way. I've found that for beginning students, the structured way works immeasurably better. I start with oral exercises, and we work all the way through a number of other things. And what that accomplishes is that if they're doing pieces for me and not emanations from their souls, they are

able to look at them. Whereas if it's emanations from their souls, it's so close to them that it hurts and it's almost cruel to say, "I know what you mean is that you are suffering very deeply, but this is the way you've written it, and it comes out funny." So, I would rather make it into an exercise so they can be objective about it. I also find that they write a lot more if you do that. They write a lot more. If you leave it up to them, they're either afraid to show it to you, or they are afraid to write it because they feel it's they, themselves, who are being judged. You are making a judgment on the quality of their personality, or their being. Whereas if you have them do an exercise, you are just making a judgment on the quality of the exercise. So, I prefer to do that.

Question: What are some of the exercises that you start with?

Atwood: For poetry? For poetry, I start them pounding the table because I find that the way they have been taught poetry in the high school has usually been "intellectual." That is: "Analyze this poem. Give the meaning in twenty-five words or less. Do a précis of it. Analyze the metaphors, analyze the similes," etc. But nobody has really done very much basic work on rhythm with them at all, and for me, that's where a poem begins; and that's where it begins for small children—it's with rhythm, not with the intellect. So we go right back to the pre-school rhythm band or primitive tribe, whichever way you want to look at it. We do a certain amount of chanting, and we record that and listen to it, and it at least gets them not to write iambic pentameter lines without knowing it. Because what a young student will do almost always—he'll slide into Shakespeare. He'll slide into iambic pentameter, and then you say, "Did you know that you've written an iambic pentameter line?" Then he'll say, "No, what's that?" So, you might as well begin by realizing that words have certain rhythmic values.

Question: Do you use nursery rhymes?

Atwood: I don't need to because I can have them make it up right in the classroom.

Question: You just count it out?

Atwood: Everyone pounds the table. No-body feels like a fool … by the end. They all feel like fools at the beginning.

Question: What sort of exercises would you recommend for a beginning fiction class?

Atwood: Oh boy. I've never taught a be-ginning fiction class, but I think I could probably think up something pretty inter-esting—if I put my mind to it. But I don't know what I would do right at the very beginning because it would have to be something comparable to what I've just described to get them to look at sentenc-es—to get them to realize that there is more than one kind of sentence and that they sound different ways. I don't know how I would do that. Once I got into plot, I think one of the things I would have them do, which I also do for poetry class, is I take a couple of *Grimm's Fairy Tales*, which happen to be very good to work with because they are very heavy on the emotional content.

There are two that I like to work with. One of them is called "Robber Bride Groom" and the other is called "Fitcher's Bird." They are both very heavy plots. They both have female protago-nists. If I were teaching an all-male class, I would probably teach a different one, one with a male protagonist.

"Fitcher's Bird" is a variation of "Blue-beard's Castle." A wizard steals young girls and puts them in a basket and takes them to his castle, and then he says, "I'm giving you some keys and an egg, and I want you to keep the egg with you all the time; and the keys open every room in the house, and you can go into every room but *that* one." So they always carry around the egg, and finally they can't re-sist the temptation to go into the little room; and they open it up, and in it is a basin full of blood and a lot of cut-up bodies. Of course, they are so horrified that they drop the egg and it gets a blood-stain on it, and the wizard comes back and says, "You've been into the room." Then he takes them in and cuts *them* up.

But then there is the third sister, who is very clever. Instead of carrying the egg around with her, she puts it on a shelf. Then she immediately goes into the room and sees what's there. But, of course, she doesn't get found out, and she puts the bodies together and they reunite and come back to life, including her own sisters. She hides them in a cupboard and the wizard comes back and says, "Let's see the egg." She shows it to him, and he says, "You're the only one who passed the test. I'm going to marry you." [Laughter.]

She says, "Okay, but I get to invite the guests, and you have to take all this gold to my family." So she weights up his basket with what he thinks is gold and sets him on his way, but she has put her sisters in the basket instead of gold. She puts a skull in the window with the bridal veil on it. Every time the wizard stops—because he is so tired because they're so heavy—the sisters say, "I'm looking out the window and I can see that you are stopping. Will you go on?" Because, by passing the test, she now has all this power. He looks behind and sees the skull and thinks that it's her.

Meanwhile, she has taken off all her clothes, opened up a jar of honey, rolled around in it, cut open a feather bed and rolled around in that, and disguised herself as a bird. She escapes that way. The wizard comes back and goes into the house, thinking the wedding is going to be celebrated, and all the bride's relatives and family come and burn down the house. Okay, the problem is: Transpose that plot into a modern story using modern characters. You may use only part of it if you want to.

The "Robber Bride Groom" is a little bit easier to do. That's a real puzzle. That will keep them busy for quite a long time.

With poetry, it's wonderful because you tell them: Choose any character out of the story and write a poem from the point of view of that character. One person wrote a wonderful poem from the point of view of the egg. It was terrific. Some of them write from the point of view of the wizard, others from the dead sisters, others from the central character sister, others from the sister disguised as a bird, which is even more terrific. Anyway, that's one thing that you can do that makes them concentrate on a problem rather than themselves.

Question: Have you ever written for children?

Atwood: I've done one children's book, which was in verse—for very, very small children.

I ENJOY [WRITING] MORE THAN ANYTHING ELSE. AT THE SAME TIME, I'D RATHER DO ANYTHING ELSE.

Question: What kinds of themes do you find sell best for children maybe twelve to fourteen?

Atwood: I've never written for that age group, and I don't think I could. I don't know what would sell the best. I think you would have to ask a publisher that. I think that would probably be the adventure story—juvenile adventure story category. That seems to be what kids of that age like.

Question: When you were talking about people who were writers and people who are not writers: Are there any universal characteristics of writers that you could name that distinguish them from non-writers?

Atwood: They write. That's the only one I've ever found.

Question: Non-writers sometimes write, too.

Atwood: They don't keep it up. They don't continue writing.

Question: Why do writers continue? What are the rewards or motivations for you that keep you doing it in spite of the fact that you said it was so hard?

Atwood: I don't know. I enjoy it more than anything else. At the same time, I'd rather do anything else. It's more challenging than anything else, more painful and more rewarding, and I do it partly because that's what I am. I've been doing it since I was sixteen, and I've never found anything more compelling, including working with films, which, to me, is a kind of sideline. It's just really what I do, but I feel that I will know when I come to the end, and I will then stop and do something else. Before I kept sheep, I used to think that, like Beatrix Potter, I would be a sheep farmer. But having done that, it's not going to be sheep. [Laughter.] Whatever else it is, it won't be sheep. It won't be cows, either—something quite different.

Question: Do you have any theories about the function of a writer in society?

Atwood: Well, yes. But I come from a generation that was always told that it had to behave a certain way, and thinking up theories about what the writer ought to be doing immediately becomes, to my way of thinking, another version of that.

Question: But what do you feel?

Atwood: I guess what I really feel is that the writer should write, and the society should then make its own decisions about that. I think that once a writer decides, "This is the party line. This is morally what I ought to be doing. Let me dedicate myself to this," and if that's in violation of what their real direction as a writer is, you just get postcard art or something that isn't real. You see, we always have to struggle with that in my country because people are always having theories about that.

Question: I was thinking something more along the line of the writer as oracle, someone who has greater insight than other people into the complexities of society.

Atwood: Shall I say that artistic things of all kinds, including painting and dancing and so on, seem to be a characteristic of all human societies. In other words, I think that what we call "creativity" is a human activity, and the queer thing about our society is that some people do it and some people don't. Whereas, in other less divided and specialized societies, everybody does it. Everybody tells stories. Everybody sings. Everybody dances. Everybody decorates—does decorative things. Now, some people may do it bet-

ter than others, and some of it may be sex divided—you know, women weave, men pound sticks on gourds, or whatever. But everybody does it.

The real question to be asked is: Why *doesn't* everybody do it in our society? What is it that we do to people that makes them stop? That, to me, is the real question. It's not why you do it, or even what function it performs—because it obviously performs a very important human function, or all these human societies wouldn't be involved in it. In more primitive ones, it's connected with religion, and I think we've lost that connection. But I think there probably still is a sacramental connection of some kind.

Question: Do you feel while you're fishing around in your own head as you write the first draft, do you have a sense of there being people outside of you who you are writing to—a potential audience?

Atwood: I don't at the moment I'm writing, but an interesting thing has happened to me. I used to think, *Well, if I were put in a rocket and shot to the moon and there's nobody else there and the earth blew up, would I still continue writing?* And I think I probably still would, simply because I'm compulsive. On the other hand, I've often tried to write journals, and I have never been successful. I think the reason for this is that it's a conflict for me. If it's

Margaret Atwood, smiling after receiving the St. Lawrence Award for Fiction for *Dancing Girls*, her first collection of short fiction. Making the presentation is *Fiction International*/St. Lawrence Writers' Conference director Joe David Bellamy, 1978.

a journal, then it's supposed to be private. If it's supposed to be a diary, who is it for? If it's for me, what do I need it for? If it's for somebody else, who is it?

Question: So writing fiction is a neat way out of that trap?

Atwood: Well, I don't know if it's a neat way out of that trap, but it is something that is possible for me to do. Whereas a journal seems to be impossible for me to do—except the kind that I am now keeping, which is, "I planted the garden in April, and then there was a cold spell, but by the middle of May, such and such, such and such, and such and such should come up. I then planted so and so, so and so." And then next year I can look and see when I planted those things. That seems to be about as far as I can go with a journal because it's performing a function. I know what it's for. Whereas if I'm just writing down: "I felt crummy today. What am I going to do about, you know, whatever?" Why write that down? I don't know. I'd like to talk to somebody about that some time and see why they do it— because I've always thought it would be a nice thing to do. But I could never do it. I can write letters because I know who I'm sending them to.

Question: So you do have a sense of writing for somebody else?

Atwood: I must have. But I'm not conscious of it. I don't know who it is. I think that any person who writes fiction or poetry is writing for someone, but they don't know who. It's like writing a note, putting it in a bottle, throwing the bottle into the sea. You have faith that somebody will open the bottle. You don't know who it may be. It may be someone who can't read the message!

Question: Would you assume then that somebody like Virginia Woolf was writing her diaries for posterity?

Atwood: I don't know who she was writing them for. This is a puzzle for me, but she must have known. She must have known that somebody would read them, and I think people who do write journals do feel that, even if they write them in cipher, eventually somebody will read them.

Question: Do you think it is best to stop writing each day at the point where a lot of action is going on or at a point where not very much is happening? Does it matter? I mean, do you choose to stop during an exciting scene with the idea

that you can pick that back up more easily the next day?

Atwood: Well, my life is so determined by the activities of other people. So, I usually have to stop when it's time for me to go back to the house. I write in a log cabin, which is at a distance from the house. And I have a certain number of hours during which I can do that, and after that, I have to go back to the house—because I have a young child and this child's activities cannot be postponed. You cannot say, "Wait until nine o'clock tonight to have dinner because I'm writing." So, I pause when I have to. Sometimes I pause when I come to a natural stopping point—when I've finished a section dealing with the character, so I think I can knock off early because I don't want to start the next person right then. But mostly I stop when I have to.

Question: I find it extremely hard maintaining the right sort of a mood as I write. I'm often affected by things around me. I mean, you might feel a certain way and you take three months to write something, and then three months from then maybe you're in a car accident or somebody may die, and you don't feel the same way. How do you keep the right mood?

Atwood: Keep the momentum?

Question: Yes—how do you do that for the length of a novel?

Atwood: Well, if I were you, I'd stop at an exciting point and then pick it up and go on to the end of the book and then rewrite the whole thing. But, you see, I'm not you. So I don't know how you should do it. That's something you'll just have to find out. The thing about talking about writing is that it's talking about an unknown. Nobody really knows anything about it. They do all these studies on creativity and so on, but none of them may apply to you.

Question: Do you find it difficult to write from a male point of view?

Atwood: It does make a difference. It is more difficult. But that doesn't mean you shouldn't try. Of course, it's always going to be a "this is a poet's novel" problem, because if they know that you are a woman and you're writing a male character, it's very easy to say, "This person does not grasp the essence of maleness." I think it's historically been a lot easier for men to get away with writing female characters than it has been for women to get away with writing male characters. Although, in the nineteenth century, it was easier because there are a lot of things you didn't have to put in. George Eliot did a pretty good job in *Middlemarch*, for instance. But sexuality was taboo. So she couldn't write about that anyway.

I think it's historically been easier for men to write female characters because everybody, including women, had fairly limited expectations of what a female character was. You know, you could have her menstruate or have a child—a few things like that, and that was it. And everybody would say, "How realistic." [Laughter.] You didn't have to have her thinking about politics, or having ideas, or even thinking about much at all.

I mean, Molly Bloom is a case in point, if you actually look at what Molly Bloom thinks about during the whole book. She thinks about her lovers, she thinks about bodily functions, and she thinks about her child. That's it. She didn't think about anything else much at all—a little bit about singing. If you did a man like that, everybody would say, "This is a caricature!" You know: "No man is this limited. He doesn't think about just weightlifting and bodily functions and screwing women. It's a caricature!" So that's why it's more difficult. Two-dimensional women are acceptable; two-dimensional men aren't. Maybe I should say "were."

Question: What makes a character interesting?

Atwood: Ah—that is a question that should be asked of the reader, not the writer. The writer, of course, thinks that all of his or her characters are interesting. The other thing about the reader is that there is no such person. Readers come in many shapes and sizes, and one reader will say, "This is the most fascinating book I've ever read," and another reader will say, "This is a pile of crap." So, I wouldn't worry about the reader. You know that there is one.

Question: What do the readers want?

Atwood: I'm not a reader. I *am* a reader, but when I'm writing, I'm a writer. And I don't think that you should worry about that because it's like the filmmakers who try to second-guess the audience. Somebody makes *Easy Rider*, and a lot of people say, "A-ha, let's make another *Easy Rider*." They try and they fail—because the film viewer is already somewhere else.

So I think the only thing you can do is to try to make your book the best way that you can make it, and then it's the message-in-the-bottle problem. You put it in the bottle, you throw it out, and there are people out there who are to read your book. Sooner or later, they will read it. It helps to have a publisher who will distribute it properly. But apart from that, you can't do anything. You can't say, "Readers are this way, and I'm going to cater to them." You just can't do that—unless you want to write best-

sellers. Unless you want to write some kind of predictable sub-genre. If you want to write gothic romances, I can tell you how to do it. I can even tell you why the readers identify with the characters, but I hope that's not what we're talking about.

Question: What do you have to accomplish, do you think, to justify calling yourself a writer?

Atwood: I was very pig-headed as a child—well, not as a child, as an adolescent. I became pig-headed when I started writing. Before that, I was kind of wishy-washy. But, in fact, there was *no* justification. But I think you have to have that because there is nothing that is more easily put down or more easily condescended to, or patronized, than somebody who says, "I'm going to be a writer." Everybody says, "Oh, yeah." If you say, "I'm going to be a doctor," everybody says, "Good for you. Going to medical school—how admirable. Hope you make a lot of money." Things like that. But if you say you're going to be a writer, everybody finds it quite pretentious of you.

But I think you just have to grit your teeth and do it. I got a lot of that put down and so on. Of course it bothered me, but it didn't stop me. The fact is that you might as well go through it because once you publish, people are going to do it to you in reviews anyway. You might as well prepare yourself for it.

Question: There have been a great number of literary critical approaches suggested for *Surfacing*. How do you feel when you read one of those? Does it seem as if they're talking about something else or someone else?

Atwood: Sometimes they're talking about something else.

Question: They obviously don't know what you intended, but do you sometimes discover things that surprise you or that you were unaware of?

Atwood: I was quite surprised when I saw a religious interpretation of *Surfacing*. But this has now become, I find, fairly standard. People are teaching this book in religion courses. Now, this was not at the top of my mind, shall we say, when I was writing the book. But I can't become too perturbed about any of that because, as I say, all readers are different and if somebody can take that book and make a plausible analysis of it that does that, and it *was* quite convincing to me when I read it. I thought, *Gosh, did I really do that? Yeah, sure enough—chapter and verse—there it is.* I have to say, "Okay, let them do it."

I can't stop them anyway. So, why get an ulcer? You can't determine, you can't control, critical reaction to your work. You can't do it.

Question: I was asking a group of academics once, "Why do you teach Margaret Atwood and why not Marge Piercy?" And they said, "Well, Margaret Atwood is so much more lit-critical."

Atwood: [Laughter.]

Question: It was pleasantly stated.

Atwood: That's because they're going about Marge Piercy the wrong way. I could do a good course on Marge Piercy, using books like, for instance, *Woman on the Edge of Time*. I would teach it as a utopian romance. I think it's perfectly "lit-critical." But I see what they mean. You can play games with your students with *Surfacing*. But, I don't know. Does that bother me? I suppose it does. I can't let anything bother me too much because there's so much of it that if I were going to be bothered by that sort of thing, I'd be bothered all the time. I'm the world's greatest worrier anyway, so I just try to shut it out. That's why I live on a farm and have an unlisted phone number and only read the mail once a week.

interview with

JOYCE CAROL OATES

Joyce Carol Oates has published more than thirty novels, including *Expensive People*, *We Were the Mulvaneys*, *Blonde*, and *Them*, which was a winner of the National Book Award for Fiction. She has also written some twenty collections of stories, including *The Wheel of Love*, *The Poisoned Kiss*, and *Heat and Other Stories*, in addition to many novellas, plays, poems, and essays. She is the Roger S. Berlind Distinguished Professor of Humanities at Princeton University and a member of the American Academy of Arts and Letters.

This interview was recorded in June 1977 at the Saranac Lake Center.

< Joyce Carol Oates at Saranac, 1977.

Joe David Bellamy: Good morning. This is a question-and-answer session, and Joyce will be happy to answer whatever you have in mind …. Well, she may *not* be happy to answer. She may *not* answer, in fact. But try her.

Joyce Carol Oates: Well, I'm open to any questions …. I write with a pen …. [Laughter.]

Gail Godwin: One has read so much apocryphal gossip about how you work. I even read something once about how you took a typewriter into the bus station. And I'm just …

Oates: Where did I plug it in?

Godwin: Would you be willing to just answer that most pernicious question on your habits?

Oates: Well, my habits have evolved over a period of years. So what I do right now doesn't necessarily represent what I did when I began. I think we have different phases of personality, which I'm sure are evidenced in something as obvious as our conversation or the letters we write to people; so a writer, I think, does go through different phases. Right now, the way I write is in longhand, and I accumulate many notes because my novels and stories are really prose poems now rather than more cinematic works, as I think they tended to be some years ago. Ted [Weiss] was saying yesterday that there is a fear of poetry, and people are not buying it.

You will be amused to know that my most recent novel, *Childwold*, is really a prose poem, and it was conceived that way with strange margins and things like that. It was all written in longhand, very lovingly, and with a kind of sacramental feeling one gets writing poetry; and I mentioned this to my publishers, of course. They thought it looked funny—rather a suspicious kind of set up. They are very fine people. My editor is a wonderful person, but she wrote back rather hurriedly and said, "We must never *say* it is a prose poem." I was thinking for the blurb it would sound instructional to say that this is a prose poem and that people would then not buy it, thinking it was Harold Robbins[1] or something. But she said all the book dealers would be very nervous about that. We must never use that word. Keep the word "poetry" out of it.

But *Childwold* is somewhere between being a novel and a prose poem because it has characters and an evolving plot. Things do happen in time and space,

---

1 Harold Robbins (1916–1997) was an American novelist of commercial fiction whose books, including *The Carpetbaggers* (1964), sold more than fifty million copies.

which, I think, is perhaps the definition of a novel. But I do write in longhand, and I really enjoy it. If I have a few minutes at this conference to just go back and write a scene or something that is evolving in my mind, I really love that. It's so enjoyable. But if I were faced with a typewriter in the Greyhound bus station or whatever that was—if I had to write something in this cold sterile kind of print, then it wouldn't be quite as exciting.

So I accumulate this mass of notes, which are very romantic or elemental in some ways, I think, and then I transpose them. I can have maybe a thousand pages. *The Assassins* almost did me in, an ugly duckling of a novel, and it's one of those things that you have to love because it's so awful nobody else will ever like it. I must have had a thousand pages of notes. So then—what is it?—the right brain or the left brain?—had to start percolating, and it was transposed into some sort of linear and coherent form, *semi*-coherent. The kindest reviewer noted that it was an "unreadable" novel. That was *The Yale Review*. I think he was really trying to be nice.

Question: I've studied your novel *Expensive People,* and I've always wondered how it must be very difficult to get into a first-person sense of this character ….

Oates: This fifteen-year-old boy? No, it's very easy. Absolutely.

Question: Was it based on something you heard about or read, or how did you get into it?

Oates: Well, I'm very fascinated by different aspects of life and *not excluding* the social adventure that Proust and Fitzgerald and other people have embarked upon. I think that's a legitimate adventure—you know, the social world, the upper middle-class, and so forth. One would not want to stay there for long, but I was interested in that for a while; and in a city like Detroit (near where I live), the suburbs are in some instances very wealthy. One sees all these strange examples of breakdown, which, since 1963, have become almost national. But at that time, they were rather prophetic and were happening in certain suburbs of Detroit where the automotive millionaires lived.

So I'd heard these strange tales of fragmentation and breakdown. One of them was of a boy who had killed his mother with a gun … belonging to his father. He'd just fired through the window as if she'd been shot by a sniper. Then, later, he came in the house and the police were there, and he acted too casual. He saw his mother lying there, and then he went to his room and did his homework. He was trying to be very cool. But, you know, it didn't work because that's not how one would act. His scenario wasn't too professional.

So this story was kind of floating around in that suburban area where right now you know what's going on around the same area—that child killer! He's called "The Doctor" or something because he kidnaps these children—he's taken seven of them—and he does things to them. Well, it's sexual abuse, but they are perfectly clean when they're found. They're usually naked. Their clothes have been laundered and folded neatly. Everything about them is perfectly clean. The fingernails are just perfect … they're cleaner than they've ever been. Now that's happening in the same area, and if you live around there and you have friends there, they're all thinking and worrying about their children, as they should be, including some of my students who are older who have children. But something that is in this consciousness strikes very deeply into the North American consciousness as a whole. Bad things start happening in some areas that then branch out in a few years. I hope it really won't happen, but one can sense it as prophetic.

No, it was very easy for me to do. I think part of our psyches contains twelve-year-old murderers. Nothing human is alien to us. The most disgusting thing I ever wrote was called "The Triumph of the Spider Monkey," which was so disgusting I could barely read the galleys—and whenever anybody mentions it to me,

I kind of look away and pretend I don't know what they are talking about. Some of my students said, "You have a new novella out?" and I changed the subject. It's the first-person confession of the maniac Bobby Gotteson to Joyce Carol Oates. It was written as a vicious parody of a kind of *National Enquirer* tabloid. *The Antioch Review* was going to bring it out. Then they ran into all this legal difficulty. I'm sure you've heard about it. They didn't run into difficulty because of the tabloid, but I don't think that helped matters.

It was a disgusting thing with lurid sectional furniture ads, you know, like in the Sunday feature. The three-section sofas and foldaway things. And "We're looking for fresh, young talent"—the kind of little ads that you see in really bad Sunday supplements. It was a vicious satire, which never got published in tabloid form. All the tabloids I think were bought up, and some more circulated underground. It was really *supposed* to be disgusting. It came out when there was a lot about possible censorship.

So, I have all these words in there that I didn't fill in. I don't really write obscene things—I don't care necessarily to read them. But this was so much fun because I had all these blanks, you know, the sort of things that Norman Mailer would feel. When I used these blanks instead of the words, I thought, *Well, the*

THINGS DO HAPPEN IN TIME AND SPACE, WHICH, I THINK, IS PERHAPS THE DEFINITION OF A NOVEL.

horrors that are in the readers' minds are just projected on to this, and they are just filling in all the blanks themselves.

So, this is Bobby "Gotteson," which has suggestions of Charles Manson, and I ran together Manson and Richard Speck. I thought, had they met, they might have liked one another. [Laughter.] "Born to kill" or whatever the strange tattoos are. I ran them all together with Howard Hughes, I think. He rides in a helicopter. It's a fantasy. It's very surreal, and I wrote it very quickly in a white heat. And I repented in leisure, as one does with things like that. But it was so easy to do I really wonder sometimes about myself. Somebody is killing all these stewardesses,[2] you know. These things are going on. It seemed very easy. Then, when it was all done, I saw what I had done and I put it away up in the drawer for some weeks. Then I rewrote it. Recollected in tranquility, it got transported into something that approached structure and approached art, I suppose.

But it never came out in the tabloid version, which I think was really very funny—because I had this kind of silly photograph of myself, my husband, and Bob Coover[3] and his wife. We were coming back on the SS *France* together, and they kept coming around and taking pictures of people at tables, and we were there and we were all kind of happy and silly and so they took this. I sent the photograph in and that was in there and we have, you know, the little black-out: "The maniac enjoying himself." [Laughter.]

But then Bob Coover! They didn't have the black-out on Bob Coover so he's kind of looking sideways, and so it would seem that the maniac was actually Bob Coover. I had told the publisher not to do that. I said, you know, "Put the little blank things on all of our faces." Then I wrote back and I said, "Now, Bob Coover does have a sense of humor, but he's not going to like that, maybe." So

---

2 Here, Oates is referring to one of the plot elements in her story "The Triumph of the Spider Monkey."

3 Robert Coover (1932-), author of *The Origin of the Brunists*; *The Universal Baseball Association, Inc., J. Henry Waugh, Prop.*; *Pricksongs & Descants*; *The Public Burning*; and others, is one of the most highly regarded experimental writers of his generation.

From left: An unidentified student, Ursula Hegi, another unidentified student, and C.E. Poverman.

we stopped the presses or something. But it was too late.

Anyway, all these things wound up in the warehouse or basement, and then later on, Black Sparrow brought it out in a different form. I changed it around. It's much more approaching art now, and originally it was supposed to be a really sleazy, disgusting thing that you might actually read. Very prurient. There were all these little footnotes like: "The film of this disgusting thing will be made and released on December 26," you know, starring all these awful people. The Manson/Gotteson character dies, and all these people rush forward to write their memoirs. They're not ashamed of all the things they've done. As soon as he dies, they come forward and make millions of dollars. He made nothing. It was a parody of what probably has been happening and will continue to happen in southern California and elsewhere. Yes, the Gilmore thing[4] and then after the Watergate thing—the same sort of phenomena where nobody's ashamed. They rush forward with their contracts.

---

4 Gary Mark Gilmore (1940–1977) was a career criminal who was convicted of killing a motel manager in Provo, Utah. Gilmore refused all appeals of his conviction and became the first person legally executed in the U.S. after the death penalty was reinstated in 1976. Gilmore's story was documented in a best-selling book of narrative nonfiction by Norman Mailer, *The Executioner's Song*, in which Mailer utilized Gilmore's letters, interviews, trial transcripts, and statements that Gilmore gave to the press. The book appeared at a time when the "nonfiction novel" was still revolutionary.

So that was very easy to do, and yet I have no interest whatsoever in Charles Manson. I don't want to meet him. I don't want to read about him. I have *no* interest. If he came in the door, I'd move to the other side of the room. I don't have any interest in these people except as fictional possibilities or explorations of the psyche. But in no way would I say, as Freud might try to, that this is some compensatory thing, that I really want to meet these people. It's not true.

The madmen that I have met have been very few, and I agree with what was said earlier. These people have been very boring because they are monomaniacal and obsessive. They are not interesting. Neurotics are very boring people. Psychotics even more so, but neurotics—if you are one or are thinking of becoming one—it's just like you are one note. Like when you first meet a neurotic, he (or she) may seem interesting at first because they are always talking about how they want to murder their father or grandmother or cut off their thumbs or something. Bake them in a pie. You know, there's all this phony mythic stuff. But then the second time you meet the person, you know, you've changed a little and you want to talk about the movie *Annie Hall*. They're still talking about their grandmother or their father, and they're kind of mumbling and trembling. Then the third time you

meet them, now you want to talk about the St. Lawrence Writers' Conference, and they're still talking about their father! The most boring people in the world are these neurotics. So we move on.

The same is true with their poetry. People really liked Sylvia Plath for a while. But then you re-read her and maybe teach her and you see the truth. Because the test of any literature is how it works with a group of intelligent, bright people. You get through it and there is a point where Sylvia Plath is so incredibly boring that you go to read Immanuel Kant and he's exciting. He's scintillating. But there is something about the neurotic—this one note, you know, this repressed anger—which is really a facade of a childhood dismay. The child is so frustrated and dismayed and terrified, it comes out as a false anger and it becomes very dull-looking. Are there any other questions?

Question: Could I ask you about your story yesterday? I'm intrigued by this taking of factual material and bringing it into fiction, yet, in a sense, still preserving the aura of the original. Can you say something about what goes on in your mind as you translate these things?

Oates: Oh, I love to do that. In fact, I would suggest for young or new writers who don't have any overwhelming projects that you try this kind of thing. I see it as a sort of marriage or wedding with the consciousness of another, let's say, greater personality, or maybe not greater.

Let's say you meet Yeats. There may be some interesting kind of wedding there. One of the things I did last summer seemed so, so exciting, and I never completed it, so it's open for anybody. I was going to re-read and complete in some other form the works that writers had been working on when they died. And I did *Felix Krull*. I loved that. I loved it. It's called "Further Confessions."

I have always felt that Thomas Mann did not, in a weird way, understand Felix Krull. You see, Mann, at the end of his life, became very Olympian and very sardonic and comic. He's a good comedian, but really, his temperament was tragic. *The Magic Mountain* is a marvelous, marvelous novel, and its tone is elegiac. It's a great work, and *Doctor Faustus* is even better—and that's tragedy.

So then at the end of his life with *Felix Krull, Confidence Man*, he runs through again very quickly all the same themes that he worked with so deeply when he was younger, but this time, it's comedy. Felix is such a deep and subtle character, I think. But Mann treats him like a puppet. He gets more and more superficial, and as his little fragment comes to an end, I just think that Mann's dangling him around. I thought I would

take Felix Krull away from Mann. He's not treating him well. [Laughter.]

I re-imagined Felix Krull as he is on the day after the novel ends—it's a fragment. He's going to be leaving for South America and he has money. He's a confidence man. He has a false identity, which interests me very much, too. This was just so exciting. I remember sitting in our courtyard in the sun and re-reading Mann and arguing with him. "Felix wouldn't have done this. Felix is more subtle. Why are you doing this to your character?" I wondered: Did Mann know that he was going to die? And things suddenly seemed less important and he was writing more quickly?

It was a strange fragment because he began when he was fairly young, put it aside for twenty years—or was it forty?—a long time. Then he took it up again near the end of his life and continued right after where he had ended previously, which is a feat in itself.

But I made Felix Krull into an artist. I thought he really was an artist. I set him on his way and he meets all these ghouls—because my next book is about parapsychological experience where the dead come and we don't know whether they're psychic projections or real, that sort of thing. He meets Thomas Mann, his creator who wants to take him back to the underworld to die because Mann dies. Felix gets away from him and I felt such excitement that this character got away from his creator, and he gets away from me, too.

He gets very interesting. He sits there in these cafés in Lisbon reading newspapers, and he sees the futurist manifesto, which was going to be reprinted at this time, and something clicks with him, and he goes to Italy then, and he gets mixed up with these futurist artists. They were so experimental but, as you know, they really didn't develop their own iconoclastic ideas. They were very experimental, but then nothing happened. It was taken up maybe forty, fifty years later by other painters, and so that's the end of that story, which was so much fun to write. I couldn't have written it without Thomas Mann. You know, really, it was so good.

Question: This is the other side that is fascinating. I mean, in the Joyce story, you explored the actual life and turned it into fiction. Here, it seems to me you're taking fiction and turning it into life.

Oates: Well, the many things that I do in the story have their analog in the Mann fragment. But the James Joyce story is very fictional, too. There's another one I had so much fun writing but nobody really knew what it was, even the reviewer. I guess they liked it well enough, but they had no inkling what it was about.

It's the "Meditation on the Death of Shelley by Lord Byron." I set it in Maine. I love Maine and I love the atmosphere. As you may know, Lord Byron had to go identify the body of the drowned [Percy Bysshe] Shelley. Byron was the lover of life and women and wine, and he didn't really want to do this, but they came to get him and—he had to.

Shelley's body was washed way far away, and it was many weeks before it came ashore. He had been a very beautiful young man, as you know. Byron described him as so graceful. He was like a flame or like a snake gliding in on his tail. That's a marvelous description that Byron has of Shelley. But when he was washed ashore, he was just a hunk of something. Byron looked at him and with a kind of hysterical, nervous laughter said, "That's not a man—it looks like a sheep. The jaw is gone." He was really traumatized, and something about the way Byron talked as he saw the body of this beautiful, young man just went through me. You know something about that?—Byron, Shelley, the way he was denying what he saw, the way the beautiful face had been all eaten away by fish or something. So I wrote that and had fun writing that. It's called "A Posthumous Sketch."

I don't think many people know what it is—even though the Byron character has a different name, there are these gross hints. He's trying to write this poem, and it's a Byron poem, you know. He's got the first couple of lines, and we all know what the other lines should be. He can't get the rhyme and he's drinking beer and it's two o'clock in the afternoon and he hasn't had his breakfast. I thought now any literate reader is going to say, "Come on, the next line is, you know, give him a quote." But sometimes there are these odd, obtuse clouds in the reviewers' heads, and they don't get these things.

The one I couldn't do, which I throw out to any of you—I tried to read that dreadful ghastly boring novel, I'm sorry—*The Sense of the Past*, Henry James. I know why he died before he finished that. It's so boring! I was going to try to finish that, but I just couldn't. I mean, I couldn't read it, let alone rewrite it. And my whole project came to a premature halt with that particular book, so I just stopped doing it. But really I advise you to try this sort of thing if you're not completely committed to something that you *are* doing. This is so much fun. Really.

Question: I want to ask about your plays. I see the list of plays here, and I haven't seen any of them. What kind of experience have you had with these?

Oates: One play has been published at Black Sparrow, and another will be coming out. I don't see my own plays. At one time, Bob Coover was having a play produced at the American Place Theater—I think right after mine—and we were writing back and forth, and Bob was going to all the rehearsals and he really enjoyed them. I said to him, "I didn't go to mine, and I don't think I'll go to the play itself because I don't like that kind of play!" [Laughter.]

I prefer Chekhov. No, I don't like this modern sort of theater. I want it to have a plot, and I want to know what's going on, and I don't want strange people addressing the audience and odd, oblique, surrealistic things. As a theater-*goer,* I don't want to see my own plays!

Question: Not even after you've written them?

Oates: But maybe that was being a little facetious, I don't know. I don't see myself as a playwright.

Question: We saw one of your plays and enjoyed it.

Oates: Which one was that?

Question: The Halloween play.

Oates: Oh, *The Sweet Enemy.* That goes way back. That was the Actors Studio—Frank Corsaro, who is now directing opera and is quite well known in New York City, a very inventive man, very imagi-

Joyce Carol Oates at Saranac, 1977.

native. Frank wanted me to write a play. He had read my first book of short stories. He wrote to me and he said, "Write a play." And I said no. It seemed very ridiculous. I'm not interested in the theater at all. You have to have it in your blood.

So finally I wrote something, and he said, "Come to New York." He went through this play with me, and he said, "You know, Joyce, in the short story and the novel, you can have paragraphs where nothing happens—because it's psychological and it *is* dramatic. But why are your people just sitting around on stage? They sit there. They've got to *do* something." And I said, "Oh." [Laughter.]

Suddenly, it dawned on me that the visual is so different from what most of us are writing. There's psychological movement, but the motion that's visual has to be concrete—like people come and go, and they walk around on stage, and they *do* something. So it was educational for me.

Question: Some poets who were not playwrights were doing great drama in the nineteenth century.

Oates: Yes—like Yeats. They're meant to be done in the drawing room. Yeats's plays are almost like masques—with dancers. They are more like rites than plays, sacred rites in a religion that nobody remembers any longer, so they are very difficult to follow. You have to know and love and to have forgiven a great deal of Yeats before you can sit through one of his plays—then, it is beautiful.

I like plays. I like to encourage my students to write them and put them on because one thing you really learn is how economical you have to be. You're not supposed to have any wasted dialogue, and the action moves very fast and it's exciting. When I meet with my writing students this afternoon, I want to talk about how it's a good idea to envision a story or chapters of a novel in an actual, visual way.

A piece of student writing that I read recently for this afternoon, I thought was really very successful when it had an objective and visual dimension that even in a sense could be filmed. When it wasn't doing that, it had to fall back on language alone; and when you fall back on language, you had better be Samuel Beckett or James Joyce, because to do it on the strength of style alone, you have really got to be good. There are not many people who are that good. I think even William Gass at times is not actually that good—that one would read that much of

his prose without there being any objective referential dimension to it. I know people would disagree with me, and I do admire his work; but you have really got to be right up there with James Joyce or Samuel Beckett to exist on style alone. But if you want to write a novel and it's not going to be all a feat of style or experiment, a good way is to block it out in your daydreams and actions, so that it has a concrete dimension ….

I do a lot of this when I'm driving. It seems the perfect time for meditation. You're all alone and the phone cannot ring; and assuming you don't suddenly run into a bridge abutment or something, you can do this wonderful meditation.

Question: Which of your books do you like the best?

Oates: I always like the one I finished most recently. I'm very, very absorbed in what I do at the time. What I'm writing right now will seem to me all absorbing—absolutely. I don't even think about the other ones. By the time my novels come out and reviews appear, it is almost as if somebody else wrote them.

People say that I'm detached or cold, or that I don't have the right attitude and I'm not human enough. That's not true. I'm very human and very warm—my pulse, my heart's blood is beating into a work of art, but it's not that one. It's another one. I'm very connected with another one.

Question: Are you able to work on more than one thing at a time? To get away from something if it's too intense?

Oates: Yes. If it's very intense, I should get away from it. My writing is all autobiographical in an emotional sense, and I try to hook up with this private, emotional *something* that's happened in the real world.

Now, Gail [Godwin] spoke of getting some letters. I get a lot of letters, and many of them are very disturbing—and *disturbed*—letters. They are from strange people out there. In fact, Robie [Macauley] knows one of them. In a sense, he's the strangest one, that guy who kind of threatened my life for a period of years. One of them even showed up in a big class—I have about 150 students—and this odd man showed up. He telephoned my teaching assistant and said he was going to kill me. I didn't know who he was. We'd never met, and he was hanging around the department. Everybody could give a description of him. They were saying how much he weighed. You know like you give to the police, as if people in the department were getting ready; and they had this wonderful, very professional attitude. They obviously had seen *The Godfather*, and they were going to give the police

the real color of his eyes, the clothes he was wearing, and all that. He was hanging around for a couple of days.

So when you have these things happen, either you're going to worry about it and get nervous and all that, or you try to say, "Well, my experience is not that unusual. Have there not been many other people whose lives have been threatened? Who receive strange letters with smears of blood on them like I got one day?"

My students were coming in, and I have my writing workshop in my office. I have a large table, and I was just opening my mail as one does in a sort of absent-minded way and talking with them. I looked at this letter, and it sort of fell down on the table, and one of the students saw it and there was a smear of blood on it. I took it back, and I said, "It's a fan letter." [Laughter.]

This guy in northern Michigan—I don't know what his problem was, but he said, "I want you to know that I am serious." He was going to come down and see me or something. So I thought, you know, look at the Kennedys. Look at people who have been assassinated, who really lived through all this. Why should I mull over what I'm going through? I'll write about the external. Or I'll write a novel like *The Assassins* where a person is actually assassinated. He is killed, and it's marvelous how it cheers you up, you

I FIND IT'S IRRESISTIBLE TO WORK WITH PRIVATE EMOTIONS WHEN THEY'RE TRANSPOSED INTO SOME SORT OF PUBLIC DIMENSION.

know, because like you think *you've* got troubles! [Laughter.]

It's like you come in to show your operation scar to somebody, as Lyndon Johnson did, and the person says, "Oh, I've got terminal cancer. You think you've got troubles!" Everything becomes a Woody Allen film eventually.

So I have this autobiographical dimension. I was telling some people last night about the private meaning of my story "Daisy," since there is insanity in my family. I don't think it's on that level—I don't think this person in my family would have been a genius. But who knows? But I think, you know, she was rather bright and became insane and really never developed in any way, and this person was born on my birthday and looks just like me. So the theme of "the double" means a great deal to me. And the babbling, the way the words get all skewed around, phrases that could almost be poetry but instead are babbling, and it's such a tragedy.

So that story, for me, has the objective Joycean dimension and a very private

one that nobody would know about. So I find it's irresistible to work with private emotions when they're transposed into some sort of public dimension. That's the only way I really like to write. I don't care about my own life that much—to write just about my own life. I'd rather write about something going on out there in, say, North America. However, I couldn't write about these external things just in themselves. They wouldn't interest me. I have to have the private connection.

Question: Have you done a biography?

Oates: No. I love to *read* biographies. I have never done one.

Question: Have you thought of writing one?

Oates: No. I'd have to do so much research.

Question: How about an autobiography?

Oates: Oh, an autobiography. I keep a journal. Oh, maybe I have and I've forgotten! [Laughter.]

Question: You write, after all, in many more forms than most writers—poems, stories, criticism, novels, novellas. Can you say something about how you decide, or how you come to one rather than the other?

Oates: I think the great divine form is the novel. I think there we approach as close to divinity as we'll get. As Lawrence says, "It's the great book of life." Everything's in it. Your philosophy—throw it in and see how it turns out in the scrimmage of life. Your religious beliefs—if you're a scientologist, throw that in a novel—as Gail [Godwin] did. You know, let it knock around, and so clearly its inadequacies are shown up. So the novel is my great consuming interest, and other things, I think, are perhaps peripheral, though when I'm working on them, I like them very much.

I find poetry quite hard. Poetry is difficult. I couldn't do the poetry riding in a car. I'd have to have the piece of paper and I write it in longhand, and it seems to take so long for the poems to have a shape. Poetry does call for a different consciousness—much more musical. While it can be intellectual, I think, in a strange way, it's non-verbal. Poetry is almost non-verbal. It's physical. There is something about the rhythm. Prose poetry is like that, too. But great scenes in

novels that tend to be visual are not really imagined in terms of language immediately—not by me. I *see* them, as in visions, and then I write them in language—as if I were reporting what I'm seeing. Poetry has to be language first. It *is* language.

Question: How do you cope with the volume of possibilities, between your own work and review requests and that sort of thing? Do you do it all, or do you have to be very rigorous in selecting what you do?

Oates: What I review?

Question: Reviewing or whatever. You seem to have so many imaginative possibilities in your own work.

Oates: Oh, it's very interesting. I believe in strange synchronistic events. Oh, it happens so often with me. I was just finishing a novel on religious experience where a man is very ascetic, and I have that inclination, actually. I think we all do—the strange, almost deathly pull toward asceticism. You know, denying the body and all that.

I worked through this, and it was very strange for me to be in that world of this fundamentalist religion, where this man was really hooked into the divine and it was like a heartbeat. Then the divine presence left him when he was about thirty-three years old because he had become arrogant and he is, like a tragedy, full of hubris and divinity left him. Now, I don't know whether objectively God leads people or whether it's a psychological phenomenon that just clicks off and they can't bring it back. It interests me so much. I can't begin to tell you how fascinated I was with that. And I'm still homesick for that novel. I dare not read the Bible again. It was getting to be too much. I'm not going to read it for a long time.

But immediately when I finished that, like a couple weeks later, *The Simone Weil Reader* came. And I was asked to review that. And, as you know, Simone Weil took the path of negation—a time-honored heresy, actually, at least in the Catholic church. She aspired toward Catholicism in a way. She flirted with Catholicism, but she did not get baptized. The Cathars allowed that one could starve oneself to death as a form of meditation, I guess, or

Joyce Carol Oates conducting a lecture as part of the St. Lawrence program at Saranac Lake, 1977.

"getting back to God," the idea of de-creation, that God creates you in the flesh, as Eve, for example, and all this puritanical stuff, which I don't really believe in. Flesh is evil, and eating and drinking and carnal experience is so bad, and … you've heard it all before. You can play it through on your own computer.

So to de-create the flesh, you just starve yourself and then you get more spiritual and you start hearing visions and the spirit flies up to wherever it's going. So I reviewed Simone Weil, and I re-worked all these things in re-reading her. I re-read that big book twice, and I was having all these arguments with Simone Weil in my mind. I finally wrote a review, which I think was supposed to be regular length of two or three pages, and it was, like, fifteen pages! I don't know whether it will come out.

So, it's an example of how I think the book just came, and it spoke to something I was really obsessed with at that time. Had the book come a year before when I was writing something else, I would have said, "Fine, I'll read it some other time. I can't review it right now. Thank you." But the reviewing usually ties in with something that I'm interested in.

Question: Do you think there's ever a possibility that a time comes when the writing becomes a substitute for really living?

Oates: For living. Yes. Yes.

Question: I'm talking about *instead* of really living.

Oates: Oh, yes, I think that's true, but I think that writing is not a substitute for living. It *is* living. Writing is a form of living. It's a form of experience. Anything that our consciousness partakes in is a form of nature. I don't see myself in my little bubble of consciousness to be any different whatsoever from the fish or the birds or all these creatures that are supposedly in tune with the universe—and humanity isn't? I think that's nonsense. I think whatever we do is human. Whatever we do belongs in the universe—simple as that. We are all part of this protoplasmic essence—perhaps it's divine, perhaps it isn't. But we're all part of it.

So if I write, if I want to write eighteen hours a day and not see my friends, that's living. That is just as legitimate as hanging out in the pub and talking with these people. I do not think, however, that a writer should be a cocoon or a host for the larvae of the work. That is, I don't think a person should allow himself to die because some parasitic kind of work is going to be written. Ezra Pound said, "Great poems must be written. It doesn't matter who writes them." That's a demonic theory—because it means that there are great revelations struggling to come into consciousness, and they will come through a certain fabric. It could be anyone in the room—and they will rent you or violate you to get through. Say, the Darwinian theory of evolution. You know how very neurotic Darwin was. Or Freud's theory. Or Jung's theory. Jung had to go through hell. He had to harrow hell to deal with, to integrate, his own theories, to be able to accept them.

Jung said that the great visionary artists are artists in one part of their psyche, and the humanity that's attached is secondary. It flows through you, and you are a vehicle; and if it's flowing through you, it means you're not controlling it. Rilke felt that way when he was writing these great mystical poems so quickly and they were coming *through* him.

If this happens to you, there is nothing you can do about it. You're just going to wake up in the play and you look and you see that the playbill is *King Lear* and you've got the starring role, and you're going to go out and have the revelations on the heath and then you're going to die. There's nothing you can do about it—it's fate. It's your destiny. I don't think you can control it. And you're in another play and you're eating and drinking and having a good time and you're Falstaff! You know, if you're Falstaff, you're not going to be Prince Hal. There's Hotspur and there's Falstaff, and they're just different.

Question: Unless you're Shakespeare.

Oates: Unless you're Shakespeare, and then you're "all in all," as Stephen Dedalus said. Yes, and since Shakespeare was the great arena for all these people, we think he could handle them all, but maybe not—maybe they were all handling him.

But anything you do is part of your life. Freud had a very simple-minded idea of human psychology. I'm going to say that without any fear of embarrassment. I really believe this. He thought that the extroverted personality was healthy and an introverted wasn't. That's ridiculous! The average extrovert has a very shallow soul. The average extrovert is miserable and just completely restless if he doesn't have a group around him. He's all alone in a room with a book or without a book. If he's alone at all, he gets very nervous. To me, that's neurotic. An introvert can go in a group for some periods of time and really have a good experience, and then an introvert retreats and goes into his own psyche and there communes with some other deeper level. To me, the introvert is a more healthy form, a higher form, of consciousness.

Freud thought that if you spent a lot of time away in your room writing or reading, or brooding out on the lake, that you were neu-rot-ic. If you were maybe in kindergarten, your kindergarten teacher would fill out this form and say, you know, "Little William Carlos Williams is sitting in the corner [laughter] and he's not playing with Buster and Billy out on the playground and let's send him out for therapy!"

You know, this is the American fallacy that the extrovert is healthy. The extrovert is not. The extrovert is like a child compared to the introvert. The extrovert does physical work in society and organizes things. Most politicians are a combination of both. Businessmen, too. Athletes are a combination. The average extrovert is somebody who does a lot of physical labor. Extroverts build the pyramids that introverts have designed. Architects, poets, visionary artists designed civilization. These other people carried it out. Somehow, it got turned about that the extrovert or physical or Hemingway-like character supposedly is healthier than the introspective person. But this is absolutely untrue, and we should reject it. You know, in the annals of American psychology, it is absolutely false.

Question: I can really appreciate what you're saying. I have a neighbor whose child is very quiet, you know, and likes to read. She said that she's trying to get him over it—as if it were an illness!

Oates: That is so American. It is so tragically American and so futile. The only good thing that comes out of it is that the isolated child in conflict with this peer group will develop a strong personality. You really do. You develop a hide like a rhinoceros.

I was talking with Ann Beattie yesterday and saying how when you first begin writing, I think, most people have a rather sensitive skin. It's natural. But then as the years go by, and the fifteen-thousandth review comes in, and they've said for the fifteen-thousandth time that you're a Gothic novelist or something—your hide is rhinoceros-thick. You know, nobody can get you upset except maybe with a flame-thrower at that point, or a buzz saw. I mean you've just got this tremendous hide all around you, and you have great elephant feet and tusks and a plutonium mask. You sit there and, not that you want to invite it, because you don't want that, either, but it is increasingly hard to wound a person who is scarred all over.

So the introvert develops interesting strategies for dealing with the extroverted world. Look at the great works that have come out of this, all these great works, the classic maybe being *Portrait of the Artist*. The real James Joyce was actually kind of extroverted. He was called Sunny Jim. He was very cheerful. It was his brother Stanislaus who was really introverted. When he wrote *Portrait of the Artist*, James Joyce said, "You know, I can't really make Stephen Dedalus a hero like me because I won medals in track." He was an athlete.

So, he went back to maybe his more essential personality, which was deeply introverted. He did away with the extroverted side so that *Portrait of the Artist* is a masterpiece of claustrophobia, where everything is filtered through this brilliant consciousness. It's an ambiguous portrait of an artist. I think that Stephen's brilliant. Other people say, "Well, he's a young man." It's true. But for a twenty-one-year-old man, he's rather brilliant. But he's not concerned with people out there whom he loves or hates. He's only concerned with love and hate in his own psyche.

Auden said, "If you are a young woman and you're in love with a poet, and he's writing love poems to you, be very careful. He's not writing about you, he's writing about his feeling." Moreover—I don't think Auden said this—but I would say, "He's not even writing about his feelings. He's writing about how he's going to structure his feelings in the poetry." So that the beloved is two or three steps over there, and by the time he's writing about it (and if it's all these evolutions that poetry goes through), it becomes something very different from the one-to-one relationship. All these are the absolute riches and rewards of an introspective life, an introverted life. The Kingdom of God lies within.

Christ said ... Christ was certainly an enlightened person who I think did have

problems …. [Laughter.] I don't want to sound simple about this because I've dealt with the whole thing over the past year. What happened with Christ? What was that? Christ means enlightenment. Like "the Christ"—"Jesus the Christ, Jesus the Enlightenment." He said the Kingdom of God is within, and that's true. The Kingdom of God *is* within. Whatever you mean by God—it *is* within. When you meet somebody else, it is the extent to which the divinity in your own soul is developed that allows you to relate to this other person. If you fall in love—and love and respect and honor someone very deeply—that love does not lie in the person, or floating in the air, but it's *your* quality. It's your own depth, which you are projecting. So that the quality of a person's love does not attach itself so much to the object (though naturally one needs an object that deserves it) so much as it is a reflection of the depths of one's own soul.

Question: Joyce, doesn't everyone also have to stress the other?

Oates: Yes. But I don't think you can even see the other person unless you've developed your own depth.

Question: Yes, but think how often the other makes that development possible.

Oates: That's true. It is an inner penetration. But, say, a very superficial and arrogant or even ignorant person confronted with a deep person will not begin to value that person. Let's have some examples from literary history. I think we could all come up with any number of lovers who were much deeper than the beloved. You know, characters who wasted their energies and their time, who pined away, because the beloved was really not worth it. It's because the one had developed the inner self so well or it had been developed in that person, and the object was not worthy of it.

Question: Do you think that's true in *Madame Bovary*? Her husband was boring. He was just boring.

Oates: Charles becomes very, very complex in that novel. He's a masterpiece of characterization. *Madame Bovary* is a brilliant novel. I can't read it without being moved. There are scenes where Emma is just walking her dog and the wind is blowing and the scene is this long, and it could be a scene in a movie by Bergman. Flaubert doesn't tell you what's going to happen or what is happening. He just describes the way she goes out with her dog. What kind of dog is it?

Question: A greyhound.

Oates: Greyhound! Yes. And the greyhound's restless and it's a sleek beautiful dog. (I haven't read this novel for ten years.) She goes out and it's beautiful, but then the wind starts blowing and her ribbons are sort of whipped around her bonnet and she starts home. Suddenly, that one page is so beautifully done that I get shivers reading it. It's all laid out there.

Emma has a very fine personality. I think that Emma Bovary is very deep. I think in her tragedy we are all potentially present. I think we all are very much like Emma Bovary. We are searching for the lover, the savior, who is in the outside world. At the end of the novel, Emma is completely distraught, and yet she thinks in her hysteria—before she goes in to get the arsenic—she thinks, *But maybe there could be a lover yet—somewhere a handsome man, a poet, maybe.* She dies really unenlightened.

I think that's the tragedy that we have to hold before us, those of us who may think that we know what we are doing. The Bovary tragedy, the search, the insatiable search, which in literature often symbolizes nymphomania is, in fact, a false search—a search for an outside confirmation of one's own self. I think that's a possibility of psychological despair for everybody.

JOHN HAWKES
& GAIL GODWIN

Before his death in 1998, John Hawkes wrote sixteen novels, including *Second Skin*, *The Blood Oranges*, *Adventures in the Alaskan Skin Trade*, and *The Passion Artist*. He was considered to be one of the most important experimental novelists in the postmodernist American pantheon of the latter part of the twentieth century. Educated at Harvard University, at the time of his death he was the T.B. Stowell University Professor Emeritus at Brown University.

Gail Godwin is the three-time National Book Award nominee and best-selling author of twelve well-received novels, including *The Odd Woman*, *Violet Clay*, *A Mother and Two Daughters*, *Evensong*,

< John Hawkes and Gail Godwin
at Saranac Lake, 1976.

and *A Southern Family.* (For a more complete bio, please see her interview beginning on page 167.)

This conversation took place during the conference at Saranac Lake in June 1976. The mood of the day was upbeat, and the jocular tone of the conversation between these two old friends brought forth much more laughter and general hilarity than can easily be captured in print.

Both writers opted to take extreme positions in order to show their primary alliances, but in many ways this was a mock argument, staged to highlight the dialectical aspects of the issue of autobiography versus pure style and invention in fiction. John Hawkes's position was actually more fashionable for the time, but, in fact, we have learned since that his own work was more autobiographical in some ways than anyone supposed at the time.

John Hawkes: Gail and I have decided that we'll each make a brief statement and then see if we can carry forward from the statements. We are supposed to argue. I have a particular problem with the subject, and I guess the reason I'm speaking first is inverse alphabetical order.

Gail Godwin: That's right—yeah. [Laughter.]

Hawkes: Right. I have a particular problem with the subject of "the place of autobiography in fiction" because I have no memory. The reason that I mention that I have no memory is that Gail assures me that she and I once had a very, very fervid, violent discussion on this subject, but I can't remember it. I hope you will be able to reconstruct it.

Godwin: I will. [Laughter.]

Hawkes: In my youth, in my lovely lost youth, when I was energetic and totally self-confident, and totally self-preoccupied, I would have said that there *is* no place for autobiography in fiction. That would have been my position—pure and simple. The reason I would have said that is out of a concern for purity in fiction. It has to do with what we want fiction to be, what we *expect* fiction to be. I expect it to be *vision*, pure and simple—the pure utter vision that focuses us back on the properties of the created work itself, in effect, on its structure and on its language.

In those main areas I find the essential delights of fiction.

I expect fiction to do something along the lines described by Nabokov when he said that he is not interested in any fiction unless it gives him "aesthetic bliss." The question is whether or not autobiography in fiction in some way threatens the possibility of aesthetic bliss, or whether autobiographical fiction is just as secure as any other kind of fiction in creating aesthetic bliss. I make it sound as if most fiction is not autobiographical. Now, in my middle age, I must say that, of course, I cannot hold such positions of purity, that obviously almost all fiction is in one sense or other vaguely autobiographical. I say that with great reluctance, and I'll retract the statement. [Laughter.]

It's hard to try to think of fictions that tend to be truly pure. I suppose Kafka, Poe perhaps. I was thinking of *Henderson the Rain King*. If we took a single writer—and Saul Bellow is probably essentially an autobiographical writer— Henderson in *Henderson the Rain King* did have a model in real life. Yet, *Henderson the Rain King* is a fiction, which when you read it would never call your attention to the role of the author within it or to authorial self-preoccupations within that fiction. You have only the vision of the fiction itself, and that seems to be part of the joy of it.

Such a novel as Djuna Barnes's *Night-wood* is, to my mind, pure fiction. It's a kind of work that when you read it, you simply have a shock and delight of the total immense creativity that goes into this neat little work. There is a phrase in it: "'Love,' she cried, and put her heart on a plate like the lopped leg of a frog." That's wrong. "Her heart *twitched* on a plate like the lopped leg of a frog." That, to me, is what fiction ought to do. It ought to make us feel our own hearts flopping about on a plate like the lopped leg of a frog. It ought to be just that great a shock, an illumination, a surprise, a pleasure, which always comes back to language itself.

But, on the other hand, much of the great fiction that we know—Conrad, Fitzgerald, Hemingway, who else?—all of these writers in one sense or another are autobiographical writers. And, in certain cases, some of the really great novels, like Malcolm Lowry's *Under the Volcano,* are magnificent simply in the sense in which they overcome autobiography and turn the life of the writer, or aspects of that life, into monumental gigantic fictions that we can all appreciate. I've probably said enough. Don't you think? I think I've said it all. I'm going to go home. I'm going to go home. [Laughter.]

Godwin: I think you did quite nicely for both of us. Now we can get right down

to the point, the place of autobiography in fiction. How much is a good thing? When does it destroy the illusion of fiction? And when does it give you that necessary emotional involvement with the writer? Now, I should state my predilection. I admire things like *Nightwood,* but I can't get involved when I read a sentence like "Your heart twitched on the plate" because I can see the author writing that and saying, "Boy, isn't that good." [Laughter.]

Hawkes: Oh, come on. That's an outrageous thing to say. [Laughter.]

Godwin: No. But there's another kind of fiction that I find myself more and more interested in, and that is where the author simply gives himself completely. Gives himself completely. Not a memoir. It doesn't have to be "bad," either. Something like, do you know Rilke's novel, *The Notebooks of Malte [Laurids Brigge]*? Well, here's probably a perfect marriage of autobiography, poetry, and fiction. What Rilke did—it took him ten years to write this—he decided he wanted to create a character, a young man becoming a writer, and you never know if he does become one or not. What he did—he was an Austrian, as you know—he decided he would make his character a Dane. When he finished the book, it was a completely imagined character, but the experiences in that book, he had taken from his own letters. He wrote to his wife, Clara. He spent most of his time away from her, apparently, because they had voluminous letters, and he asked for all the letters back. Who was that other one? The famous one—she was with everyone. Salome? Yes. And he got all *their* letters back. And then he went through them, and, for instance, the opening segment of the book in which he's living in the little hotel across from a hospital, that was taken out of his own letters. So he just took some experiences of his own, his preoccupation, for instance, with the prodigal son at the inn, that was also his own. But he gave them to this other character, this Danish man with a strange family. Ghosts would wander through the dining room. That seems to me a perfect blend.

Then you get something like Frank Conroy's book *Stop-Time*. Does anyone know that? Now that's another interesting case. That is, I think, pure autobiography. (I don't know him.) He just had to sit down and make sense of his life, and it took him a lot of effort. And since then, he's never written anything else except for one story that I've read—correct me if I'm wrong. It was in *The New Yorker*. It was about a man who had written one thing and couldn't write anything else, and he went to a psychiatrist and, I believe, the upshot of the story was that God

had told him he couldn't write anymore. He plays a piano in the Village now.[1]

Then you get another extreme case—Harold Brodkey. I'm doing extreme cases to sort of balance it out. Has anyone heard of him? Now, he seems to be able to perform these feats of memory. I've only read three things of his. One of them is quite powerful, about a boy who was raised by a foster mother and she kept saying to him, "Why don't you imagine what it's like to be me." He's a good boy, so he goes out in the forest one day and says, "I'm going to imagine what it's like to be this woman." And he has to start by being a girl. So he tries to imagine what it would be like to have breasts, and the only way he can do that is to find some fatty part of his body. So he takes his buttocks and he imagines them up in front and then he faints. It's a very powerful rendering of Harold Brodkey's own experience of doing what his foster mother asked him to do. That is an extreme case.

---

1 Frank Conroy (1936–2005) did eventually write a novel and other books. The novel was called *Body and Soul* and was well-received. He also published a collection of stories, *Midair*, and two collections of essays, *Dogs Bark, But the Caravan Rolls On: Observations Then and Now* and *Time and Tide: A Walk Through Nantucket*. But *Stop-Time*, which was a huge success and has become a classic of the memoir genre, was a hard act to follow. Conroy also served as director of the literature program of the National Endowment for the Arts and as charismatic director of the Iowa Writers' Workshop for many years.

What would interest me, and interests me, and interested me when I began writing, is the question: Why is it that in some fictions we don't mind when the autobiographical element sticks out at us, and at other times, it's just plain embarrassing or it sits up there like a wart or something? Now how can you assimilate things in your own life that you want to use? How can you put them into fiction?

Hawkes: Which comes first? The fictive-making impulse or the things in the life?

Godwin: That's hard to say.

Hawkes: Don't you think that, generally speaking, you *can* say? You can't say, "for instance"?

Godwin: Can you say?

Hawkes: Since I have been trying to argue against autobiography in fiction, which I obviously can't do … [Laughter.]

Godwin: Yes, you can. You did perfectly.

Hawkes: No. You just destroyed me. [Laughter.]

Godwin: I couldn't destroy you.

Hawkes: Last night, Russell Banks reminded me that thirteen years ago, he and I were both at Bread Loaf, and he reminded me that I had a similar discussion with Nelson Algren, who absolutely demolished me on this subject of autobiography in fiction. I was trying to argue the purist line, and Algren was saying that every writer must get out and research his fiction before he writes it. He was arguing this in a marvelous way. Nelson Algren was a terrific man. I don't know where he is now. His ghost must still be walking ….

Audience: He's not dead.[2]

Hawkes: No. I know he's not dead. But he was a ghost then. I think he's a ghost now—by which I mean any time of day or night Nelson Algren, in his black suit, is simply wandering through the trees, through the houses, drinking, whatever. I mean he was always there. He was a magnificent presence. I simply couldn't argue my purity line against him. Now, what was the point of all of this?

Godwin: Wait. Let's stop right there. I would love to know about your purity.

Hawkes: I was trying to say that now I have attempted, or at least stated, that I believe that the most interesting fiction is fiction in which the autobiographical impulse tends not to be visible at all, is not even of interest, *Lolita*, say, or *Pale Fire*, or *The Songs of Malderoar*, or some such weird

2 Nelson Algren, author of *The Man with the Golden Arm, The Neon Wilderness*, and *A Walk on the Wild Side*, died in 1981.

_I_'M LOOKING FOR THE PASSION THAT COMES OUT OF THE RECOGNITION OF HOW THE DIFFERENT ELEMENTS IN FICTION WORK.

fiction. But at any rate, let me say that we promised to talk about our own work, and as you were talking, it seemed to me that, in a sense, what we're talking about is the difference between the imagination as a transforming medium and the imagination as something that makes something new "out of whole cloth"—that ugly phrase that we used earlier out on the deck.

I believe, in a sense—as opposed to all physicists—I believe, in a sense, in the mystery of the imagination. I believe that it is, in fact, possible to write fictions which are so shockingly complete and new unto themselves that it is very difficult to find their sources in memory, if you try to do it. I'm now speaking out of personal experience, which means that you won't know what I'm talking about because I'm about the least-read novelist in the United States. But anyway. [Laughter.]

I wrote a novel called _The Cannibal,_ which is pretty much a vision of a hallucinated Germany, a neo-Nazi Germany, rising out of the ruins of itself at the end of a mythical Second World War. It's not autobiographical in any sense. But I want to confess that since my own interest is in fiction as self-made and self-standing rather than transformational, rather than coming out of a transformational imagination, I want to confess that the very first fiction I ever wrote, a short, surrealistic novel called _Charivari,_ came about when I had athlete's foot in Montana. [Laughter.]

The fact of the matter is that I had been trying to write poetry up until that point. Suddenly my wife, the girl who was about to become my wife, gave me a book to read while I had my feet in a bucket of potassium chromanganate, and I said, "I can write a fiction more interesting that this." So I began to write prose on a child's tablet. And ever after, I've written only on lined ruled paper like a child. Sophie and I were about to be married, you see, and we were twenty-two years old. So I wrote a novel about a middle-aged couple who were childlike. We were really childlike people about to get married. So my novel was about people who were middle-aged and had

John Hawkes and Gail Godwin
at Saranac, 1976.

been married for a long time but who were childlike and were childless. Had no children. And my father-in-law, my father-in-law-to-be, was a major in the Army. So in the book, the wife's father is a general and the mother is called the generaless. The father's father, my father, was not a parson, but my family was, in some sense or other, always religious to me. So I turned the husband's father into a parson, and the novel was how the parson tortured his son by making him lie on the kitchen floor, this forty-year-old man, and drop drops of water on his forehead. But, at any rate, it was a highly autobiographical novel.

Godwin: Did someone really do that?

Hawkes: No, of course he didn't do that. But emotionally I felt drops of water on my forehead. So I'm just confessing. We're all autobiographical novelists.

Godwin: I really am interested in getting back to your purity. I read an article or an essay on you, Jack, in Scholes's book *The Fabulators*.[3] In that you say that when you write, you sit down and you just kind of put words down to see where they're going to take you. Then, at some point, you're able to arrest your unconscious and then pull

3 *The Fabulators* by Robert Scholes, published in 1967, was one of the seminal critical books on what came to be known as postmodernism in American and British fiction. Scholes considered the work of Durrell, Vonnegut, Southern, Hawkes, Murdoch, and Barth.

it up, unaware, and then shape something. Now, I think that's utterly fascinating because I work in a completely different way. Yet I would love to try yours. In fact, I think I'm going to try it this week.

Hawkes: But it's utter nonsense, Gail. I've never said that and never done that. [Laughter.] I couldn't do that. I've never just put words down and then seen if I can make something out of the words. That isn't true.

Godwin: Well, then how does it go? What is your process?

Hawkes: Whatever I've written starts from a visual image or a fragment of a sentence, in a *sense*, overheard. Perhaps even a theme. I mean, *The Lime Twig* is based on a newspaper article that I read about legalized gambling in England, and I thought how disastrous that an entire country should base its economy on buying the dreams of its people. So I simply became obsessed with that idea. I had never been to England, and I tried to write a novel. I began about two young people whose lives are destroyed through the buying and selling of dreams. So I wrote a novel about a racehorse gang. But it isn't true that I … that sounds like automatic writing, you know.

Godwin: No, no, it's not meant to. In other words, then, you take an image …

Hawkes: I don't think it's in that book.

Godwin: It *is* in that book. [Laughter.]

Hawkes: Okay.

Godwin: Well, will you talk about your purity a little bit? This pure fiction that is not transformational and it's written with aesthetic bliss as its end. Talk about that a little bit.

Hawkes: What do you want me to say about it? It's hard to talk about it.

Godwin: Is aesthetic bliss enough?

Hawkes: Oh, yes. Is aesthetic bliss enough! I mean, is it possible to achieve aesthetic bliss? That's the question. I'm only looking for the passion, the excitement that comes out of the recognition of how the different elements in fiction work—the beauties of the language itself. I mean, that's what I care about—the language, the language, always the language, I suppose, as a poet cares about language. But you care about language, too.

Godwin: But, as I said in our walk yesterday, if it's necessary, I will risk a page of clichés to find out something that I didn't know.

Hawkes: See, that's a kind of risk. I think I take different risks. I assume, when I begin to write, that I don't know exactly where the fiction is going or what the fiction is going to be about. The last three short novels that I've written—*The Blood Oranges*; *Death, Sleep, & the Traveler*; and one called *Travesty* (which has been totally overlooked in this country—it's on sale now)—these fictions all began when I didn't know what I was going to write. I had nothing to write. Then, in each case, an image or an idea or a kind of phrase would come to mind, and I would begin to try to write. *The Blood Oranges*, for instance, is about two married couples who mingle their lives and their loves (as I will say in my reading on Sunday night), according to the jacket copy, in a kind of mythical Mediterranean country called Aleria. At least, this is a sex novel, but it's really about the imagination, not about sex.

We use the phrase "aesthetic bliss," but I think it's no accident that Nabokov is using sexual terms to describe imaginative products. I think there is a very close relationship between sexuality and the imagination. I think they work in similar ways—that's why pornography is necessary and justifiable and exciting and useful to talk about. It's part of the reason that *Playboy* is justified, too, I suppose. At any rate, what was I trying to say?

Godwin: I don't know.

Hawkes: I forget. You see, the beauty of the thing is that Gail can always be clear. I talk about purity ....

Godwin: I can't be clear.

Hawkes: I talk about purity and become completely muddled and obscure, and she tries to talk about something called "autobiographical fiction" with great lucidity.

Godwin: That is such a—you're just getting off the subject.

Hawkes: No, you were being extraordinarily lucid as you talked about those three novels and different ways that personal experience or memory functions within fiction, and I find it extremely difficult to be very lucid. I can only say that when I write, memory hardly functions at all. I do not write from memory. As I write, the vision itself seems to take shape and suggest where the narrative has got to go, and I try to pursue it. And try to make it. But it's not based on memory at all. Let's ask you how much of your ...

Godwin: No, I want to find out a little more about this process. You say you start with an image, and then you write and let it take you somewhere. Now some people, including myself, if they tried that, they would come to a great big halt ... after about a page or so. I've tried that and I would like to try it again. For instance, we were talking about Robert Coover this morning, who does this. He will write a story about the process of the story.

fiction international
St. Lawrence University
Writers' Conference
June 13-20, 1979

Joe David Bellamy (left) presents an award (a track trophy) for endurance to Robie Macauley for his five years on the faculty at the *Fiction International*/St. Lawrence University Writers' Conference at Saranac Lake, 1979.

In 1975, I was convinced that I'd done my lifetime servitude teaching at university writers' conferences. North Carolina, Colorado, Utah, Florida, Santa Clara, Squaw Valley—each one had its pleasant moments, its tedious stretches and, generally, a feeling of hopeless repetition. Thus, when Joe David Bellamy invited me to teach at the St. Lawrence/*Fiction International* Conference at Saranac that year, I had a hard time persuading myself.

My misgivings were wrong. What I'd arrived at, by sheer good luck, was a combination of one of the most beautiful settings in America and the most intellectually stimulating conference of all. I've now gone back to Saranac two more years. Meetings of this kind often tend to be over-organized imitations of academic routine. Saranac is like a week in the country with a company of friends carrying on an informal, continuous, frequently brilliant conversation about the creation of literature. People sitting and talking around a fireplace at night; people gathering on a verandah or a sunlit boat deck; a leading novelist such as Joyce Carol Oates giving a reading from her new work; the poet and Princeton professor Theodore Weiss speaking unceremoniously about poetry; another gifted fiction writer, Ann Beattie, talking about her *New Yorker* stories—these glimpses give some small sense of what the Saranac experience is.

And that Saranac conversation is very hard to leave at the end of the week. All year long, I have letters, snapshots, short story manuscripts, telephone calls from writers I first met there. They have a feeling of community and stimulation that other conferences seem unable to offer.

St. Lawrence University has added something new and original to American literary life and the teaching of writing. And everyone connected with St. Lawrence can take some pride in it.

—**Robie Macauley**

Hawkes: We were talking about Coover's story "The Magic Poker" in *Pricksongs & Descants*, and the story is simply about the process of writing a story. You think that's precious. I don't think so.

Godwin: No, no. I think it's precious ....

Hawkes: You mean his *concept* is precious.

Godwin: No, no, no. The *practice,* which is sort of out now, but in 1968 it was in, the *practice* of writing a story about writing a story—Barth, for instance.

Hawkes: Yes. It's a bit boring. But the problem is this: If you insist on the value of fiction, of those fictions that depend on memory, it seems to me that there is a presupposition that the value of memory involves verisimilitude or reflecting a reality that really exists around us. And that's the proposition that seems to me questionable. I don't think that it is very safe to assume that there *is* a reality around us that we want to reflect. There are those writers—and, of course, I should have mentioned Barth immediately—there are those writers who don't believe in that at all but who believe that fiction *creates* the reality, that whatever reality we know is, in fact, created by ourselves as people or by ourselves as fiction writers. So it's a question of what kind of reality are we talking about. "Memory" does seem to imply *reflecting* reality that is discoverable and tangible all around us. This other position assumes that, in a sense, there is no such thing, and you start out in a void and then try to create life to fill that void. That's what I think real life does anyway. It's all in a void—sometimes filled with lovely music—but it's a void nonetheless, and it's terrifying!

Godwin: Yes. Memory can be a trap. For instance, take a sentence: "We took a rowboat out to the island."

Hawkes: That's Coover's story.

Godwin: Is that the beginning?

Hawkes: More or less.

Godwin: Okay. "We took a rowboat out to the island." Well, here we're all sitting, and *there's an island out there* ....[1] Now, if you were writing this story, what *is* it that would make some of us say, "Well, now, let me see. What's going to happen on this island? Let's go with no preconceptions." And others of us would say, like Virginia Woolf, "Once, we went to the lighthouse." What *is* it? And can one do both?

---

1 Godwin is referring here to a small island that does, in fact, exist. It sits immediately across Upper Saranac Lake from the Canaras Conference Center, where the *Fiction International*/St. Lawrence University Writers' Conference was held.

fiction international
St. Lawrence University
Writers' Conference

June 13 - 20, 1979

On Saranac Lake in the Adirondacks

E. L. DOCTOROW is one of America's most respected novelists. Born in New York and educated at Kenyon College and Columbia University, he established a career in publishing, eventually becoming editor-in-chief of The Dial Press, while writing **Welcome to Hard Times** and **Big as Life**, before turning to a teaching career at schools such as University of California-Irvine and Sarah Lawrence. His third novel, **The Book of Daniel**, was nominated for the National Book Award; and his most recent novel, **Ragtime**, one of the most widely praised books of the decade, won the National Book Critics Circle Award. In 1978, he made his debut as a playwright with the N. Y. Shakespeare Festival Public Theater's production of **Drinks Before Dinner**, starring Christopher Plummer and directed by Mike Nichols.

DANIEL HALPERN is the well-known editor of **Antaeus** and the American Poetry Series published by the Ecco Press. He also edited **The American Poetry Anthology** and is Director of the recently established National Poetry Series, an endowed program to publish five books of poetry annually through participating trade publishers. His poetry has been published widely in magazines such as **Esquire, Partisan Review,** and **The New Yorker** and in the volumes, **Traveling on Credit, Street Fire,** and **Life Among Others,** published by Viking/Penguin. He has taught at Princeton and The New School and teaches currently, and is Acting Chairman of the Graduate Writing Program, at Columbia University.

JAYNE ANNE PHILLIPS is co-winner of the St. Lawrence Award for Fiction for 1978 for **Counting**, published by Vehicle Editions. She has also received a National Endowment for the Arts grant, Fels and Houghton Mifflin awards, and a Pushcart Prize for her work, which has appeared in many magazines, including **Gallimaufry, Iowa Review, Ploughshares, New Letters, North American Review,** and **Fiction.** Her collection of prose-poems, **Sweethearts**, was published by Truck Press; and her forthcoming story collection, **Black Tickets,** will be published this fall by Seymour Lawrence/Delacorte. A native of West Virginia, she has taught creative writing courses at Humboldt State University in California and at the University of Iowa.

JOE DAVID BELLAMY is publisher and editor of **fiction international**, a consulting editor for the University of Illinois Press' Short Fiction Series, and Director of the Conference. A widely published critic, reviewer, and anthologist, his books include **The New Fiction, Super Fiction, Apocalypse,** and **American Poetry Now;** and he has written for **The New York Times Book Review, The Washington Post, Saturday Review, Partisan Review, Harper's Bookletter, Quest, The Atlantic Monthly,** and many others. His collection of poetry, **Olympic Gold Medalist,** was recently published by the North American Review, and his poems have appeared in magazines such as **Paris Review, Iowa Review, Ploughshares, Prairie Schooner,** and **Poetry Northwest.**

CAROLYN FORCHE was born in Detroit, Michigan, in 1950. Her first book of poetry, **Gathering the Tribes,** won the Yale Series of Younger Poets Award in 1975 and was published by Yale University Press in 1976. Her poems have appeared in **The New Yorker, Antaeus, American Poetry Review, Ms., Dacotah Territory, Virginia Quarterly Review, Chicago Review,** and elsewhere, as well as in **The American Poetry Anthology** (Avon, 1975). She has been the recipient of National Endowment for the Arts and Guggenheim fellowships. For the last several years, she has been teaching at San Diego State University; and in the fall of 1979, she will begin teaching at the University of Virginia.

CHARLES SIMMONS is the author of three novels: **Powdered Eggs**—winner of the William Faulkner Award for a notable first novel, **An Old-Fashioned Darling,** and this season's widely reviewed and successful novel, **Wrinkles,** published by Farrar, Straus and Giroux. Mr. Simmons is an editor, and writes frequently, for The **New York Times Book Review.**

WILLIAM KITTREDGE is co-winner of the St. Lawrence Award for Fiction for 1978 for **The Van Gogh Field and Other Stories,** published by the University of Missouri Press. His stories have appeared in **The Atlantic, TriQuarterly, North American Review, Antioch Review, Iowa Review, Carolina Quarterly, Northwest Review, Ploughshares,** and elsewhere. He has been an editor of the literary magazine, **Cutbank,** and co-editor of two mass-market anthologies, **Great Action Stories** and **Great Detective Stories,** published by NAL. He has held a Stegner Fellowship at Stanford University and a National Endowment for the Arts Award and has taught for many years and served as Director of the Creative Writing Program at the University of Montana.

ROBIE MACAULEY, currently Senior Editor at Houghton Mifflin, was formerly editor of the distinguished literary quarterly, **The Kenyon Review,** and former Fiction Editor of Playboy. His long awaited new novel is forthcoming from Alfred A. Knopf. His other work includes **The Disguises of Love,** a novel, and **The End of Pity,** a story collection, as well as **Technique in Fiction,** a study of the craft of fiction widely used for college writing courses. His stories have appeared frequently in the **Best American Short Stories** and **O. Henry Prize Stories** anthologies and in magazines such as **Esquire, Playboy,** and **Cosmopolitan;** and his reviews and articles, in **Vogue, The New Republic,** and **The New York Times Book Review.** He has been a recipient of Fulbright, Rockefeller, and Guggenheim fellowships.

General Information

Special Guests: In addition to the resident faculty, several special guests appear each year for various lectures, workshops, or readings. Among this year's visitors will be: **Seymour Lawrence,** president of the Boston publishing house Seymour Lawrence, Inc. and publisher of Vehicle Editions, NYC; **G. E. Murray,** poet and an editor of The Paris Review; **Annabel Levitt,** poet and publisher/editor of Vonnegut,Brautigan,Donleavy, and Tillie Olsen; **Annabel Levitt,** poet and Poetry Columnist for Chicago Sun-Times Book Week; **Maxine Groffsky,** literary agent and an editor of The Paris Review.

General Information: The **fiction international**/St. Lawrence University Writers' Conference is designed for aspiring writing students and those seriously interested in writing as a career, for students of literature interested in how writers practice their art, and for free-lance writers seeking to sharpen their skills and gain insights about the current publishing situation. Instruction will focus on the art and craft of writing as well as on the editorial needs of fiction, poetry, and nonfiction markets and provide guidance toward producing marketable manuscripts.

Daily workshops in the novel, the short story, and poetry.
Lectures and panel discussions of: Recent Poetry; Writing a First Novel; Literary Agents; Women's Fiction; Book Reviewing; Magazines: Big and Small, Popular and Literary; The New Fiction; and other topics.
Eminently qualified staff of widely published writers and editors.
Close personal contact between students and staff in an informal setting.
Individual attention to manuscripts.
Unusual range of recreational opportunities.
Lovely natural lake-and-forest site and relaxed atmosphere.

...ference Center of St. Lawrence University—originally, family camps of the ...offers spacious accommodations for 70 guests on the ...nter include a central lodge with enormous ...comfortable residential ... are two

Financial Aid: No general scholarship aid is available for summer work. However, regularly matriculated college students taking a minimum of six credits during summer sessions at SLU or elsewhere, may be eligible for loan-funds. Inquire at your Financial Aid office.
Faculty members at colleges, universities, or at secondary schools, are frequently eligible for reimbursement-aid from their resident institutions for attendance at the Conference.

Houghton Mifflin Award: Established by the Boston publishing firm to encourage young writers of promise through their participation as Fellows during the Conference. Recipients are chosen on the basis of fiction submitted for consideration by **fictional international** magazine; and they must be presently enrolled in, or recent graduates of, selected graduate writing programs in the United States.

Seymour Lawrence Fellowship in Fiction: Established by publisher Seymour Lawrence to encourage fiction writers of promise through their participation as Fellows during the Conference. To be considered, a candidate must be nominated by an editor, publisher, literary agent, well-known writer, or college teacher. Nominations may be made informally in a letter to the Director. Supporting manuscripts of eligible candidates must reach the **fiction international** office by May 15th.
Fellowships pay all regular conference expenses, exclusive of travel.

Registration: Individuals wishing to attend the Writers' Conference should complete a Registration Form (or a facsimile) and return it with a $50 deposit to: **fiction international**/St. Lawrence University, Canton, New York 13617. Make checks payable to St. Lawrence University. The deposit will be applied to the tuition cost. Balance of tuition and fees will be collected at registration on June 13th at Saranac.

Register early: Conference size is limited. Students will be notified of acceptance on receipt of application and deposit. Deposit will be returned in full if enrollment is closed.

Room & Board

Fees: Tuition: $235 non-credit
$285 undergraduate credit (4 hours)
$310 graduate credit (3 hours)

The conference was a great thing for me. I was afraid of a whole week of writing, writers, thinking. But I enjoyed it. I really enjoyed it. I feel good about myself being able to enjoy this kind of thing. The food, environment, and people made it an experience that excited even a lazy bum like me.

—Mitch M., White Plains, NY

A good book, a pipe, and a wicker sofa.

There was a marvelous sense of community there,
a true harmony of personalities ....

—Joyce Carol Oates

interview with

ANN BEATTIE

Ann Beattie was born in Washington, D.C., and educated at American University and the University of Connecticut. She has taught at Harvard and is currently the Edgar Allan Poe Professor of Literature and Creative Writing at the University of Virginia. She has been a frequent contributor to *The New Yorker*.

At the time of her appearance at Saranac Lake in 1977, Beattie had written and simultaneously published two books, *Distortions*, a collection of stories, and *Chilly Scenes of Winter*, a novel. Since that time, she has published eight collections of stories and seven novels. Her collections include *Secrets and Surprises*, *The Burning House*, *What Was Mine*, and *Perfect Recall*, and her novels include *Falling in Place*, *Love*

< Ann Beattie at Saranac Lake, 1977.

Always, and *Picturing Will*. Her work has been included in four O. Henry Award collections and in John Updike's *The Best American Short Stories of the Century*.

Commentators from the audience include Theodore Weiss (bio footnoted, page 90), Gail Godwin (bio, page 167), Robie Macauley (bio, page 122), and conference director Joe David Bellamy.

Ann Beattie: When I started teaching writing at the University of Virginia, I noticed that a lot of the students' work was very neat, and it sort of frightened me in its neatness. What I mean by "neat" is not "technically perfect," but simply that the writing seemed to be very contained, unambitious, and *small*, in all senses of the word. People weren't taking enough risks, and these efforts didn't at all resemble my first attempts of writing, which were very sprawling and disconnected, with a lot of stuff going on in them that never finally tied up. (I didn't know how to tie them up when I first started writing.)

I began to try to think of some corrective or something that I could say to so many people who were doing what I thought was a mistake—limiting themselves too much at the beginning of writing, editing themselves before they got all the material out. I started thinking what was probably happening was that they were afraid. They were afraid of taking risks and making fools of themselves, and so they were editing in their minds before they put anything on paper. In encouraging them not to do that, I started talking about the *mystery* of the writing process and urging them not to be afraid of that mystery. If you pour out that mystery on paper, you can edit it *then*—but don't be afraid to put it down. Don't think of something large

or bizarre or important and then make it neat in your mind and *then* put it down—because that won't work. You have to get it *all* out—on paper—and then work with what you've written.

I started looking through statements that writers had made about how they write and about their art, and what I'm going to talk about today is the way that writing is an *unconscious* process—how much in the dark writers are when they write. Although I realize that there are some people who conceive an idea and then sit down and make a lot of note cards and make outlines and things like that and write perfectly well in that manner, I think a lot of people have the mistaken notion that you *have* to do that, that somehow because writing is a craft, it obligates you to do all those things and to outline the story or the poem as though you were taking notes on a history lecture. But I don't think that's the only way.

Here is some commentary by Joan Didion. She talks about how she writes, how she wrote her books. She talks about the pictures in her mind, and she says that she focuses on visual images and she follows the impulses, the directions, the pictures take her. Didon says:

"When I talk about pictures in my mind, I am talking, quite specifically, about images that shimmer around the edges. There used to be an illustration in every elementary psychology book showing a cat drawn by a patient in various stages of schizophrenia. This cat had a shimmer around it. You could see the molecular structure breaking down at the very edges of the cat: The cat became the background and the background the cat, everything interacting, exchanging ions. People on hallucinogens describe the same perception of objects. I'm not a schizophrenic, nor do I take hallucinogens, but certain images do shimmer for me. Look hard enough and you can't miss the shimmer. It's there. You can't think too much about these pictures that shimmer. You just lie low and let them develop. You stay quiet. You don't talk to many people and you keep your nervous system from shorting out and you try to locate the cat in the shimmer, the grammar in the picture.

Just as I meant shimmer literally, I mean grammar literally. Grammar is the piano I play by ear. Since I seem to have been out of school the year the rules were mentioned, all I know about grammar is its infinite power. To shift the structure of a sentence alters the meaning of that sentence as definitely and inflexibly as the position of a camera alters the meaning of the object photographed. Many people know about camera angles, but not so many know about sentences. The arrangement of the words matters, and the arrangement you want can be found in the picture in your mind. The picture dictates the arrangement. The picture dictates whether this will be a sentence with or without clauses, a sentence that ends hard or a dime fall sentence, long or short, active or passive. The picture tells you how to arrange the words, and the arrangement of the words tells you, or tells me, what's going on in the picture. It tells you—you don't tell it."

What Didion is saying here relates too to something that Flannery O'Connor emphasized over and over again when she commented on writing, which is that writing comes at us through the senses. When we write, we are writing through the senses, too, and almost everything that Joan Didion is talking about has to do with feeling. I think that maybe opening yourself up in that way and letting things come at you through the senses and writing *about* them through the senses is important.

The idea of mystery is important, too, and, most of all, the mystery that overwhelms the writer. Didion talks fur-

I'M NOT A SCHIZOPHRENIC, NOR DO I TAKE HALLUCINOGENS, BUT CERTAIN IMAGES DO SHIMMER FOR ME. LOOK HARD ENOUGH AND YOU CAN'T MISS THE SHIMMER. IT'S THERE.

ther in this piece about her floundering around with characters. She doesn't know why they're there. She writes scenes that, at first, seem random, and she includes small details (like emerald rings) that she doesn't know what she's going to do with. All that material starts out as a kind of mysterious confusion to her, but if you've read any of Didion's writing, you know that she doesn't communicate her uncertainty about that. Rather, she communicates a sense of inherent mystery very well. We feel that we're looking at something very mysterious when we read her, and the kind of spooky undercurrent that you sense in the writing is because she was spooked when she wrote it. She didn't know what was going to happen. It's like being possessed by something.

I have lots of quotations about being possessed. One of the best, I think, is from William Blake, who says:

"I am not ashamed, afraid, or adverse to tell you what ought to be told: That

I am under the direction of messengers from heaven, daily and nightly. But the nature of such things is not, as some suppose, without trouble or care. If we fear to do the dictates of our angels and tremble at the task set before us, if we refuse to do spiritual acts because of natural fears or natural desires, who can describe the dismal torments of such a state? I, too, well remember the threats I heard. If you who are organized by divine providence for spiritual communion refuse and bury your talent in the earth, even though you should want natural bread, sorrow and desperation pursues you through life, and after death, shame and confusion effaces to eternity."

It's good I can claim that Blake said that. If I came in here today and told you, "I am not ashamed, afraid, or adverse to tell you what ought to be told," it wouldn't sound so good. But it's true. Voices had better be talking to you in your head, and

Rapt audience in the Boathouse at Saranac.

that's scary. You don't go around saying, "I heard five voices today before breakfast. How many did you hear?" But, as Blake indicates, if you're going to write, you'd better be hearing them.

I taper off with Robert Frost: "Like a piece of ice on a hot stove, the poem must ride on its own melting. A poem may be worked over once it is in being, but may not be worried into being. Its most precious quality will remain its having run itself and carried away the poet with it." I think that is what Didion is saying, too—that all these images were coming to her. They were really running on their own legs, and she caught up with them.

She became the embodiment of them. She became a conduit to what was running underneath them.

I feel this way about my own writing. When I started writing, I thought it was sort of weird. I guess I was, to some extent, doing what other people did, even though the rough drafts of my stories were pretty large and sprawling. But they should have been even larger and more sprawling, and the legs should have been not only running this way, but this way, and this way, and this way, and this way, and all over the place.

There are so many directions that you can follow, and I think it's best to put it all out there and pick your direction rather than pick it in your head. Because when it's down on paper, it looks differently from how you've perceived it, and then you can choose more wisely. Because that's the way you're coming at people, not through your head but through this piece of paper with these little black marks on it for the words, the language.

Frost also says, "No surprise for the writer, no surprise for the reader." Flannery O'Connor emphasizes that, too, that there has to be some point in the story at which you're surprised, you're overwhelmed. Otherwise, your readers are not going to be surprised and overwhelmed. It clearly doesn't have to be somebody suddenly—*wham!*—jumping out of the bushes. It doesn't have to be quite that dramatic. But in effect it does. There has to be something that really does spring forth.

One thing that took me a long time to learn about writing—I think it probably took me about five or six years to learn—is pretty simple. I'm not the sort of person who writes with the beginning, middle, and end in mind. I'm writing with a character's name in mind or a line of dialogue or some feeling that I can hardly localize. I write very messy beginnings to my stories. I put a lot of things in there. I put in a sun that looks like a jar of paste. I put in a particular kind of wild flower. I put in an Irish Setter. I put in all this stuff that means nothing to me when I'm doing it. And then when I get stopped at the middle of a story and I don't know where to go, I flip back and I look at all that stuff. At that point, there will be some way I can start bringing those things in and tie the story together. Perhaps everything will disappear in the editing but the Irish Setter. But if I hadn't put it in there in the first place, the dog wouldn't have been able to save me. So. So much for my salvation by Irish Setters ....

If there are any questions that you want to ask, I'd be happy to answer them. After telling you about my professed ignorance of this whole artistic process, I'd be happy to try to answer your questions.

Joe David Bellamy: What writers who are in sympathy with your sensibility are alive and writing now?

Beattie: Let me consult my list—a writer named Stanley G. Crawford. [Laughter.] I won't tell you the titles, or you'll really start laughing. I was giving somebody a list yesterday of books to read, and the titles were indeed very strange, and the people's names were unusual—such as A.G. Mojtabai, who wrote a wonderful novel called *Mundome*.

Somebody commented that I had extremely long finger-nails and that I seem to be very unwilling to identify myself as a writer—which is true.

But, really, Stanley G. Crawford, gosh, he's wonderful. He's a sheep farmer in Arizona. He's written a couple of novels and a new one that's just being submitted now. His novel is called *The Log of the S.S. The Mrs. Unguentine.* For all the good that does you, I feel very much in sympathy with it. It's about, well, it's awfully surreal, but to say something reductive about it, it's about people who have a boat and who pull around a whole world with them, and it's not some nice fairy tale.

There are so many writers that I like now whose names are probably not well known. A.G. Mojtabai, I think, is an excellent writer, and her second novel is called *The 400 Eels of Sigmund Freud*—a great, bizarre, surreal thing. Another writer who I think is possibly the most brilliant writer writing today is Steven Millhauser, who wrote a first novel that was very well received and won a prize in Paris and was very well reviewed in the United States, but I'm not sure how

it sold. The novel itself was called *Edwin Mullhouse*,[1] and he's just written another that will be out in September or October, which is called *Portrait of a Romantic.*

Bellamy: Name three who are more recognizable.

Beattie: Well, Donald Barthelme. I enjoy a lot of his writing. Some, I must admit, I still don't get. But every now and then, he just knocks me over. That story that you mentioned, "Zombies," I thought was just wonderful. Then he had a story called "The School" that was out during the past year that I thought was marvelous. He keeps surprising me. I mean, when I think I have Barthelme pegged, suddenly he publishes another story and I realize that I really don't. He's worth the effort. Let me think who else is recognizable.

Well, I like a good number of Grace Paley's stories. I like Grace Paley's endings.

---

1 *Edwin Mullhouse*, published in 1972, is perhaps the best-known novel by Steven Millhauser, who won the Pulitzer Prize in 1997 for his novel *Martin Dressler*.

She's done a neat thing. She's done the same thing that O. Henry did that we all look at now and realize is a cheap shot. She's withheld evidence to the last minute, and then she lets emotion rush in. She suddenly just goes bang, and then the story's over. But she does it so uniquely. O. Henry often did it in a heavy-handed way. She pulls the same trick, but she's such a delicate artist, to my way of thinking.

Who else might you recognize? I like Joy Williams's short stories, and her novel *State of Grace.* There are so many others.

Gail Godwin: Tell us more about yourself and the *place* you work. I love this business about the Irish Setter. If that's not too private, could you give us a little picture of your going there—wherever there is?

Beattie: I'll tell where "there" used to be until two years ago, when my husband and I lived with two other people in a four-room house in Connecticut. I used to write on a *footstool,* and it was so cold in that house in New England. I had a three-cornered pillow, which was up against a radiator, and my typewriter sat on the footstool, and I would just sit there, with the plant gro-lights sending off an eerie lavender glow, and write.

Then I got a little money, then I moved, and now it's a room with six windows curving around it and about two hundred

plants. Actually, now it's down to about a hundred and fifty because I'm moving. Gesneriads have been propagated with great success. I have a desk facing out the windows, which I never look out of, and a huge electric typewriter, which is how I compose even first drafts. I rarely write anything by hand. Those of you who have seen my handwritten comments on your work will know that it's indecipherable.

Question: What about your fingers?

Beattie: My fingers? They type on the typewriter in the room with the plants. After midnight. Fingers come into action. Fingers go like this after midnight: "Get ready." Left hand makes this sort of a gesture. [Laughter.]

Question: I just meant—because your nails are so long.

Beattie: I type poorly. [Laughter.]

Question: Is it that you don't want your fingers too close to the words?

Beattie: Somebody was interviewing me—I hate to find out these things about myself because they're absolutely true. (My nails actually aren't too long now. They're usually longer.) Somebody commented on the fact that I had extremely long fingernails and that I seem to be very unwilling to identify myself in terms of being a writer—which is true. When I'm at a conference or something like this, I really feel weird. I feel like an imposter because it would seem just as likely to me that somebody would want to talk to me about the propagation of plants. Or, you know, washing dishes and, you know, how do you do it? I mean—anything in the world. But this seems a weird thing to have isolated—to appear as what I am appearing as here.

But the questioner said—very rightly—that it's my own personal attempt to distance myself from that image, not just that I don't want to present myself to other people as that. I don't want to be that in my own thoughts, so I grow these long nails, which provide a physical barrier between me and the keys—between me and the artistic process. Damn questions. I hate 'em. They pass judgment on my furniture. Ridicule my dog! [Laughter.] "The dog she thinks so highly of is a mongrel with one brown ear and one blue eye." [Laughter.] Glad *he* can't read!

But as for the actual writing process, it sounds odd to say I write at night, very late at night. It seems a spooky thing with the angels coming in the dark and hovering over the back of you or whatever. But I am really very lethargic until night. I'm just one of those people who have to build up energy all day, and I don't start going good until about eleven or twelve at night.

I usually write from twelve to three or four or something like that—but very sporadically. I don't work on a regular basis. I'm incapable of it. The most I ever worked on a regular basis is the few times I've been unfortunately overwhelmed by the necessity or impulse to write a novel, and I just want to get it done. So I just sit for eighteen hours a day until the thing gets done. Two out of three fail, and that should tell me something: I should take a break! But I don't. I don't have very regular work habits.

Theodore Weiss:[2] You speak very eloquently of mystery. Can you say something about the revision process?

Beattie: Yes. Sometimes the stories that I write really go through almost no revision at all—unless I write a long story. I don't usually write long stories. Most of my stories seem to be fifteen to eighteen pages, which I don't do consciously. The writing just seems to take that length. Those stories really don't require extensive revision, but when I get to thirty to thirty-five pages, I think I'm getting more toward a

---

2 Theodore Weiss (1916–2003) was editor and publisher of the *Quarterly Review of Literature* for nearly sixty years with his wife, Renee Weiss. He also was an award-winning poet whose works include more than a dozen books of poetry. In 1987, he retired from Princeton, where he was the William and Anne S. Paton Foundation Professor of Ancient and Modern Literature.

From left: Robie Macauley, Raymond Smith, Joe David Bellamy, Theodore Weiss, Joyce Carol Oates, and Gail Godwin at Saranac, 1977.

novel, which I know so much less about. It really does become very confused, and I try with those thirty-page stories to cut them down to fifteen, yet it seems if it hasn't come out as fifteen pages initially, it's almost impossible to edit to that.

But a lot of my editing is really throwing out whole pages rather than the kind of editing which is "this word is wrong" or "leave this sentence, strike this one, leave this one." I don't really do too much of that. Almost inevitably, the exact words that I think of when I'm writing the first draft are the exact words that will appear in print—with maybe one or two exceptions per story. But it's *the whole* I'm focusing on, the whole plot and the kinds of transitions that I make and the time, and maybe the tense will be changed from present to past. But I'm

really not one of those people who stares and stares at something and finally finds the actual words for it.

Question: You don't throw out whole pages—*now*, do you?

Beattie: Yes. I still do all that. I wouldn't know what to do without that working method. I just edit out what I'm not going to use.

Question: You were talking earlier about stories coming from images, a collection of images. Do you remember what they were, or could you tell us more about how you got started from there? With *Chilly Scenes of Winter*, for example?

Beattie: I'm probably more in the dark about that than with most stories. I think I'm pretty much in the dark about all that until people explicate these things for me. I don't really remember. *Chilly Scenes of Winter*—it's a good question. First of all, I guess, was the idea to use songs.

When you're writing, if you want to put music in, it's difficult because all songs seem appropriate. You know, it seems too contrived. If you're about to profess your love to someone in the story, "True Love" starts playing on the radio. It looks like a terrible contrivance on the writer's part, but you and I know that when we're about to profess love, "True Love" suddenly does come on the radio. I actually had one of my characters say this in *Chilly Scenes of Winter*—bespeaking my own dismay that this is the case. The character says, "You know all songs are always appropriate," or something like that. All those songs from the sixties were still knocking around in my head—that was one thing that made me write the novel. A lot of them didn't get in. Most of them didn't make the final cut.

The novel got titled *Chilly Scenes of Winter* because my husband had always liked Cousin Emmy's song called "Chilly Scenes of Winter," but that was nowhere in the book; so he wrote in a little scene where the character goes and plays that particular record, and then he wrote in a few lines so I could title the novel *Chilly Scenes of Winter*. It seemed like a good idea to me.

Other things, I don't know. The house that we lived in with two other people—I think the interaction between the two of them resembled aspects of the relationship between Charles and Sam in the novel. The eating scene at the table goes on for about eight pages, and they're leaving to get wine glasses and they're questioning whether they need spoons or not. Do you get a napkin and let the vegetables get overcooked, and in any case you forgot to bring water. These two people that we lived with were pretty fascinating. The meals were hours long, but it was never sitting and enjoying food. It was always running for spoons or bringing milk or taking something back that was burned and cooking it again and while he was waiting for that to cook, eating some bread, turning on the radio. These meals would just go on and on into the night with Beckettian dialogue. Actually, their whole lives resembled *Waiting for Godot*. I was in the middle of it and, I thought, functioning very sensibly while everything just stayed like this from day to day to day.

Weiss: You didn't know what you were getting into when you moved in with them?

Beattie: I knew. They moved in with us.

Weiss: May I ask you ... I'm a little puzzled listening to you read "Shifting" and watching the adroitness of that story. It's very hard for me to believe that that was all mystery [without revision].

Beattie: Sure was.

Weiss: I mean it's too, too artful, unless your mind by now has reached such a pitch of art that you don't have to revise—that's what we all hope for. Some of us were talking in here earlier. I said the athlete, who was a real athlete, doesn't watch his feet while he's running, of course. But before he runs professionally, he works very carefully *not* to.

Beattie: Oh, I'm sure [the apparent absence of self-consciousness comes from] all the writing that I've done. I imagine I've written two hundred stories. I imagine they taught me a lot, and I don't really realize as I go along what they're teaching me.

The thing is that these stories *are* coming from my subconscious, and I think that the subconscious can be a surprisingly organized thing. You know, when you dream, it's all there. I don't think there are many extraneous elements in dreams. Things really fall into place. I mean, there's obscurity—you have to wait until you wake up to analyze them. But it's all there. I mean, it's all there, as it should be. The subconscious has edited it—because you're not dreaming everything at once. So I think that, really, things do come out pretty "logically" from the subconscious. If you're lucky, things come out pretty logically and pretty much the way they're *going to be* from the subconscious.

When I started to write "Shifting," for instance, I had no idea why the woman was learning to drive a stick shift car, and I certainly had nothing in mind about using shifting as a metaphor and the sexual element that appears. In fact, I was thinking of my attempts and failure to learn to drive a stick shift. But why it should become fiction—that story—is unknown to me. That's not a story where I hid many things deliberately as I wrote. That was the only thing—that car—I just didn't know what to do with it. I started really caring about cars and writing about cars when I read Raymond Carver's stories. I was raving yesterday to somebody about what I think may be my favorite story of all time, a story called "What Is It?" by Raymond Carver, about a couple who's going to sell their car and declare bankruptcy—but the story's about much more than that. Cars are surpassing dogs in my imagination.

But some of these stories just do come out the way they come out, and the longer ones seem more confused. You know, it's hard to work with them and hard to know even when you look back what to throw out and what things carry the right connotations at the beginning.

Bellamy: Do you think of yourself as an absurdist?

Beattie: No.

Bellamy: And neither is Diane Arbus?

Beattie: She's not an absurdist. She's a great realist. Arbus's photographs really fascinate me, and sometimes I have scenes in my stories I imagine as parallels to Arbus's photographs. In my story "Dwarf House," there *is* a dwarf. In fact, there *is* a dwarf house, a house full of dwarves, and there is one giant who lives in the house. He's just there—no explanation. The way society *does* that if you're an outcast .... The way if you are, you know, in an orphanage or something like that, they'll also bring in some kid who has the measles because they don't know where else to put that kid. But, at any rate, suddenly there was a giant there, and I did have a particular giant in mind. He was the one from Arbus's photograph that's titled "A Jewish Giant at home with his parents in the Bronx, N.Y. 1970." It's a terrifying picture of a very sad, huge giant and little parents standing around a depressing living room that might be too small for him, but that could annihilate anyone's soul.

Weiss: When you're not writing, do you do anything—other than live?

Beattie: Well, I don't go around consciously thinking about what I might write. I don't do any of that. I become more and more tense if I don't write. I

mean, not necessarily biting my fingernails type of tense [laughter], but a kind of tension in my mind. [Laughter.] Bad analogy. They're not that odd! [Laughter.]

Weiss: No, but you will admit they don't look bitten.

Beattie: [Jokingly] I nibble on them with long teeth that curve around to the side.

I think I can only go so long without writing, and it doesn't bother me for a week or two. Sometimes it's not bothered me for six months, and then suddenly, "You better get at it." Also, my husband's very good about that. He trails me around the house and keeps a record of exactly how many hours and places I've been since I've written something to amuse him.

Chilly Scenes of Winter would never have gotten written if it hadn't been for my dear friend David Wiegand because I wrote about fifty pages, and I knew that was a very unmanageable length, and I knew my editor in New York was just going to beat his hands on the desk and then crawl under it when he got something that length. I didn't know what to do, so I read it to David and said, "How can I edit this?" He said, "Don't do that, just write 'Chapter Two' and keep going."

So it got to be every night's bedtime story. You know, *read the bedtime story*!—the chapter that had been knocked

I'VE RIPPED UP MORE THINGS THAT LOOK LIKE THEY MIGHT BE THE STARTS OF NOVELS THAN I CAN TELL YOU.

out over eighteen hours that day. One of the best compliments in my life also was when I was reading something that I thought was a pretty funny section of *Chilly Scenes of Winter*, and I looked over and my husband had put the pillow over his head and pulled all the covers up. He didn't want to hear it. "That's enough of that book." [Laughter.]

It's funny when something hits me and, as I say, I don't know when it's going to. When school let out at the University of Virginia, I wrote two thirty-page stories in one week. Before that, I hadn't written anything for four or five months. That's the way it goes. Once I get going, it's hard to stop. I stop myself simply because of fatigue. I need to write a lot. I hate to write a lot. I literally, you know, go like *that* with the typewriter and get up and leave it because I could stay there and just keep doing it. I've ripped up more things that look like they might be the starts of novels than I can tell you. Or failed stories. I have the beginnings, and I must have a stack two feet high, of

things that didn't work out that I knew by page two or three weren't going to work out. But things that are even two or three pages long that I think might have the possibility of being a novel, I actually rip into confetti. I really don't want to write novels.

Weiss: Do you ever go back to some of these?

Beattie: No. No. I think maybe once or twice there might have been a line or something like that, but really in a pile that big, that's all it's ever been for, using that material that's put away.

Question: Do you feel pressure to write novels?

Beattie: Pressure to write novels? No.

Bellamy: If it weren't for *The New Yorker*, would you?

Beattie: If it weren't for *The New Yorker*, would I? I guess so. Yes. I guess I'd be one desperate creature if it weren't for *The New Yorker*. Guess I'd feel the pressure to be a waitress at night and everything else that writers do to live.

Weiss: When you deal with students, when you tell them to get loose in their imaginations, do you give them any help to loosen them? Because it's one thing to tell people "Don't be afraid," but when you push them in the water, what do you do?

Beattie: I guess I don't. Individually, I'll back people into a corner as much as I can, but I don't have any manifesto, like "Learn yoga" or something to tell the class. I wish I did, and I probably should have something. I mean, there are a lot of people I know who teach writing by assigning exercises that *they* consider to be liberating exercises. But I just won't do that because I think if you're serious about being a writer, you should be a writer. You shouldn't have somebody concoct exercises for you to do. I'm very suspicious of that way of teaching writing.

I'll sit down with a student individually and say, "Bullshit, this isn't what you really think. What would the situation really be like?" If they don't start telling you the truth after that, I think they probably don't know the truth, and the best thing to tell them is just to give up the story rather than to keep rethinking .... I don't know how to teach writing.

Question: You say there are certain ways of loosening that you do approve of?

Beattie: Oh, he [Ted Weiss] was going back to what I said when I started talking about how things seemed to be coming out automatically edited, which seemed to me unfortunate because they were losing so much. I really approve of writing a lot and then editing it, rather than editing in your mind. People are so afraid of making a mistake, but the real mistake is one of too much caution. It's a natural mistake to make and is a hard one to get over. I just don't know any easy way to get over it.

Weiss: We have more and more workshops to tell students where they're going wrong .... It's quite paradoxical, I think.

Robie Macauley: Don't you think that's a reaction against the early workshop tendency to be very precise and learn how to write the well-made story?

Question: The tidy story. Yes—the tidy story.

Beattie: If you really think about it, though, what can your imagination do to you? I mean, there is no reason you should be afraid of your imagination because it can't hit you, it can't take food away from you. It can't do anything ....

Weiss: No, but as Gail was saying, it can take you over the edge.

Beattie: Yes, I guess. When people were talking about that a couple of days ago, I was listening with great interest because I really have never felt that close to the edge.

Weiss: I haven't either. But I see people.

Beattie: Yes. I see people.

Bellamy: I'm sure this is a very naive and subjective statement, but it seems to me that different people have very different attitudes when they look down or dive down into their unconsciouses. I was struck last year with John Hawkes's feeling about his own unconscious. He seemed to feel that whatever was there was *terrifying*, and he embodied that fear so thoroughly, it made an impression on me. It was especially striking because I realized I didn't feel that way myself. I feel the unconscious is nothing to be afraid of, and somehow it's even a funny place.

Beattie: Yes. That's interesting. I do think of my unconscious as being out of a cartoon strip or something. What's running around in my unconscious are dwarfs and giants and spacemen and things like that—not anything that's going to get me.

Weiss: But reality is catching up with you.

Beattie: Then again, I think of those things as being like a comic strip. I keep seeing things in frames.

Bellamy: All those images of drowning, or going too deep and perishing, going mad and all that stuff really seem alien to me.

Beattie: Yes.

Weiss: Certainly Joyce Carol Oates made it sound convincing, from her point of view.

Question: What about dealing with things that are painful to you? Everyone has stories that need to be written, yet they are so intrinsically painful or horrifying that you avoid them, if possible. Yet those may be the most mysterious and most interesting occasions of your life.

Beattie: Well, personally, the way I write, my stories are not very autobiographical at all. They're a lot about things that have happened to friends or that I know have happened to people. Those things are painful, but because it's not really me that I'm writing about, it's easier, automatically, for me to write them. I also don't write the story exactly as I heard it. It's fiction.

Question: Are you evading those other things?

Beattie: I don't think so. No. I don't think that if I were to write autobiographically that I would have anything very interesting to say, and I don't think that's because I'm evading anything. I think it's because I get up in the morning, I drink a cup of coffee, I teach my classes, I clean my house, I go to bed. You know, what's there? Where are the dwarves? [Laughter.] Where are the little ones stalking me?

Question: But you haven't learned to drive a stick shift yet?

Beattie: I certainly have *tried* to learn many times. Yes. [Laughter.] Many, many times.

Question: You haven't found the right instructor.

Beattie: That's the good way to look at it. That's the way I like to look at it. Bad instruction. I think now it's something mystical I'll never grasp. [Laughter.]

I certainly admit that there is a lot of pain in my stories, but it's just not my personal pain. I guess that's why I can handle it. If I do have a great deal of personal pain, it's on such a level that it's not conscious enough to me—even in the unconscious—to write about. There may be little bits and pieces. There are things that I put in my stories that I know would be painful for people to read—I mean, things people have told me that I've taken out on rare occasions.

There was one thing that I took out of a story that I consider to be one of the best scenes I ever wrote, which was at the end of a story. It was about

one of my relatives, a woman I've al-ways thought of as being very cold and formidable. My mother said to me once, something in passing. She had lived with this woman for a while, and this woman had been married for a period of about two weeks. Nobody knows what hap-pened, but my mother said that one of her memories—and this is my mother when she was six or seven years old—was coming home in the day and seeing the new bride, with her long hair flying out behind her in the sunlight, being chased around and around the dining room table by her husband. I thought, *Wow.* I mean, not only did it completely alter my perceptions of that relative, but what a scene.

I took that out, not because I thought the person would recognize herself as the one who had been chased. But it was just too horrifying. It was too close to me, because it was a relative, even though a distant relative. Or maybe, in some way, I thought there would be a possibility that she would recognize herself, even though it seemed a really outside chance.

Other times, I've put terribly painful things my friends have told me in stories and then forgotten them until that mo-ment when they call me and curse me for having done that to them. One case is the ending of a story I wrote called "Tuesday Night," which is about a woman who is divorced who's living with another man, and by the end of the story, it's pretty clear that the other man is going to leave. As he is getting ready to start the dis-cussion about leaving her, she suddenly thinks back to her first husband and how he said he was leaving. He had been in such a terrible state that he was riding on a country road, and as he came to the top of the hill, he looked at a huge yellow tree and realized for the first time that it was autumn. Period. End of story.

This is exactly what a friend told me about a bad period in his life, and he happened to be at my house when *The New Yorker* arrived, and he read through it and threw the magazine down, and said, "Damn it, I never knew I told that to anybody!"

You have to be nasty and just grab ev-erything that's material. Your unconscious may not get you—your friends might.

Question: It's not something you would do if your friend told you not to?

Beattie: No. I wouldn't do that. That's playing unfair. But other things. I have to think that people tell you those things because they want you to remember them. So why not remember them in the pages of *The New Yorker*?

Bellamy: What would you like to accom-plish over the next forty years?

YOU HAVE TO BE NASTY AND JUST GRAB EVERYTHING THAT'S MATERIAL. YOUR UNCONSCIOUS MAY NOT GET YOU—YOUR FRIENDS MIGHT.

Beattie: I don't have any sense really that I'm going to *be* here for the next forty years. I don't have any sense of that. If I live through Harvard [where she was going to teach] next year, I'll be happy. I don't know really—you mean in terms of writing? I'd like to learn how to write a novel. I'd really like to do that. I don't know how to write a novel.

Chilly Scenes of Winter really doesn't please me as a novel, because I look at it as just another story. It was written in such a quick period of time, and I devoted no more time to that novel really than to a long story I had in *The New Yorker* called "Colorado." It's funny, too, to be identified as Ann Beattie who writes short stories and *a novel*. You know people have that sense of it: You write poems or you have a *book of poetry*. You know, that whole thing that people do. But *Chilly Scenes of Winter* seems just another one of my stories, and certainly not one of my most accomplished.

I was also very displeased because when the reviews started coming out of *Chilly Scenes of Winter,* people kept picking up on the hype Doubleday had given it as being a novel of the sixties, which was so far from my intention. I suddenly realized they were doing this, in part, because people desperately wanted a novel about the sixties. Had I known that, I fancied that I could have written one. I should have written one. I mean, it just never occurred to me to do it .... Too late!

Bellamy: It's not too late.

Beattie: Well, I mean, the other novel that I would write about the sixties would be too similar, to my way of thinking, to *Chilly Scenes of Winter*—because there is some of it in there, but it's such a minor thing.

Question: Chekhov couldn't write novels either. I wouldn't worry about it.

Beattie: I *do* worry about it. It doesn't help me to hear of Chekhov's problems.

Question: How did you get started being accepted at *The New Yorker*?

Beattie: Hmmm—I don't know.

Weiss: You were accepted quickly?

Beattie: No. I started mailing stories off to *The New Yorker*. I probably mailed them stories for two years. I had twenty consecutive rejections from *The New Yorker*—but very polite. I mean, from the minute I sent something in, I didn't have an agent, I didn't know anybody. I simply put a story in an envelope. It was actually done for me. My friend put a story in an envelope and mailed it off to *The New Yorker*, and I got back a letter from Roger Angell, who is my editor, saying there were things he liked in my writing but that they weren't printing it but to send

everything in the future directly to him. So I sent him twenty stories. He wrote on and on about what good stories these were and how he wasn't printing them.

Letter number twenty said, "Dear Miss Beattie, You must realize by now that you're an excellent writer. Clearly *The New Yorker* is not your market, but there are others. Best of luck in the future. Sincerely yours." I was *enraged*. I figured, what more do you want? This is … this is impossible to expect a writer to be anything but excellent. The hell with you, buddy. So I fired off a letter, sent him another manuscript, figuring well, at least I'll take five minutes of your day. So they bought it. [Laughter.]

Question: What did you say in the letter?

Beattie: Oh, I said that there were *not* other markets and listed to him what was happening with magazines and told him while I did appreciate very much the time he had spent with me. One of my favorite letters came from Gordon Lish, who was fiction editor of *Esquire*: "Dear Miss Beattie, I believe it is the writer's obligation to do more than chronicle the dreary days of her dreary characters. Sincerely yours." [Laughter.] I *loved* that. I think it's wonderful. He writes me now saying, "I have received your latest dreary story." [Laughter.]

Weiss: That's the kind that should go in your *Collected Letters.*

Beattie: It's really funny, though, because I have all the letters from the first "Dear Miss Beattie" letter to the ones now that say "Look Ann." They start out "Look Ann." Occasionally, letters now say, "I enjoyed your story very much. You're really going in a new direction. To save you embarrassment, I have not circulated it around the office." [Laughter.]

Was I ever vindicated, though, because when John Updike reviewed my novel, he sneaked in praise for one story, and it was a story the magazine had rejected: "It's Just Another Day in Big Bear City, California."

Question: But they didn't help you?

Beattie: In editing? Yes. Very helpful. Roger is an excellent editor. I can't imagine having written the way I write without his editing. He's really a great editor. I imagine that can also be terrible, though, if a person isn't in sync with his or her editor.

Question: Well, how much can they do to you?

Beattie: Well, how much *do* they do? Sometimes they do a lot and sometimes, as I say, I'll write a story with little revision and they'll print it with only a little more revision. It just depends. Sometimes they think it will be better to put something in the past tense rather than the present tense. They don't do the kind of "take out this word, put in this word" editing. But I write a lot of stories in which, initially, there's a confusion in the time sequence. I have trouble going from past tense into present and present into past. I don't work hard enough on it, I guess. They're very meticulous about such changes.

The other thing is that, to my way of thinking, they ask for a great number of specifics in terms of exactly what people look like and where something is happening. I didn't used to think in terms of whether a story was happening in Manhattan or the Adirondacks. But I think it's really helpful to have this sense of where exactly it's happening, and they've sort of insisted upon that and have beaten that into me. I guess, in a way, they've beaten "spacemen who come to Earth to take pornographic pictures" out of me.

Question: What happened to the twenty stories they rejected?

Beattie: I guess they're around somewhere. I mean, they're not being sent out now.

Weiss: You didn't send them elsewhere?

Beattie: Yes, I finally got an agent, and she did send them elsewhere, but nobody bought them. Almost no publication buys anything from me now except *The New Yorker.* I rarely sell anything anywhere else.

Question: Do you have a sense of the difference between the twentieth story and the twenty-first?

Beattie: No. I think when I first started sending stories to *The New Yorker*, they were all right. I mean, I think I deserve to have gotten their attention. But I think the twentieth is better than the first, though maybe from the fifteenth to the twentieth, they were all on an even par.

Weiss: Do you think it was attrition or actual improvement? This is a serious question.

Beattie: Attrition—no. No. Never. No.

Weiss: No, but it's a serious question. Because if you bombard a magazine, after time, a fix occurs. You know, they anticipate what you are going to do, and probably if you go beyond it, they may not recognize it. On the other hand, you clearly are proving that it does pay to keep beating after them.

Beattie: I think if you're talented, it pays to keep beating at them. But if you're not, I mean, there's just a lot of beating done of poor editors who …

Weiss: What writer knows that?

Beattie: Yes. Well, I don't know. I mean, I think, for instance, Donald Barthelme's being the success that he is now is that he's educated the American public. He's educated editors. There's one case in point. I think that having written that much, he's taught people how to read him.

Weiss: And you probably did that on your own behalf.

Beattie: Well, I might have. I must say, Roger Angell was more skeptical about things that I was writing [early on]. If I wrote those same things today, maybe I wouldn't get the same objections from him—or perhaps I'd be handling those things much differently now. I was sending him spaceman stories and dwarf stories, and he kept writing letters about how he wished I would write out of my own experience. Now I write things out of my own experience, and he says, "So and so is going to know that!" You know. "Take that out!" [Laughter.]

It's funny, too, at *The New Yorker*, fact checking always seems to have the attitude that you're putting one over on them, and a lot of times they'll actually become very adamant that I change the name of a minor character because they *sense* that that might be a real person who's going to cause problems and object. Inevitably, those are made-up characters, and the things that I *do* slip through …

There are occasionally mentions of real people, sometimes even with their first names and actual situations that have happened to them, but I don't know these people directly—I've heard about them from a friend, for example, and their story has stuck in my mind. The magazine doesn't tend to question those stories when I mention them. I never make those people or those stories my main characters or situations. I sometimes sit there *just like this* when the story is being edited by *The New Yorker* now. Are they going to see? It's like the kid with the cookie behind his back. Are they going to notice my arm's bent? [Laughter.]

interview with

ANNIE DILLARD

Annie Dillard first came to national attention with her 1975 Pulitzer Prize-winning book, *Pilgrim at Tinker Creek*, a narrative set in Virginia's Roanoke Valley. Since then, she has published *Holy the Firm*, *Living by Fiction*, *For the Time Being*, a memoir about her parents titled *An American Childhood*, and a novel called *The Living*. Her new novel, *The Maytrees*, was published in June 2007. As a poet, Dillard is author of two collections, *Tickets for a Prayer Wheel* and *Mornings Like This*.

This interview was conducted during the conference in 1978. Commentators from the audience included Rosellen Brown (bio, page 150), Margaret Atwood (bio, page 21), Robley Wilson (bio footnoted, page 112), and conference director Joe David Bellamy.

< Annie Dillard.

Annie Dillard: Everybody is smart. Every Tom, Dick, and Harry is smart. You see so many people trying to slide by because they're smart. They are smart enough to learn that they're smart. They're not quite smart enough to have discovered that everybody else is smart, too. Everybody is smart. The whole race is smart. The only difference between people's abilities is in the raw materials they have in their minds. That's how educated they are.

Now, it's a cruel thing to insist that there is no such thing as talent. We all want to believe—at least I do—that being selfless was easy for Albert Schweitzer, that Faulkner just naturally poured out the novels that came popping into his head, that Rembrandt and the people who paint, paint because they have to. We want to believe all these nonsensical things in order to get ourselves off the hook. We don't have to worry about being that way because we're obviously not that. *We don't have the same habits.*

I maintain that the people who've made something of their lives, the Pasteurs and the Gamoffs and the Cézannes and the Melvilles, were neither more talented, nor more disciplined, nor more energetic, nor more driven than the rest of us. They were simply better educated. The trick to doing something with your life is to be very well educated. Some of those people did it the hard way, study-ing all these difficult works on their own alone in their homes. Others did it the regular way and went to school and went to graduate school and so forth. But you won't find any of them who haven't stud-ied. In American literature, there is a myth that the writer just pops out of no-where and spontaneously utters all these things freely on the page.

Recently, they found a big trunk of Whitman's possessions, and it was a trunk in which he had all his papers he had col-lected during his entire life. They dis-covered, reading these papers, that what Whitman had done his whole life was never leave the house. But he would go over and over all these little pieces of paper and study things and read things and write things down and write endless journals. He wrote emotional journals about how he could make it seem to other people that he was always outside. He was completely conscious of doing this all the time. He never left the house! He was a scholar. He spent all his time with his papers.

The same with Thoreau ... Thoreau was this very well-educated man who read Greek, whose reading was almost entirely in the Greek classics. Everybody thinks he came along and, with the blunt end of a crayon, wrote *Walden*. He was a Harvard man!

I'm trying to think of the ones where the myth is really strongest. Hemingway!

THE ONLY DIFFERENCE BETWEEN PEOPLE'S ABILITIES IS IN THE RAW MATERIALS THEY HAVE IN THEIR MINDS.

You know, Hemingway spent all of his time studying Turgenev, studying Sherwood Anderson. What else did he study? Chekhov. So, for some reason, people think that in order to be like Hemingway—instead of doing what he did that pertains to his writing, which is learning about something—they think they should do what he did in his leisure time, which is completely irrelevant. I mean, it is totally and utterly insane. You know, it's like saying if you want to write like Jane Austen, comb your hair.

People often ask me if I discipline myself to write, or if I work a certain number of hours a day on a schedule. They ask this question with envy in their voices and awe on their faces and a sense of alienation all over them, as if they were addressing an armored tank or a talking giraffe or Niagara Falls. We all want to believe that other people are natural wonders. It's no discipline! It's no hardship on you! You do it … you do it for love. You care about the thing by then—your stakes in it are absolutely enormous—and you do it for love.

If you had a baby and the baby couldn't sleep through the night, and you had to get up once or twice a night to feed the baby, it would be a total drag. But it wouldn't be this horrible discipline you would impose on yourself. You wouldn't say, "I've got this externally imposed regimen. I must feed this baby. I'm a human wonder." It has to be done. Somebody has to do it, and you do it.

People lift up cars for love. It's a possibility for life to work that hard. It doesn't mean that you have to work that hard all your whole life or you're not real. It's just a possibility for certain times of life. You're not going to spend your whole life lifting up a car. Your baby's going to outgrow its needs. Pretty soon, your baby's going to sleep through the night. You don't choose that as a way of life because you're Superman. It just comes along that you can, yes, that's a possibility, you can work that hard. But it's no incredible discipline that super writers impose on themselves because they're real writers.

If you learn something, then you love it. Then after you love it, then you'll do it. So the people have the relationship wrong, I think, when they keep saying that you learn by doing. I think you do by learning. First you learn something, and then you love it, and then that love will tell you what to do about it. So if you feel crummy and don't like anything, then you should go learn something. Then you'll love it, and then love will tell you what to do, and then you won't feel crummy anymore because you'll be doing something. In a profound way, we *are* what we love—it individuates us more strongly than any other thing. Our emotions are all pretty much alike. But the loves that are very, very specific to us—those are our strengths, those are why we are here.

If you guys are going to be writers, it's all very well to have the sound of literature in your heads. Most of the problems with stuff I see in the students is just a matter of literary judgment. That's what the book reviewers say—*literary judgment.* "This person's literary judgment is impeccable." What they mean is taste, which is a damnable term. It's a class term. It's a horrible term, taste. But the fact is, you know, if you're cringing when you're reading something, the writer needed more literary judgment, and that's a product of an educated mind. It doesn't matter in the whole world what it's educated in. Computer terminology used to say: "Garbage in, garbage out," referring to, you know, what you feed a computer. A computer can only process what you have told it about the world. That's all your mind can do, too.

So if you sit around reading every little new novel that comes flying off of the world, then you write one of those flying little novels that comes off of the world. You can't do anything more than what's in your mind. Where your treasure is there should your heart be also .... That's about it.

Question: What about motivation? When you talk about loving what you're doing and that becoming the motivation ...

Dillard: First you learn it. You can't wait around to be hit by love. You can't wait around to be hit by anything. That's how you let your life go by. You go learn it first, and then you'll love it.

It's just like a course of study. "Oh, seventeenth-century poetry, well, I didn't like it at first, but now I like it." That's what you say when you're in college. "Oh, I didn't like this course at first, but now I like it." What it means is: I'm getting to learn this material to see what it is. Now I like it. Your heart then enters. Then you can understand the thing. All of life is that way. Life is sort of a dreary course, which gradually improves as you get to know the material. [Laughter.] If you can write a sentence, you can write a book. [Laughter.]

Rosellen Brown: She's right. It's not funny. It's true. A novel is pasted together. It's clerical work.

Dillard: It's material work.

Brown: You say, "Where should I put this?"

Dillard: In the life of the mind, everything is connected somehow insofar as it has being. But you just sort of browse in your reading, and you have all these years. I mean, I'm only thirty-three. I'm pretty well read, and it doesn't take very many years—if you just read all the time. Don't do anything else. [Laughter.] It's really fun. You'll love it. You get to lie down. [Laughter.]

One time, someone asked me, "How did you become a writer?" I said, "Well, I used to be a painter (which is true), and I was standing there painting one day, and I'd been standing there for some time working on this very difficult painting, and I suddenly looked around and thought, *I could be sitting down*." [Laughter.]

Question: Do you think there are pockets of reading desires you can't indulge? I'll give you an example. I especially like books on biology like Sagan's books and

books like *The Selfish Gene*. I don't think I'll ever use any of those. And also, I have a horrible compulsion to read about baseball. What can I do? [Laughter.]

Brown: We're all such damned Calvinists. We have such set ideas abut what is or isn't appropriate in reading. The best part of this, I think, Annie, is that at a certain point you can begin to say to yourself, "I want to use this." Maybe I will, maybe I won't. But it's okay because most of what I see I use somehow. If that Calvinist part wants to express itself, I don't really have to worry about it—I'm not wasting my time.

Dillard: For eight years, it never occurred to me that I was going to use any of that. I am not talking to you as writers, essentially; I'm talking to you as people. I never thought I would use any of it. I was just reading. It never occurred to me in a thousand million years I was going to *use* it. I was just lost in my own ramblings.

Brown: But that's not true anymore—probably.

Dillard: No, and life is no fun anymore, either. [Laughter.]

Margaret Atwood: Just an observation—because *we* Canadians don't believe it. In fact, we're probably too much the other way. America has this wonderful belief that everything can always be changed.

I think it goes back to the Revolution or something: Get rid of the king and have something else, and also *that every individual is infinitely perfectable.*

Dillard: You are right. I have that belief. You're absolutely right. Where's Rob? Rob [Wilson] noticed that about me the first day. He said, "Oh, you don't correct your students' punctuation, do you?" And I said, "I do." He thought that was a psychological phenomenon—that I thought people's punctuation could be improved.

Atwood: Yes, of course it can. It can be improved. But when you say that everybody—that any Tom, Dick, and Harry—is smart, for instance, I mean it's possible to improve everything, yes, but surely only up to a point, in some cases. What we're stuck with is the weather, right? We know we can't ever do anything about the weather. We have to live with it.

Joe David Bellamy: So what you're saying, Annie, is: "Use your strengths."

Dillard: Yes.

Atwood: "And don't be dismayed by your weaknesses."

Dillard: And don't write yourself out of the ballpark because you're not Faulkner, or because you're not Sherwood Anderson. You've got something you can do.

Atwood: Yes, okay. I'll agree with that. I don't believe that everybody is the same.

Dillard: Anyone will tell you that in order to be a *real* writer of fiction, you have to be able to tell a story. The essence of fiction is to tell a story. Well, I'm sure it is. But I feel like writing fiction anyway, and so I'll try it. I have a few things I can do. I can write sentences.

Robley Wilson:[1] There's a kind of a sub-surface edge to what you're saying. It's driving me up the wall. I think it is not the case that doing or being exposed to or getting involved in various art forms is essential because life is some sort of marvelous self-improvement trip. I think that the intelligence that makes art and the intelligence that puts commas in the right place are two different things. I don't know what the relationship is, but they're two different things. Now, I could drive my students crazy by talking about semicolons. I know how to use a semicolon. I could lay it on pretty heavy.

---

1 Robley Wilson edited *The North American Review* for more than thirty years. His novels include *The World Still Melting, Splendid Omens,* and *The Victim's Daughter.* His collections of stories are *The Pleasures of Manhood, Living Alone, Dancing for Men, Terrible Kisses,* and *The Book of Lost Fathers.* His poetry collections include *Kingdoms of the Ordinary,* which won the Agnes Lynch Starrett Prize.

But they're students; they're between eighteen and twenty-one years old. They've been brought up in a school system, which has persuaded them that they can't write anyway without making fools of themselves. So even if they can write, at this point in their lives, they're reluctant to because somebody is going to jump on them and say, "You've got a messy line." You talk about garbage in and garbage out. My students, in particular, are at an age when they don't know when they have ideas, but they know if they do have ideas, they aren't worth anybody's time. You're eighteen years old, you're at a large university. You say to yourself: "What do

From left: Rosellen Brown, Robley Wilson, Eleanor Bender, and Joe David Bellamy discuss magazine and small press publishing during Saranac, 1978.

WRITERS BECOME WRITERS WHEN THEY ANSWER THE QUESTION, AT SOME POINT IN THEIR LIVES, OF HOW TO DEAL WITH THE WORLD AROUND THEM.

people care what *I* think?" So you keep your mouth shut.

Dillard: It just depends.

Wilson: The best student writer I ever had was the worst manager of punctuation I've ever seen in my life. I thought, *I don't know what to do.* This was an extension class in Chicago—this guy was a mechanic during the day. He wrote fantastic stuff because he had figured out how to see the world. Writers become writers when they answer the question, at some point in their lives, of how to deal with the world around them, and he had done that. Here was a guy who was turning in marvelous essays, which any good editor could have turned into publishable stuff. But he was twenty-two, twenty-three years old. He had a living to make. He couldn't afford the luxury of doing the kind of reading that would have improved his punctuation, and all I could do was talk to him

week after week and say, "You're terrific. But I don't know what to do with you, because you ought to be flunking this course hands down."

I said, "Look, I like your stuff. I deplore your punctuation. I'm going to pass you with a C. Do me one favor. Please do not come back and take the second half of this course because it's going to be a different instructor, and he'll kill you. He'll kill you, and you'll decide you don't want to write. I want you to go on writing. I don't want you to worry about where to put the capital letters. I don't want you to worry about whether you use a colon, semicolon, or comma. Write—because you see this world a helluva lot better certainly than any of my colleagues at this university, and certainly more clearly than most of the people who are writing and publishing." So I'd like to make a distinction between the kind of intelligence that makes art and the kind of intelligence that can keep house.

Brown: It's going to be boring to say this, but anybody who has a clear view of the world can take three weeks to learn correct punctuation—afterwards, *knowing* it is a separate thing. Learn how to use capital letters and punctuation! I think you're being too lenient on someone like that—when you can get through the world or this particular class because you have a wonderful sensibility. I don't think much of the sensibility of a twenty-one-year-old who can't use capital letters. I wouldn't lay that on a nine-year-year old. maybe.

Wilson: I *would* lay that on a nine-year-old.

Brown: You would? I probably wouldn't. But, here, I think you're selling a twenty-one-year-old short if you think he can't learn to punctuate in a few weeks of work.

Atwood: It depends on what kind of tacky shape he's in. If he's in very tacky shape and about to fall to pieces, then he probably can't do that right then.

Brown: Maybe. Maybe. But I think you can separate the two elements. You can say, "This is magnificent. This is marvelous. But you really might want to sit down sometime with a workbook and learn more of the basics."

Wilson: I'm not trying to make a pedagogical point, except in a general sense.

I'm trying to say there is a difference between these kinds of intelligence.

Bellamy: I think the greater percentage of students *are* capable of assimilating the housekeeping kinds of chores without a lot of destructiveness to other parts of their minds. In fact, it might even improve their vision. Certainly, some may not be able to, but I agree with Rosellen. I think it's important for college instructors to make it clear that this is one thing society expects and one thing that you expect by insisting upon it and by paying attention to it.

But the thing that breaks my heart about certain students is those who already do those things and those who, in fact, *have* what we call talent and show it in everything they do, but they seem to lack any kind of fiery need to keep doing it. They are the ones that I give talks to—something like the one you were just describing, Rob, you know: "All the fetters are off. Just get busy. Just keep doing it. Just turn out the pages." And they seem to be unable to do that. If I say, "Write three stories," they write three stories and then they stop. They seem never able to proceed on their own. Maybe this is just an accident, but it seems in the last several years that's always the case. I'm certainly not a teacher who wants to train embryonic Nobel Prize winners or anything.

But when one does see a talented student, one hopes for some kind of yearning for accomplishment. It seems that the two qualities seldom go together, and the ones who are the most talented are the least ambitious. There's not enough ambition around. What's gone wrong?

Wilson: Are you really unhappy that you have some students who have a modicum of talent?

Bellamy: It's not that. It's the ones with a lot of talent who don't seem to have any ambition.

Wilson: Well, that may not be their bag.

Bellamy: I understand that, but where *is* the desire?

Wilson: Well, if it's going to come, it will come. I think it has a lot to do with the genes, I'm afraid. If I have a student who is pretty talented and I say to him, "Write three short stories," and he does that and quits and I say, "Do you feel the impulse to write a fourth?" and he says, "Nah." I say, "Well, fine. I'm delighted." So, good. *Be what you want to be.* Don't worry about that.

One thing that *does* bother me is there are some public school systems that make a big deal out of the housekeeping, and they turn out students who, by God, can really punctuate. They really know what a topic sentence is, and they really know how to paragraph. There are all sorts of rules about these things. I used to believe them. I used to believe that you could teach this sort of thing, that there were rules for doing it. Then one day it occurred to me that you start a new paragraph when you feel like starting a new paragraph! [Laughter.] There's no goddamn rule about it. You already have a big paragraph, and you say, "This page is getting awfully *thick*. I'm going to put a little white space here." That's all there is to it.

But you get these students in your classes and, boy, they can punctuate and they do all the things the textbooks tell them to do, and you have them for a year and they write the same thing every damn week! It's impeccable. There's no way to fault it except it's absolutely dull because these kids have no idea how to write!

Dillard: My latest quotation is from J. Henri Fabre, who was just an absolutely wonderful nineteenth-century French entomologist whose work I very much admire. I just read a biography of his. It was a wonderful little tour of nineteenth-century France. What an interesting life. Anyway, he said in there somewhere, "Clarity is the sovereign politeness of the writer. I do my best to achieve it." So, you can say to your students, "Look, it's just polite." They don't want to be rude.

They live in society—that's the last thing anyone wants to be is rude. They don't want to do what you tell them until you can figure out a persuasive reason, and this is it: "It's *impolite* to be unclear."

Bellamy: Yes.

Dillard: I read in *Simone Weil* about a fairy tale that reminds me of two metaphors for the writing life—and maybe a good way to end.

I don't like fairy tales or children's literature; in fact, I can't stand them, and I never learn anything from them. But there was one that was just absolutely terrific. It was a little girl who was supposed to go somewhere, but she didn't know where. But that's where she was supposed to go. *But she didn't know where.* Her fairy godmother or somebody stepped in and gave her a big, silver, decorated, embroidered *ball* and told her how to use it. She was meant to roll it along the world and to follow it as it rolled, at random. When it stopped, she was meant to pick it up and roll it again and follow it; and when it stopped, she was to pick it up and roll it again. That was her path—where that ball ended up, that's where she was supposed to go. However, at the end of every one of those lines, she was supposed to *learn French*, then *learn Egyptology*, whatever it is. You just follow the little ball until it ends, you pick it up, and you roll it again. Do what you gotta do.

The other metaphor for the artistic life is this wonderful thing that happened on this island where my husband and I live. We live some of the year on a very small, teeny-tiny island in Puget Sound, which is a narrow, very deep channel, and *the tide rushes in*. Very high tides, very strong currents, six to eight knots, because the channels are so narrow and there are islands in between, blocking the currents and making them go every which way. Then, *the tide rushes out*. The currents are extremely strong. Fishermen have a hell of a time trying to catch salmon in this place, and their nets go drifting away.

I'll do this on the board. Here's the island. This took place about forty years ago to a man named Farrar Berne. The forty or fifty people who lived on the island were very eccentric. There's no electricity or running water. There are no resources whatsoever on the island except what floats by, and what floats by on the tides is apt to be *logs*. If you get a piece of Alaskan yellow cedar, you see it out on the water. Everybody stands in their cabins with binoculars, hoping that something is going to float by. And if a piece of yellow cedar floats by, everybody launches their rowboats and runs out and gets it. If something that *holds water* floats by, that's a very valuable thing because

there's no water on the island, so something that will hold water can act as a holding tank for your well, or a cistern for your rainwater.

So one day about forty years ago, a big aluminum pontoon floated by, thirty feet long, some sort of hollow object welded together that was a long hollow cylinder that would hold water. It held air. It would float something. It was just obviously a wonderful little thing to have— even just as an object, just like being a little kid. They didn't have any stores! So Farrar Berne, who was just a homesteader on the island, rowed out and tied on to this pontoon in, you know, a little seven-foot rowboat and started rowing it back to where he lived, which was at this point in the island, Fishery Point.

When you're tied onto something thirty feet long, it dominates you because of the tides. It has thirty feet in contact with the water, and the tide is going to take that thirty-foot object and swing you along with it. So instead of rowing this thing back home, the tide caught him. There are a few little other islands, but essentially the tide is wandering out of Puget Sound into the Pacific and the next thing is … Japan. [Laughter.] It's the next point of land you're going to hit if you miss all these islands on the way, which you're quite apt to do. Farrar was strong—all those people *live* in a rowboat, and they can row. But the tide caught him. So he got instantly turned around, so the pontoon was dragging the boat—for a Nantucket sleigh ride—and the tide is pouring out, and he's rowing three miles an hour this way, and the tide is going six or seven knots that way.

So he's drifting out toward Japan at a furious rate of speed, but he points his bow back toward Fishery Point, where he belongs and where he wants to tie his pontoon up. He steadily keeps rowing for Fishery Point while ahead of him this pontoon is dragging him to Japan. [Laughter.] He rowed all night. The sun went down, and he's in the rowboat, and he rowed steadily toward Fishery Point all night long. He kept looking over his shoulder and kept his bow pointed all night toward Fishery Point. Well, along about morning the tide changed, and he didn't change what he was doing at all. He just kept rowing toward Fishery Point, and the tide took him back. Jeez, he was clear down here, and it took him back and put him here, and he was able to beach the pontoon and to come home.

That is such an absolutely, totally dandy metaphor for the artistic life. You go where you're supposed to be going, and it will take you here, and you'll be going the exact opposite direction from where you're supposed to be going. But just keep trying. Just keep rowing toward where you're going, and you'll be led every kind of which way. But just keep rowing toward where you're going, and *you'll get there.* [Applause.]

on moral fiction

WILLIAM KITTREDGE, ROBIE MACAULEY, CAROLYN FORCHÉ & JOE DAVID BELLAMY

This panel discussion took place at the June 1979 conference at Saranac Lake. The panelists were Robie Macauley, Carolyn Forché, William Kittredge, and conference director Joe David Bellamy. Respondents in the audience included Jayne Anne Phillips (bio, page 229), Daniel Halpern (bio, pages 211–212), and Charles Simmons (bio, pages 187–188).

The term "moral fiction" was made current at that time by the appearance in 1977 of a highly controversial book, *On Moral Fiction*, by the novelist

< Top: Carolyn Forché.
< William Kittredge.

John Gardner, author of *October Light* and *The Sunlight Dialogues*. Gardner's book struck a cultural nerve because it criticized many of the premises of postmodernist thinking that were in vogue among fiction writers just then, plus Gardner rankled many because his discussions of individual writers pulled no punches. He seemed to some commentators to be proposing a lofty, somewhat dubious aesthetic on the one hand, and using the opportunity to savage his competitors on the other.

Robie Macauley was a senior editor at Houghton Mifflin at the time of the conference, one in a long line of starring editorial posts he held during his lifetime. He was also the author of two novels, *The Disguises of Love* and *A Secret History of Things to Come*, a collection of short stories, *The End of Pity*, and (with George Lanning) a widely used text, *Technique in Fiction*. He died in 1995.

Carolyn Forché won the Yale Series of Younger Poets Award for her first poetry collection, *Gathering the Tribes*. Her second collection, *The Country Between Us*, was the Lamont Selection of the Academy of American Poets, and her third, *The Angel of History*, won the Los Angeles Times Book Award. Her fourth collection, *Blue Hour*, was published by Harper Collins in 2003. She has also published widely as a translator, critic, anthologist, and reviewer.

William Kittredge is the author of two collections of short fiction, *The Van Gogh Field and Other Stories* and *We Are Not In This Together*, and several collections of nonfiction and memoir, including *Owning It*, *Hole in the Sky*, *Who Owns the West*, *Balancing Water*, *Taking Care*, and *The Nature of Generosity*. His most recent novel, *The Willow Field*, was published by Alfred A. Knopf. Well known as an environmental activist and philosopher on behalf of the American West, he co-produced the award-winning film *A River Runs Through It* and was, for many years, the Regents Professor of English and Creative Writing at the University of Montana.

Joe David Bellamy is the former editor and publisher of *Fiction International* magazine and press, former director of the literature program of the National Endowment for the Arts, and the author of fourteen books, including the novel *Suzi Sinzinnati*, a collection of stories, *Atomic Love*, and a collection of essays, *Literary Luxuries*.

Joe David Bellamy: Not too long ago, I had an idea to do an issue of *Fiction International* magazine on the theme of "moral fiction." This was partly because we had to have a theme for a grant we were writing, but also at that time I was reading John Gardner's *On Moral Fiction* and feeling that it was interesting but also very wrong-headed. I felt that his indictment of current American fiction ought to be answered. At one point, I had the idea that we would have this lineup of all the authors he had panned in his book, talking back to him. Then I decided, "No, that's really too similar to what Gardner was doing." Instead, we'll have a huge collection, an anthology of fiction, which is in some way either moral or immoral, as a way of trying to illustrate some of the ideas that are brought up in *On Moral Fiction*.

Certainly if we consider it as a philosophical issue, questions surrounding *moral fiction* are immense in scope. What we're going to do today is talk to the larger questions of moral fiction (and poetry), and if John Gardner comes into our considerations, that's okay. But we do hope to do more than simply reply to *On Moral Fiction*—although I do want to say a few things about that book.

I'd like to start off by reading a kind of humorous reply from the writer Clark Blaise. I wrote to Clark, asking him if he would like to contribute an essay on moral fiction to the issue of the magazine we're contemplating. Here's what he said: "I can't think of a topic more likely to reduce intelligent people to idiots. Either you're a pagan: passion is piety, redemption is goodness, whatever enhances the love of life is moral, and morality is merely the action of pleasure enhancement. Or you're a Christian: morality is contributing to the pool of goodness in the world. It is guidance, the reduction of evil or harm or brutality. Or you could be a psycho-moralist, where morality is linked to understanding. Or a Marxist—and I suppose there is an omnibus morality, which tries to choose all those motherhood issues without sounding dreary." Then he goes on to ask for more information and then finally he signs the letter, "If it feels good after ya done it, it's moral, right?" [Laughter.]

Well, taking a quick tour of literary history, I think first of all we should dismiss the simple-minded idea of moral fiction as thought of in the eighteenth century, the Samuel Richardson model that is so often talked about. This is the

< Top: Robie Macauley.
< Joe David Bellamy at Saranac, 1978.

idea that if the work supports behavior that you approve of, it is moral. If it supports bad behavior, it is immoral.

In those early days of the novel, you have Richardson writing, in *Pamela*, a novel that is mainly a long chase scene where Squire Booby is pursuing Pamela. Pamela is forever resisting his advances because the moral premise of the time is that you should preserve your virginity if you are a female. After two volumes of Pamela's eluding Squire Booby and of Squire Booby's proving beyond doubt that he is a total cad, he finally agrees to marry Pamela and Pamela agrees to marry him. This marriage somehow saves the novel from immorality, in Richardson's view.

Henry Fielding thought this was a crazy idea, of course, and satirized it in *Shamela* and in *Joseph Andrews*, where he presents his brand of morality, which is much more libertarian and lustful and what Fielding considered normal and healthy-minded. Joseph Andrews is a normal young male, and Fanny in that novel is a normal, healthy young female; and they aren't especially prudish. But many people in the eighteenth century, of course, called Fielding's novel immoral and Richardson's novel moral.

One of Gardner's ideas that I wanted to call into question is his idea of simple or simple-minded affirmation, which perhaps takes too much from the Richardso-

nian model. Gardner presents a number of theories in *On Moral Fiction*, and then he tries to show how various writers who are alive now succeed or, mainly, fail to embody his theories of morality. Some of the theory is interesting, but in most cases, the writers themselves, I think, are unfairly treated. One of them, in particular, is Ed Doctorow. In about two pages, Gardner takes my favorite passage from *Ragtime* and describes why it's immoral because he claims it's unrealistic and implausible. It also seems to me that his criticism of that particular scene is essentially prudish, although he doesn't bring up that element of it. It's the scene where Little Brother comes out of the closet.

My main problem with Gardner's premises is that he pushes the idea that the novelist should be simply affirmative to the extent that he leaves out many of the writers I admire, and many modes that I think are viable modes of thought and imagination, as well as stylistic modes. For example, his arguments leave out the idea of presenting nightmare or surrealism or almost anything that is anti-realistic or any kind of art that seems to be a kind of exorcism.

Some of the writing of Joyce Carol Oates, I'm convinced, is a kind of nightmare vision that functions as a form of exorcism. There are instances where hideous things are presented in art of all periods, which are meant to be exorcistic. To present something negative in a work of art—a character who is evil, for example—does not mean that you recommend that behavior to the reader, after all.

It seems to me that Gardner takes the position that if you present those things, you are immoral. He is very much like a Russian social realist in that sense. We can't look at the sordid, we can't look at evil, we can't open the Pandora's box of the unconscious at all—because it's too dangerous. I would argue that great art has always done that, and must do that. So I think that imaginative freedom is far too limited by Gardner's premises.

Jayne Anne Phillips: If you are speaking through or about a character who is doing something, or who is experiencing or advocating immorality (or what's considered decadent), but you're illustrating tremendous loss through that—that is something that comes about through distortion of an accepted morality—are you, in fact, then writing moral fiction? Because what you're writing about is what happens when an accepted morality is either exploded or distorted, or something else is being experienced either through the choice of the character or through the culture the character is involved in.

Bellamy: Well, I would say that you were. Is the artist obligated to consider morality at all? I think that's a question worth asking.

I want to try to finish up what I have to say very quickly and let other people say their five or ten minutes worth and then open it up for general discussion. I'm sure there are more ins and outs of this discussion than we'll ever explore in the time we have.

There are several elements of the imaginative process that creates fiction or poetry that I want to mention as relating to this subject. One is the idea of character. If I were trying to define what moral fiction is, if I thought that was an important issue and that the writer *should* try for morality as one of his goals, I guess I would say that there are many aspects of creating fiction, or creating art, that are moral, inherently moral, and one might even say that all art is inherently moral—if it is art. In fiction, I would say this comes about in one way through the creation of character.

I take it as an inherently moral event when a writer creates a character in all its complexity, particularly in a society, in a culture, where there are many attacks upon complexity of character. We come too easily to accept stereotypical, superficial, and empty ideas of one another because they are all around us, and our imaginations are corrupted by journalistic and other kinds of simple-minded ideas about one another, about the complexity of our own natures. So fiction is a corrective influence against those kinds of immoral corrupting effects.

Point number two: I think that fiction, at its best in the novel, provides a rare integrative experience because it shows us a whole life. The eighteenth-century novel begins with this idea of the whole life on display, and there are still novels of that sort being written, though the form may change. Charles Simmons's *Wrinkles* is one of them. I think our lives are so fragmentary and evanescent as we go along through them that we very much need the integrative, all-inclusive vision which shows us an entire life and allows us to think about an entire life. That is inherently a moral perspective. The novel is one of the few places we get such a view of ourselves.

My third point has to do with what I call the healing powers of dreams. I feel that dreams are mysterious, unexplainable. The scientists have not told us yet what they are all about. Dreams are healing, and nightmares are as healing and sometimes are more healing than pleasant dreams. I assume that art that creates dreamlike structures is ameliorative at least, and essentially beneficial, humanistic, supportive, and, in that sense, moral.

Finally, I take it that art is truly (and in a healthy sense) consciousness-expanding. Great art is an epistemological process

or quest, a search for truth. That is an inherently moral aspect of great art.

Robie Macauley: I feel a little more sympathetic towards Gardner's book than Joe does. It seems to me that this is a book on the side of the angels, but he doesn't really know who his angels are. Writing a book on moral fiction is redundant in the sense that the whole history of American and British fiction in English is essentially moral, almost by definition. I was trying to think of the great books that are exceptions, and I can't think of any books that are except for a very few, such as *Tristram Shandy* or *Finnegans Wake* or *Nightwood*, and a few others that don't fit into some big moral perception. I think that that's what Gardner is really saying, and it doesn't really need to be said. It seems to me, then, that when he becomes more particular and tries to define things, he gets in a lot of trouble because he tries to define the difference between a moralizer and a moralist, and the definition of "moralist" or "moral" in the big sense evades him.

Here's an example. Saul Bellow obviously is a moral novelist. He's constantly concerned with the right ways of behavior, the right ways of living in this world. Gardner doesn't like him. He doesn't like any of his contemporaries, and so he simply dismisses Saul Bellow by saying, "Well, he's really an essayist.

GREAT ART IS AN EPISTEMOLOGICAL PROCESS OR QUEST, A SEARCH FOR TRUTH. THAT IS AN INHERENTLY MORAL ASPECT OF GREAT ART.

He isn't a fiction writer at all!" He fits into the moral mold, but then he has to somehow get rejected on other grounds. This is true of most of the writers he is talking about. Most of the writers don't seem to fit into Gardner's scheme. I think most of that is ridiculous. It is simply because Gardner has never really considered strictly enough or severely enough what he means by moral. It is just a big, amorphous idea in his book.

It seems to me that one distinction he tries to make is a good one—and that's the difference between moralizer and moralist. Joe was talking about the traditional kind of moral impetus or the moral impulse in English fiction, which is a moralizing kind. To point to a moral in a tale was a typical sort of strategy, or at least the most obvious strategy, in the English novel for a long time. It seems to me that we learned a lesson in the middle of the nineteenth century from people like the Russian novelists and the French novelists that you could be a moralist without being a moralizer.

In other words, the moralist writer sets himself up as a judge. The novel is the case that is being tried before him. That the writer was writing on a moral subject, you might say, sets the reader up as a jury and plays out the whole case in front of the jury and lets the jury decide the more or less obvious rights and wrongs and values that come out of the case. So, I think, briefly, the thesis that Gardner is talking about is very important. It still needs a lot more definition than he provides.

Carolyn Forché: I was going to go back and retrace the two arguments. Gardner defines moral fiction as having two qualities, and one is that the writer creates characters who are models for our human behavior. He talks about making good myths, of somehow rescuing the world from its decadence by setting up characters who embody human values that are somehow able to be helpful to what he imagines as the reading world in its own struggle against chaos, perversity, confusion, despair.

Students in the Boathouse after a reading at Saranac, 1974 or 1975.

That's one aspect of this, and the other is that he defines—if I'm remembering correctly—he defines the moral act of writing. In order to be moral, the writer must engage with his imagination in a task of discovery in the course of drafts of his novel or her novel. The writer should not know the outcome, should not have an idea of what the novel will say in advance. To be truly moral, the artist must enter into the world of the novel, create it believably, and plunge himself in his imagination into the lives of each of the characters, and somehow maintain and be true to each of the characters. They would do nothing that is unbelievable, and through this process (which is revised and revised and revised), the writer comes to some understanding of what should happen in the novel to the exclusion of every other possibility. So writing becomes a mode of thought, which, to Gardner, is its value, its true form.

I have problems with both of these because I have problems with anything that is prescriptive, that limits or defines or somehow contains the artist in some mold, a way that you must view your work, a way that you must approach it in order to be moral or not moral. Gardner does see value in work that he's done without this second quality, this mode of thought. He cites "value," but he does not believe that it falls into his category of "moral." So, this is the problem that I have. I think that it is probably very dangerous to prescribe to art. However, as was said, he is on the side of the angels.

One of the elements that I wanted to bring into this discussion is not so much that we talk strictly about Gardner's book, but rather that we talk about the larger concern of how we, as writers, address ourselves to the world, and how we embrace our contemporary concerns. Maybe we should be talking about politics (in the large sense of the word) and writing, rather than morals (in the large sense of the word) and writing. In the very large sense of the words, that would be what I can address—in poetry, particularly.

I believe that American poets now are being most strongly influenced by poets particularly from Eastern Europe, Latin America, Spain, Greece, Israel. I'm thinking of Milosz and Zbigniew Herbert and Yehuda Amichai. I'm thinking of our influences now, *my* strongest influences, and the strongest influences of my peers, and I have thought for a long time about why we are so influenced—why this work affects us, and why so much of the work of our fellows in this country leaves us a little empty. That's something that I can talk about if you want to, if you want to address that specifically in questions later.

William Kittredge: I really agree with a lot of things you're saying, Carolyn. One of my methods of approaching Gardner is in the way his remarks correlate with Chekhov, who said, "Artists ask questions; they don't answer them." I really think that's true. If art has a moral purpose, it is to make us see freshly, to make us see anew, to make us see things in a way that allows us to remake our models of the world.

I have a notion that every day when we get up, our models are broken. At least mine was this morning. I got up and my model was broken. I woke up and it was nine o'clock, and breakfast was almost over. [Laughter.] We do that. It's a primary human act, and it seems to me all of us do it. All day long and throughout our lives, we make up models, which never work; and we have to remake them and remake them and remake them. We have to see the world fresh each time—if our model is going to have any congruity with the world.

It seems to me that's what good art does. If I may use the word "good"— moral or good art helps us to see the world freshly, helps us see a little bit truer.

*IF ART HAS A MORAL PURPOSE,
IT'S TO MAKE US SEE FRESHLY,
AND IT GIVES US SOME BASIS
TO MAKE OUR OWN DECISIONS.*

We probably never approach too close to "real." Who knows what real would be? In any event, it helps us see freshly.

It seems to me that talking politically, as Carolyn wanted us to do, that "good" art—if I may use that word again—is radical. It is politically radical in the sense that it helps us see the world in a different way than we saw it before. I hesitate to use the word "better" in this context, but it seems to me that a lot of genre art, for instance, is politically conservative. It makes us see the world the way we've always seen it, in a certain kind of way. If art has a moral purpose, it's to make us see freshly, and it gives us some basis to make our own decisions.

Question: I would be interested in hearing more about the influences Carolyn was talking about and why they are important now.

Forché: One thing I'm worried about is overstepping into the grounds of the talk that I am to deliver on Monday. I don't want to have to make up another one.

I don't want to use my material. I only have a few jokes. [Laughter.]

But to be serious, I think that, well, you know, in the sixties, it was Robert Bly and the Midwest Deep Image School—remember them? They're still around. They brought us a great deal of translation. The works, particularly of Pablo Neruda, began a wave of interesting Latin American work with Robert Bly's translations and others. Charles Simic and Mark Strand have an anthology that Daniel [Halpern] published called *Another Republic* that you should look at. It brings to us in translation the likes of Yehuda Amichai and Francis Ponge and others that we're interested in now.

In reading it, I began to think, "Why will I read Amichai? Why will I read Zbigniew Herbert? Why will I read Hikmet with so much interest and engagement—when the fact is that what I'm reading is translation? I'm not *reading*." I'm not really reading the music, the language that this was shaped in. So what I'm reading for is *what*, then? If I'm not reading for the original music of the language, I'm reading for content. I'm reading for a way of viewing the world—even once removed. So I started thinking about this, and I thought, "Why, *why* are we so interested?" I think Daniel probably has some ideas about it, too. But, for me, it was content.

I read Akhmatova because I wanted to read a poem like *Requiem*, where she's outside of a camp in a queue, a bread queue, and a woman who recognizes her comes up to her and says, "Can you describe this?" Akhmatova says, "Yes, I think I can." *And then a smile comes over what had once been her face.* So, that imperative, which Akhmatova brought to me, is to describe, to give witness—when we're living in a horrifying age of uncontrollable acts of terrorism, of spontaneous and sporadic terrorism, of moral depravity and confusion. I think Gardner understands this; it was the impulse for his book. I think no one would argue with the difficulties that we face, and I think that there is something that poets in translation are supplying to poets in America, and that is some kind of humanistic vision and witness.

Now, we are all very fat and happy here for right now, and so I think there is almost even a tendency of poets in America to go elsewhere for their subject matter—because they feel that they are not suffering or they are not witnessing. They are not seeing things. That's simply to romanticize, and that's *not* what I'm talking about. But I think that it's some sort of a wisdom that informs this poetry, and *that's* what we read for. I just believe that that is missing from a great deal of what is written here. Not from everything, not from our best poets. But that's why there is the hunger. That's the need, I think.

So we will read poetry in translation that is not really as well crafted. It doesn't have the technical virtuosity of poetry written in English. Marvin Bell[1] made this argument in *American Poetry Review*. Maybe some of you saw the piece on what he calls "the International Voice." He said, "We excuse in their poetry things we would never allow our own poets to say." I have a question: Why not? Why this attention to the veneer so much, at the expense so much of what we are willing to risk and say?

Daniel Halpern: Carolyn, isn't he talking about content, though—more than the writing itself?

Forché: Bell did mention the fact that it was the quality of the translation, possibly. But I know he said we will allow them

---

1 Marvin Bell is the distinguished poet and the Flannery O'Conner Professor of Letters at the University of Iowa.

kinds of language we will not allow our-selves—emotionally colored words that we will not allow ourselves. Possibly it's so bound up with content—you're right. Possibly. But this is a question that I've been thinking about ever since that ap-peared. It's a line of thought that I have. I'm just interested in why. I understand that we want to read poets in translation, but why? Why is it so?

Halpern: There can be a music if they're well translated.

Forché: Yes. There can be.

Halpern: Good translations are good poems in English, you know, even though they may not be literal.

Forché: The best are. Yes. But we're not really reading for the original, though. We can't read for that. I think the people are reading for content. I think that's true. You don't think so?

Halpern: In part.

Forché: Okay.

Question: You used the word "mystery" just now. Do you have any thoughts about the connection between morality and the sense of mystery that we don't usu-ally have with us? I don't mean mystery in the sense of "thriller," but a spiritual sense of mystery.

Forché: Is it mysticism that you're talk-ing about?

Question: Well, you used the word mys-tery, and I thought it was very interesting that you had used that word in talking about the experience of writing and the search for some other kind of experience in translations. I was wondering if you had any thoughts about the connection between the poets in our culture and their search for morality and their search for some kind of mystery in writing that was not being done in this country. When I say mystery, I think it's close to some sense of mysticism or some sort of spiritual experience—not necessarily re-ligious experience.

Forché: I would say, instead of mystery, "curiosity." I would say curiosity is why we read—to have an access to something that we cannot know in our own expe-rience. I mean we read because we are curious about things that we have no pur-chase on, and that can be a rather danger-ous kind of curiosity, in some sense.

Question: Isn't this part of an effort to go on to see something new? As Bill Kit-tredge was saying, the artist tries to see the world anew.

Kittredge: We are almost all responding to that, and it seems to me that there are pretty profound changes taking place in the world. In fiction, particularly, I see more and more edging toward a kind of romance rather than the rigidly observed tendency of fictional realism, which is really a philosophical stance probably invented in the high Renaissance. It's very dependent on notions like Newtonian physics and Descartian philosophy and so on. We all know, if we read any popularizations of contemporary physics, that what Newtonian physics tells us is simply not true.

The notion of mystery, what we were talking about, probably *is* true in a sense that the universe probably *is* alive in a certain sense and things *do* interpenetrate. Those are simply the facts of contemporary physics. We are, in fact, all part of everything, and we can't help but be. There's a whole other sense of the world emerging. It's a really interesting phase we are living in, a transitional phase. Another sense of the world that we are going to, once again, is what I call an "inhabited world" rather than an "uninhabited world"—a world in which everything but "me" is an object. It turns out that's not true—thank God.

Forché: You say, "Once again"?

Kittredge: It seems to me that almost all the people in the history of the world lived in that kind of world. Perhaps the last four hundred years or so, they haven't. It may be less than that—four hundred years in Western Europe.

Bellamy: So the Me Decade was the end of it?

Kittredge: Yes. [Laughter.]

Question: When you're reading poetry in translation and you see something political, how would you interpret that so that it affects your own work? At what point does that become political? You're saying that you're looking at the content, but at what point would that become political—how does that work? I mean, you're not going to advocate those politics, are you?

Forché: What I said about my disagreement with anything prescriptive applies to prescriptive subject matter, too. When I'm talking about "political," I'm saying that I would hope that my work would be *informed*—as we are integrated beings.

We bring our experience with us to our work. We bring with us our orientation toward the world, whether we're anthropocentric or whether we can embrace what was just spoken of here in a more real sense, an *inhabited* world. We bring everything to bear. I would hope that my work would be informed by certain political and human and moral and social values. But I do not believe that there should be a choice of subject matter that *should* be political. I mean, I do not intend to write political poems in that sense.

Question: So you would only write about your own experience?

Forché: With the experience of my imagination, which gives me just about everything, maybe! It depends on how large it is, but I don't think there is anything that could be excluded in that sense. I do not have, in other words, an exclusive view of subject matter appropriate for any writer.

Bellamy: I think the narrowest view of that was articulated by a group of SDS[2] students I used to argue with in the late sixties in a Black Lit course I was teaching in a state college in Pennsylvania. They were strict Marxists, and they argued that every piece of art is political. It's political *first* and foremost, and even if it's a haiku about a tree, it's still political. To write about a tree simply shows that the artist is …

Forché: Decadent and bourgeois.

Bellamy: Right. The author of the haiku doesn't have any sense of the importance

of politics. [Laughter.] I didn't win the argument with them, but their point of view was one I could never subscribe to. I think it's the most simplified view of the place of a political orientation in art that I've ever heard, and one that I think is ultimately simple-minded and reductive.

Charles Simmons: Is the following an aspect of the morality of fiction? I've got a sense that sometimes, very rarely, a writer means me ill.

Whenever I read Chekhov, I have a sense that his attitude toward me as a reader is a benign one—even though he may be talking in a particular story about a small life that almost comes to nothing but shows me some very human and touching aspect of an anonymous person, and then the story is over. If you want to call it moral, I think Chekhov is a moral writer. He is showing me somehow, even through a sad and an anonymous life, *that life is worth living.* That's one of the things that I take away from it.

Now, who is a novelist who I sense is malevolent toward me? I think I rarely see it. I think maybe some of these are written and not published, but one who is, is Cesare Pavase, who was a suicide. I don't know if you've read his work, but there is a glittering deadness to the world he describes, and it's transfixing. But you do come away somehow feeling that life

---

2 SDS—Students for a Democratic Society—was a radical student organization of the 1960s known for activism against the Vietnam War and in support of the civil rights movement. Because of widespread interest in these issues, the organization grew into one of the largest student movements ever seen in the U.S. But SDS became increasingly militant and Marxist in its orientation and divided by internal dissention, and it collapsed by the early seventies into various splinter groups, including the Weathermen, a group advocating violent revolution.

is possibly *not* worth it. You are transfixed by the extraordinary artistry of the writing, so you come away with an aesthetic exultation, but the true message is an evil one—to me.

Well, what about people who are in between? I think of certain Nabokov stories. Take *Pale Fire*. There's a very touching poem—a young girl is a suicide in the poem. The book is enclosed in a pseudo-academic apparatus, which pokes fun at everything. The man who writes the apparatus is a fool. To me—if this is the right use of the word—that is a "low" moral aspect of the book, but somehow I go away with an increased interest in

THE TRUTH DOESN'T, OF COURSE, ALWAYS CORRESPOND TO THE FACTS OF REALITY, BUT THERE IS A KIND OF TRUTH I BELIEVE WE HAVE A RESPONSIBILITY TO TELL.

life. So maybe it really doesn't qualify. To some extent, I'm more interested in living and staying alive after reading it. This is perhaps an aspect of the morality of the novelist, with respect to the reader, that ought to be considered.

Bellamy: Morality in fiction is hard to talk about, in general, because in many ways, books work as conversations. There is a sense of privacy in that you are alone with the writer, and I think a lot depends upon who you are and who he or she is.

Simmons: Yes, indeed. One person will read it one way, and another, another.

Bellamy: Right. For example, I've frequently taught Joyce Carol Oates's *Wheel of Love,* which I think is her most interesting collection of stories so far. I teach that in an Intro to Fiction course, and I've taught it in a Short Story course, a more advanced course. Both groups of students frequently ask me why I teach such a terribly depressing book because various kinds of visions

of mad or suicidal people are presented, and most of the stories turn out badly. A good example is a story called "Accomplished Desires." A young girl's desires are accomplished, and if she'd only known in advance how badly it would turn out, she wouldn't have wanted to accomplish them. Yet I go away from that book feeling so much better.

Simmons: Why?

Bellamy: Because I realize that my life is nowhere nearly as bad as *any* of those people. [Laughter.] It cheers me up. [Laughter.] I'm sure there must be something else. I'm sure that I'm responding to this book in the same sense that Bill was talking about. That is, I'm being presented with experience that is somewhat foreign to me, and I have a sense of greater understanding of the world around me by understanding the difficulties of these people's lives.

Simmons: Are you using her fiction according to her intention?

Bellamy: I don't know what her intentions are. I think there is also an element of exorcism and nightmare in that particular book, and in her work in general, that represents a valid ambition or direction. But beginning students seem to want to read uplifting fiction only, or fiction where things always come out happily at the end. With students who are beginning to read fiction for the first time, one must get beyond that stage of their saying that every good story has to have a happy ending in order to qualify as great art—because we all know it doesn't work quite that way. That's one reason I continue to teach that book and to try to illustrate its qualities.

I do think there is an argument to be made on behalf of nightmare fiction or tragic drama of whatever kind, where the action doesn't necessarily come out well, but which shouldn't leave you just feeling depressed or discouraged. Otherwise, tragedy might be considered immoral. Tragedy should not leave you down—right? If Aristotle is correct, it should leave you in a state of catharsis and heightened consciousness.

Simmons: I think that the way tragedy works is that you see a man who is morally superior to you, at least more demanding of himself than you are of yourself, and who will not compromise with life and suffers terribly for it. You go away from that experience and you have seen an example of moral superiority, and that gives you a sense of exultation. But there is a kind of comfortable coziness that you take away from it, too. You have compromised with life and perhaps survived thereby, and that's okay. And that's the deal that you have with tragedy—something like what you say.

Macauley: There is another thing, too. Charles, you may remember that the classical definition of catharsis is a purgation through pity and terror, and it seems to me that half of the definition has been forgotten by a lot of modern writers. That is, they purge through terror alone, and their idea is to terrorize the reader rather than to find this balance, which is the balance of classical tragedy—pity and terror. They must go together—to have art, to have a tragic art.

Bellamy: Chekhov certainly has pity, or you might call it compassion.

Simmons: You know, when I read Chekhov, I get a sense of him forgiving God almost! And I, therefore, forgive God. I forgive the world. We have so many deep inner arguments with the world and with God. Reading Chekhov does make me feel more at home with the world.

Forché: I was interested in something you were saying when you began—you mentioned what horror (or nightmare) meant to you. Now, I'm going to tell you a little story about the film *The Deer Hunter*—Michael Cimino's film. There are two ways of viewing this story that I'm going to tell.

First, what is that film that played in New York, *Warriors*? And the kids went out and killed each other afterwards. There were articles about it in the press and a furor about the responsibility of that filmmaker. An argument can be made for the fact that anything that's horrible will find the kooks in society, and they will respond in kind. But here's the story about *The Deer Hunter*. I saw it because I'm very much interested in the subject, Vietnam, and I was very deeply disturbed when I walked out of the film. I felt that the audience and I had been wrongly and falsely manipulated. The writer Grace Paley said to me a couple of weeks ago, "Don't worry whether your writing is good or not— worry whether you're telling the truth."

Now, the truth doesn't, of course, always correspond to the facts of reality, but there is a kind of truth that I believe that we have a responsibility to tell, and my story is this. A young writer, a fiction writer, in Charlottesville, Virginia, who was on a Hoynes Fellowship at the University of Virginia, was having some

trouble with his fiction, his work, his life. He was in a state of anxiety and difficulty. He had not gone to Vietnam. He had been a draft dodger in some way, but I don't know how. He went to see *The Deer Hunter* and came home and played the game and died. The game was Russian roulette—a game that Cimino used as a device that was not played in Vietnam. I believe that Cimino misrepresented the Vietnamese in that film, the war, the game, the motivations of the Americans. I believe he was condescending to the working class people from which he drew his characters, and to their environment. I believe that the film was, in a way, morally despicable. The more I thought about it, the angrier I got.

Then last week, the young writer and draft dodger died—right after having viewed it—in the fashion that one of the main characters in the film dies. Now, I don't know whether Cimino is responsible for that. I'm sure no one would say he is directly responsible for that. But I think it calls into question something that we were talking about. We do have some sort of an obligation to tell the truth, and I don't believe Cimino told the truth. I believe Cimino lied in order to fascinate his audience.

Simmons: If I may say, I was not talking about that, exactly. From what I know about the film, Cimino was making money. He was exploiting us and the subject matter, and that is evil, too.

Forche: But it was art, wasn't it?

Simmons: But my notion was about somebody who was fixing on me and didn't want my money. He was leading me—he wanted me to kill myself! He was leading me to despair.

Kittredge: I've always felt that there are certain writers who seem to be closing doors for me.

Simmons: Instead of opening them.

Kittredge: Instead of opening them.

Simmons: You can't say for sure, though, especially at first. The transfixing is a very subtle kind of thing that creeps up on you.

Kittredge: They make the world smaller than it is.

Phillips: I know what you mean about this idea about malevolence, and I agree with you. But I also raise the question: If that is true, does not that view of the world (that life is possibly not worth living) force you to redefine your reasons for living in a way that may be exorcistic? Doesn't the fact that this person has created this piece of writing, even while living under that kind of struggle (that

Buying books on the sun deck.

life is possibly not worth living), in itself provide evidence of going back from the brink, by saying, in effect, "Well, maybe it is worth it—at least today"?

Simmons: Well, it depends on how you respond to it, I suppose. If you are conscious of these intentions, you perhaps react to it as you say. If you're not, I think they have the intended effect.

Phillips: What do you mean—if you're conscious of these intentions?

Simmons: Well, not to make it abstract .... I came away rather down from Pavese, but I read more and I thought about it a

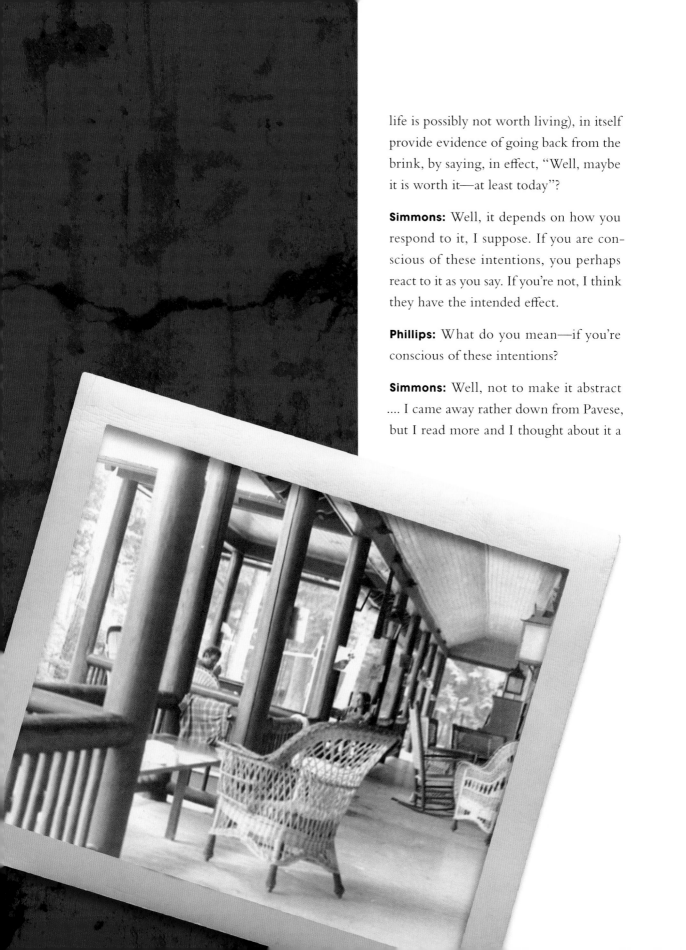

A WRITER, I THINK, IS INTERESTED IN TWO THINGS. HE'S INTERESTED IN THE WORLD, OR LIFE, AND HE'S INTERESTED IN THE PSYCHOLOGY OF THE READER.

good deal. I found out about his life and his suicide and other problems. Then I thought back—yes—he was out to share his misery with me in a depleting and lessening way! Now, could you react in another way to it? I suppose so, but I think it's more of a dramatic, or even a melodramatic, intention of his, and it's hard to escape.

Phillips: When you read someone like Isaac Bashevis Singer or some of Cheever (or you could mention several writers), they seem to use pity and compassion in such a way that they take you down. But there is this sort of light down there that they *present* to you. Then there seem to be other writers who are moving toward that same thing, but they don't *give* you the light. They just leave you down there, and the rest of it has to be completed by the reader. In a way, that could be seen as less responsible because they are forcing the reader to complete the process for themselves.

Simmons: If that's their intention, then they're *not* malevolent. I'm really talking about a very special case, I suppose, and I agree with you. Yes, if you are stimulated to do this yourself, then it does have a moral purpose.

Phillips: But some readers may be stimulated, and some may not be—perhaps depending on how close they are to that writer's despair, or how clearly they see into it. I'm just wondering about the question: Does the writer have the responsibility to give enough so that most readers will go ahead and complete the cycle back toward affirmation, or not?

Simmons: You know, the poor writer does the best he can. I don't think he thinks about these things too much. [Laughter.] Really. I didn't mean to be facetious.

Phillips: I know what you mean.

Simmons: A writer, I think, is interested in two things. He's interested in the world, or life, and he's interested in the psychology of the reader. He's going to take life as he sees it and use it in order to have a certain effect on the reader—because you're always conscious of that. Those items are the two things in your equation.

Phillips: It seems to me, too, that there is a distinction between tragedy and nightmare. This side of nightmare is very interesting to me. Tragedy probably presents a resolution, whereas nightmare does not. It is just there to perform whatever exorcism or movement is needed. Maybe it's just a matter of movement.

Simmons: Well, Joe said that it does have perhaps even a more therapeutic or ameliorative effect than pleasant dreams. I'm *sure* that's true. In my experience, I wake up from a nightmare frightened, but somehow relieved ....

Phillips: I sometimes wake up totally unrelieved. But sometimes the point of that kind of experience does not become clear for quite a while. I thought it was interesting what you were saying about nightmare and what Carolyn was saying about Akhmatova's experience in this queue. She was certainly describing a nightmare, something that perhaps had no ending to it. It had no resolution to it, at least not at that time.

Forché: I think what we're talking about then is *not* that we have to wind up permitting light, as you say, but addressing ourselves as honestly as possible to our work at every stage of it, and being true to our deepest selves.

Phillips: I think there can be sometimes a fear of descending into the nightmare, or writing in that kind of vein, because you fear you cannot really present that light. Maybe I'm speaking very personally here, but there is a danger of beginning to back off because you don't see the light looming around down there, and you don't really know what's going to happen if you can't find the light.

Bellamy: I think we're still struggling with this issue on a grand scale. I don't know how long this is going to last. I'm not even sure where it started—some critics say it started with Richardson—the idea of paying close attention to the moment-by-moment content of consciousness. But certainly we became aware of it with Freud, one of whose basic lessons was that the mystery of life lies within.

Now, as artists in the twentieth century, we are all more or less in agreement that Freud is right, and that it is, in fact, liberating and healing, and that *salvation lies* in paying attention to those nightmares, dreams, and inner visions. To censor them or to pretend they don't exist or to try to flee from them is ultimately destructive, or at least not productive.

So I think one thing we agreed upon during this session has been that Pandora's box *should* be opened. Certainly each person has to make a judgment about how far to open the door. But that's one of the things that I think, as writers, we try to do or try to cope with, try to understand—and as readers, as well.

Forché: A love of language helps. I really believe that if we are devoted to our language and to constantly reviving it and resuscitating it, we'll be performing morally.

Bellamy: One of the things that's in the box is language.

Forché: Yes.

Phillips: Language is the only thing that saves us sometimes. Writing really is a collective act. When you're dealing with language, you're dealing with something that has a collective power. You're cutting through the aloneness of whatever the vision is—by using language.

Forché: Language may be our only creation that we've made from nothing—and it's the basis of all others.

Saranac taught me that writers can be kind and generous to one another .... Thanks to the conference, I have "fresh tomatoes in the salad of my mind."

—Mary P., York, ME

I'm proud to have worked with students in the first year of the St. Lawrence/*Fiction International* Writers' Conference, and to see, as I travel around the country, that its reputation has grown steadily. I've taught in many workshops, but St. Lawrence is the most memorable—I've made life-long friends among students and staff.

—David Madden

David Madden leading a workshop at Saranac, 1974.

St. Lawrence University Writers' Conference

June 8 - 15, 1977

On Saranac Lake in the Adirondacks

JOYCE CAROL OATES, winner of the National Book Award for fiction in 1970, was born in 1938 and grew up in the country outside Lockport, New York. Her nine published novels include **Expensive People, Wonderland, Do With Me What You Will**, and **Childwold**; her nine published story collections include **The Wheel of Love, Marriages and Infidelities, The Goddess and Other Women, The Hungry Ghosts**, and **The Seduction**. In addition to five collections of poetry (including **Love and Its Derangements**) and three books of criticism (including **New Heaven, New Earth**), four of her plays have been produced in New York. Joyce Carol Oates is married to Raymond Smith, and both are Professors of English at the University of Windsor, Ontario, where they teach and edit the literary magazine **The Ontario Review**.

ANN BEATTIE is a frequent contributor to **The New Yorker**, and her stories have also appeared in **The Atlantic Monthly, Fiction, The Texas Quarterly, The Virginia Quarterly Review, Transatlantic Review**, and in the Harper's Magazine Press anthology, **Bitches and Sad Ladies**. In 1976, Doubleday published her first novel, **Chilly Scenes of Winter**, and a collection of stories, **Distortions**, on the same day. She grew up in Washington, D.C., and attended American University and the University of Connecticut. For the past two years she has taught courses in short fiction and in fiction writing at the University of Virginia, and next year she will teach fiction writing at Harvard.

THEODORE WEISS, poet, editor, and critic, has taught at the University of North Carolina, Yale University, Bard College, and MIT and is currently Professor of English and Creative Writing at Princeton. His books of poetry include **The Catch, Outlanders, Gunsight** (a long poem), **The World before Us: Medium, The Last Day and the First, The Breath of Clowns and Kings**. Since 1943 he and his wife Renee have published a critical book on Shakespeare, **The Breath of Clowns and Kings**. A recipient of such honors as the Wallace Stevens Award, and many others, he has been a poetry judge for the National Book Awards and the Bollingen Award. Formerly an editor on the Wesleyan Poetry Series Board, he is now serving as the editor of the Princeton Series of Contemporary Poets.

GAIL GODWIN is the author of **The Perfectionists** (1970), **Glass People** (1972), **The Odd Woman** (1974), and **Dream Children** — winner of the St. Lawrence Award for Fiction for 1976. Her stories have been published in **Harper's, Esquire, Paris Review**, and other magazines, and have been reprinted in numerous anthologies; and she is a frequent reviewer of current fiction for **The New York Times Book Review**. She was born in Alabama, graduated from the University of North Carolina, and received her doctorate in English from the University of Iowa. She has been the recipient of a grant from the National Endowment for the Arts, a Guggenheim Fellowship; and her novel, **The Odd Woman**, was nominated for the National Book Award. Currently, she is Writer-in-Residence at Vassar College.

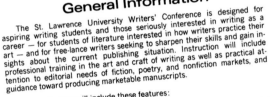

ROBIE MACAULEY is Fiction Editor of **Playboy** and formerly editor of the distinguished literary quarterly, **The Kenyon Review**. He is the author of **The Disguises of Love**, a novel, and **The End of Pity**, a collection of short stories, as well as **Technique in Fiction**, a study of the craft of fiction widely used for college writing courses. His stories have frequently appeared in the **Best American Short Stories** and **O. Henry Prize Stories** anthologies and in magazines such as **Esquire, Playboy**, and **Cosmopolitan**; and his reviews and articles, in **Vogue, Saturday Review, The New Republic**, and **The New York Times Book Review**. He has been a fiction judge for the National Book Awards and a recipient of Fulbright, Rockefeller, and Guggenheim fellowships.

TESS GALLAGHER received the Elliston Award for the best book of poetry published by a small press for her first full-length book, **Instructions to the Double**, published by Graywolf Press in 1976. Her poetry has appeared in numerous magazines, including **Antaeus, The New Yorker, The Nation, American Poetry Review, fiction international, Saturday Review**, and **Poetry Northwest**; and in several anthologies, including Daniel Halpern's **The American Poetry Anthology** of best American poets under forty. A native of the Pacific Northwest, she graduated from the University of Washington and the Iowa Writers' Workshop and has received a National Endowment for the Arts grant for 1976 and a CAPS Award for 1977.

JOE DAVID BELLAMY is author of **The New Fiction** and editor of **SuperFiction, or The American Story Transformed**, published by Random House/Vintage. His fiction, poetry, criticism, and reviews have been published in **Paris Review, Saturday Review, Playboy, Partisan Review, Iowa Review, Novel, Harper's Bookletter, The New York Times Book Review**, and elsewhere; and his interviews have appeared in such magazines as **The Atlantic Monthly, Chicago Review**, and **New American Review**. His writing textbook, **Apocalypse**, emphasizes material using fictional techniques for nonfiction writing. Publisher and editor of **fiction international**, Mr. Bellamy teaches writing and literature at St. Lawrence University and is Director of the Conference.

General Information

The St. Lawrence University Writers' Conference is designed for aspiring writing students and those seriously interested in writing as a career — for students of literature interested in how writers practice their art — and for free-lance writers seeking to sharpen their skills and gain insights about the current publishing situation. Instruction will include professional training in the art and craft of writing as well as practical attention to editorial needs of fiction, poetry, and nonfiction markets, and guidance toward producing marketable manuscripts.

The conference will include these features:

- Daily workshops in the novel, the short story, poetry, and the magazine article.
- Lectures and panel discussions of: Recent Poetry; Writing a First Novel; Magazines: Big and Small, Popular and Literary; The New Fiction; and other topics.
- Eminently qualified staff of widely published writers and editors.
- Close personal contact between students and staff in an informal setting.
- Individual manuscript conferences.
- Unusual range of recreational opportunities.
- Lovely natural lake-and-forest site and relaxed atmosphere.

The Saranac Conference Center of St. Lawrence University — originally owned, contiguous family camps of the Bentleys, Rockefellers, and deBruns — offers spacious living quarters for 70 guests on the northern and western shores of Upper Saranac Lake. Facing the sunrise over high peaks, buildings at the Center include a central lodge with enormous stone fireplaces; a recreation hall; a teahouse; a boathouse; a reading lounge and library; and numerous comfortable residential cottages — many combining architectural features of the Swiss chalet and the well-equipped meeting rooms; and Loysen Hall, a modern, air-conditioned facility. Meals are served in Loysen Hall, a modern, air-conditioned facility.

For leisure hours, there are two excellent, crescent-shaped swimming beaches of firm sand. A variety of watercraft is available: motorboats, both inboard and outboard; sailboats; rowboats; a paddle wheel; and canoes. A nature trail winds through several acres of wild forest south of the main lodge. There is a tennis court on the tract, and the 18-hole Saranac Inn Golf Course is within a five-minute drive.

Upper Saranac Lake itself is eight miles long, about two miles wide at either end, and reaches depths of 100 feet or more. It is an excellent lake for sailing and one of the best Adirondack waters for lake trout. Accessible islands offer opportunity for picnicking, exploration, or solitude.

The Adirondack Park is the largest of all state or national parks in the Continental United States. This enormous patchwork of mountains, wild forest, and lakes is the most authentic wilderness left east of the Mississippi.

Registration: Individuals wishing to attend the St. Lawrence University Writers' Conference should complete the Registration Form (or a facsimile) and return it with a $50 deposit to: **fiction international**, St. Lawrence University, Canton, New York 13617. The deposit will be applied to the tuition cost. Balance of tuition and fees will be collected at registration.

Register early. Conference size is limited. Students will be notified of acceptance on receipt of application and deposit. Deposit will be returned in full if enrollment is closed.

Room & Board: $130

Fees: Tuition: $150 non-credit
$260 credit

...non-profit organization partially funded by
...supported non-profit organization partially funded by
...for the Arts.

Conference participants on the sun deck at the
Fiction International/St. Lawrence University Writers'
Conference at Saranac Lake, 1974.

When I first arrived at the conference, I was terribly
afraid it was not the thing for me; I was wary, defensive. But
I came away with "good vibes" about it all.

—Agnes B., Oakville, Ontario

In my experience, the SLU/*FI* Writers' Conference is one of the most genuinely productive and fulfilling experiences of its kind. Frankly, the great majority of writers' conferences are usually harmless affairs, mixing appropriate amounts of angst and commiseration with zeal and ambition. There is no finer writing than that which a writer talks about doing tomorrow. Or maybe next month. But I haven't found this the case at all at Saranac, which boasts the right chemical and emotional blend of excellent people and place, pragmatism and creative instinct. I can honestly say that Saranac is a gathering of writers that works. I know the other Chicagoans who have been to Saranac feel much the same. Indeed, I believe it speaks well for any event when it is able to attract a goodly number of people from some 1,000 miles away. It's helped put SLU on the map. In all, Saranac is a place for the working writer, the established writer, the promising newcomer, and the interested amateur. Somewhat amazingly, the needs of each are perceived and fulfilled with care, sensitivity, and substance. Special bouquets to Joe David Bellamy for succeeding beautifully with such a tough task.

—G.E. Murray

MARGARET ATWOOD
& ROSELLEN BROWN

This panel discussion took place at the June 1978 conference at Saranac Lake. The panelists were Margaret Atwood and Rosellen Brown. Respondents from the audience included Robley Wilson (bio, page 112), Jayne Anne Phillips (bio, page 229), and conference director Joe David Bellamy.

Margaret Atwood has published more than ten collections of poetry, including *The Circle Game*, *The Journals of Susanna Moodie*, *Power Politics*, *You Are Happy*, and *Morning in the Burned House*, and she has written seminal criticism about the Canadian literary tradition. For a more complete bio, please see her interview beginning on page 21.

< Rosellen Brown at Saranac, 1978.

Rosellen Brown is the author of five novels: *Before and After, Civil Wars, Tender Mercies, The Autobiography of My Mother, Half a Heart*; and three collections of poetry: *Some Deaths in the Delta, Cora Fry*, and a sequel, *Cora Fry's Pillow Book*. She has also published two collections of stories: *Street Games* and *A Rosellen Brown Reader*. She has published widely in magazines, and her stories have appeared frequently in O. Henry Prize Stories, Best American Short Stories, and The Pushcart Prize volumes.

Margaret Atwood: What I would like to know is this. (I'm using this for my own education.) I can never get things straight about the United States, and people keep telling me "That's a New York poet" or "That's a Midwestern poet" or "That's West Coast."

Rosellen Brown: One of the ways I could always tell what a New York poet was, was when I was involved with Teachers and Writers Collaborative, which sends poets and writers into the schools. A lot of New York poets were working there, and there would be marvelous discussions. You would have a black poet who would say, "What I'm doing with the kids in the schools, I'm trying to get them to understand, where, you know, where they are in this world and what it's really doing to them and how it's messing them up and all the rest of it. That's what we'd do when I'd go in to work with them."

Then someone like Kenneth Koch or David Shapiro or Ron Padgett or Dick Gallop would say, "We talked about the colors of a cockatoo and, you know, the way its tail moves when it sweeps across the room." And the two of them sort of look at each other, and you have two distinct camps of poetry—camps in the sense that the covered wagons are lined up around the fire and they are protecting themselves. That's the only way I can tell New York poets when I see them.

Question: The Midwestern poets have been doing a lot of translation from Latin American poets.

Atwood: What I like about the Midwestern poets is all the disintegrating businessmen that are always in tree trunks. [Laughter.] You must realize I get my view of America almost completely through its literature, and I think I'm walking through an American woods and I realize there are businessmen in the tree trunks! We don't have any businessmen in our tree trunks in Canada. [Laughter.] No, you see, it's creepy, it's cultural imperialism, and I think they're all going to come up to die in our tree trunks.

Brown: Because all the businesses are owned by the United States?

Atwood: So that's the Midwest? What goes on farther west? What about the South?

Brown: William Stafford, in fact, in a way writes a very different kind of Midwestern poetry—full of towns and ...

Robley Wilson: Is there a point at which you "forgive" them for that because they've done something that maybe doesn't fall into a pattern?

Question: Galway Kinnell has written some beautiful stuff.

Atwood: Yes. I've heard him read a couple of times.

Brown: His best poems, or at least let's say his best known (but I think some of his best), have been about porcupines and the bear and things like that, and they're not at all regional, really.

Atwood: As a foreigner, I see all American poetry at a kind of a distance. And, to me, you can trace lines of descent, and Galway Kinnell descended from Walt Whitman, as he would probably be the first to say. W.S. Merwin is descended from Edgar Allan Poe ....

Brown: You just named two poets that I love.

Question: They are very fine poets, but so far, you haven't mentioned one woman poet.

Atwood: We're getting to that. I see the regional distinctions in the U.S. in a hazy kind of way. But it seems to me that the women poets tend to cut across those categories and do not place themselves in camps. They don't place themselves *in camps.*

I was thinking of writing something, which I probably won't because I don't have time. But certain poets in Canada use sports as a metaphor for writing poetry, particularly baseball. It seems to me that when you adopt sports, team sports, as a metaphor for writing poetry, you automatically have a team. Many have an opposing team. Many have cheerleaders, which is about all women can be in that configuration, because women aren't let into the camp. They are not let into the camp. They can be a mascot, or they can be a cheerleader or a wife. Those are the roles, and for that reason—because women don't do team sports (women are tennis players or canoeists or high jumpers, but they don't play football and baseball and hockey)—women don't arrange themselves into teams.

Question: That's changing. I've seen a lot of poets write about being athletes.

Atwood: Yes. You can be an individual athlete. But it's not that team thing. All the guys on my team are good. All the guys on your team are bad. They're the enemy. My team is going to beat your team, and I know a lot of sports statistics, as well, and anybody who doesn't know those things is really out.

Brown: The question I have for everyone is this: Is this of use to the poets or the would-be poets here?

Question: Not at all.

Atwood: Probably not.

ONE OF THE REASONS WOMEN HAVE NOT WRITTEN ABOUT CERTAIN THINGS IN THE PAST IS THAT THEY HAVE LIVED FAIRLY NARROW LIVES. I WANT TO BE ABLE TO DO ALL OF IT.

Brown: Did you have to say to yourself: "I feel like I'm writing Midwestern poetry, but I live in Maine. Should I move?" [Laughter.] You know. It is interesting to know where what you're reading was written, and if it begins to seem sort of familiar, you know you've read a lot of poets like that before, maybe you can begin to generalize.

Question: Let me say something related. My women graduate students have all been feminized, and they all think that means they have to write poems about menstruation! So everybody's talking about women as sex objects—the women, the men, everybody! The women are relating to themselves only sexually— "coming to terms with being a woman, coming to terms with my sex, coming to terms with my sexuality." The women aren't writing poems about, you know, dragonflies or the world. They're only writing about sexuality.

Atwood: Well, they wrote poems about dragonflies for a long time, and everybody told them they didn't do it as well as men did. I mean, I think there's kind of a history about that. I also think that you can't really tell people what to write about. You can only let them write through it, and then when they get tired of it, they'll write about something else.

Wilson: Is there a proper subject matter for poetry?

Brown: No.

Atwood: I don't think there is.

Wilson: It sounds as if that's what is being recommended.

Atwood: I would very much object to anybody telling me that, because I was a woman, I had to write about menstruation. I think that I can write about anything that I want to write about, but would not exclude sexuality. I wouldn't exclude it. I object to that because people did that to me when I was younger, and they said that I had to cook or whatever, and it's the same thing. I mean to say that you have to write women's things because you're a woman is the same thing as saying that you have to wear an apron. I object to that as well. But if I want to wear an apron or if I want to write about that, let me do it.

Question: Sure.

Brown: This is maybe more for fiction writers than for poets, but I just finished editing an issue of *Ploughshares* that was one in which men wrote in the voices of women and women in the voices of men. As far as I was concerned, that was just one more option. It was *subject matter*. I like to do that sometimes. I like to write as a woman sometimes. I like to write *about* women. Whatever.

And I had a real difference with the editor of the magazine who wrote a rebuttal to my introductory article in which I said, "As far as I'm concerned, this is merely subject matter, and I want the freedom as a writer to be able to write about any damn thing I please, and I want the latitude in my own life to *know* about things." One of the reasons women have not written about certain things in the past is that they have lived fairly narrow lives, for the most

part. So they haven't had access to the world at large and, therefore, they've had narrow subject matter. They've written about their kitchens. That's all they knew. I want to be able to do all of it. The editor of the magazine took exception and said people *have* their obsessions. You know. Of course they do. But it should be an entirely democratic choice for the writer.

Question: Right, especially if you're talking about something external like astronomy. Let's say you're talking about a comet. Someone will say, "Well, how do you, as a woman, relate to a comet?" I don't relate to a comet sexually! I really don't. I just relate to it as a person. We don't have to relate to everything sexually.

Wilson: Well, I think we do. [Laughter.]

Brown: You're relating to it *out of your own head*, which is masculine or feminine in some way, and is Southern or Northern ....

Atwood: Yes. But it's also just human in some way. I think she is right, that there is a part of the personality that is just human—the part that can do mathematics, for instance. There is no such thing as a *female* mathematics and a *male* mathematics. I mean, there just isn't.

Brown: Sure.

Atwood: There's no way to play chess to win that is female or male—unless you start stroking the fellow's knee under the table.

Brown: But, Margaret, there are very subtle differences in disposition between people, though they're not solely sexual. They're made up of a thousand things. There are people who write poetry who are nice people and those who write it who are awful people, and that is going to influence what you do, too.

Wilson: Should we be headed for a kind of unisex poetry, where you cannot distinguish a female poet from a male poet? My feeling is that some of Anne Sexton's poetry would be lost if she had adopted a voice which was indistinguishable from a male voice.

Question: I'm just worried about the young woman in college whose teacher says, "You are a really good poet. You ought to read Sylvia Plath and Anne Sexton."

Wilson: Why are you worried?

Question: Well, because there's Milton! There's Eliot. There's Stevens.

Atwood: If they're really good, they'll find that out.

Question: Yes. But the women are led to believe: "Okay. I'm a woman—my subject matter must be sexuality."

Wilson: There's a time in everybody's life when their own sexuality is the crucial thing, and when you're young is one of those times.

Atwood: When aren't those times, though? [Laughter.]

Wilson: Eliot said it is pointless to give a college education to anybody up to the age of twenty-five because they are totally preoccupied with sexuality and they're not really listening. If you think about your own college education: It's very distracting to be under the age of twenty-five, and you really don't get a college education. You don't really learn until you get out of college and have to do something yourself, and then you relearn it all and it finally begins to make sense.

Brown: Yes. But it's one of many common concerns. I don't believe you think about *nothing* in your college years but sex.

Atwood: I don't believe that either.

Question: It's worse for men. You know. I think more about sex *now*. [Laughter.]

In your thirties is when women start thinking about it.

Atwood: Hmmm—well. [Laughter.]

Question: What I'd like to agree with you about is what is happening a lot in universities, which is that they *only* want to teach

Poets Diane Wakoski and Tess Gallagher at Saranac, 1975.

Anne Sexton and Sylvia Plath, particularly male teachers but also lots of women teachers. They say, "Oh, here are our two suicides—we'll take a look at them." But I think what is important is for women poets to look at the history of women poets. Go from Sappho to the present. I think you can learn a great deal about who you are as a woman by doing that. So, I think we should read Milton, I think we should read John Donne, I think we should read Shakespeare. But I think women should know their history to write it.

Atwood: I had problems with Milton, myself, because of what happens in *Paradise Lost*.

I really objected to that part of it, the curly hair .... Eve has very curly hair, and it seems really a snare—for poor old Adam.

Question: Put away the curling iron.

Atwood: I know. Exactly right. Yes. I used to wear my [curly] hair in a bun because I didn't want to be confused with those ensnaring sort of evil people in *Paradise Lost*. I think, yes, read Milton, Shakespeare, and so on, but be prepared for the fact that in a lot of those books, women are the goats. You know they are, but that's okay. That's men's literature. Women do the same thing to men in their literature.

Question: Yes, but the other extreme of that is what I heard at this conference I attended at Barnard. One woman said she teaches all the great novelists and has the students rewrite the last chapters, turning them into feminist books, turning Emma Bovary into suddenly a feminist novel. I think you have to respect literature for its time. I think that can get in your way.

Atwood: Yes. But you see, we were not taught any modern literature. I went through a very classical education. I went through an ideal education—except it stopped about 1920. We started with Anglo-Saxon and we did Chaucer and we did Medieval literature.

Question: Maybe that's why you're on that side of the desk.

Atwood: Maybe, and maybe not. Because if I had only that and I hadn't gone on to discover the other stuff for myself, I wouldn't be on this side of *this* desk. I'd be on this side of some other desk. I don't mean simply discovering *women's* literature. I mean discovering *modern* literature—just modern, period. I mean, anything from 1920. We just didn't take it. It was a very, very classical education, which took you from Anglo-Saxon to 1920, and that was it.

Brown: We stopped there even in graduate school, and when I was in college, we were not allowed to read anything that was not in the language in which it was originally written, which fosters an incredible chauvinism—because it's a lovely ideal to read a Russian novel in Russian. But, you know, how many people are going to be able to do that? It's a dangerous ideal.

Question: What I would like to know is: What do you think the ideal subject matter is? What is a proper or good subject?

Brown: There is no ideal subject.

Question: What kinds of subjects do you like then—as editors?

Joe David Bellamy: Or if not that, maybe you could name names. I'd like to know what poets as contemporaries do you most admire?

Brown: Margaret Atwood.

Atwood: That's very sweet .... I'm a foreigner, and I was naturally interested in my own literature. My poetic tradition in modern times, once I'd realized it didn't stop in 1920, was very hard to discover.

I would say the difference between American versus Canadian poetry is this: What Canadian poetry has been concerned with for the past ten to fifteen years and before that, the few poets who were writing, was making a simple statement that would help us survive—mainly, "I exist." It was necessary to do that because there are a lot of people who didn't know they did exist, like the whole country didn't know that it existed.

So a lot of my earlier poetry and a lot of the poetry I was reading was really trying to articulate something that had been mute for a long time, and had been ignored and had been invisible. So there is a lot of activity that was rediscovery of a tradition, digging up buried things and assertion of existence. You know, we weren't even that worried about sexuality because we were more worried about whether we existed or not, whether we were shadows or whether we had substance. We think we've come to the point where we can now say that we exist, just

as the whole thing is about to fall apart. But we are able to make that statement, and a lot of years went into that. I find it very odd to be reviewed sometimes in the United States because they think that a lot of my poems are personal statements, and they're not. They're statements about my place.

Question: They think that because you're a woman.

Atwood: Yes. But also it's because they don't know anything about Canada, and they've no conception of what that would mean—you know, to not know that you existed politically. So they think that poems that are really about that are about myself, which they aren't. They also don't know what politics I'd be interested in. They don't know anything about that. If they live in the South of the United States, they think I make up snow and ice! I've made them up as metaphors for my inner workings. I've made those up!

Brown: Still, Margaret, the constructive thing about that is that such a confusion could exist—and I'm sure that, for you, it's not a happy mistake for people to make. You're not happy to see it made. But obviously the political poetry that you have written has not been *overtly* political in the sense in which very earnest and didactic political poetry is written. In fact, that

WE WEREN'T WORRIED ABOUT SEXUALITY ... WE WERE MORE WORRIED ABOUT WHETHER WE EXISTED OR NOT, WHETHER WE WERE SHADOWS OR WE HAD SUBSTANCE.

kind of poetry is usually boring and mostly irrelevant and not very useful for the political purposes it's intended to serve.

Atwood: Well, because it isn't only political.

Brown: Well, exactly. And that makes the difference.

Atwood: I mean, it comes out of a political context which is very clear to anybody in Canada who's reading it, and very unclear to anybody in the States who's reading it.

Jayne Anne Phillips: Margaret, can I ask a sort of lit-crit question about *Power Politics*, my favorite book of yours? I never supposed that book was personal in terms of being about you and some guy. But it just occurred to me ...

Atwood: It's about me and the sonnets of Shakespeare! I think that's what it's really about.

Phillips: I was wondering if maybe ... I know, in a larger sense, it's about the way literature is perceiving men and women and a response to that, but is it also about Canada?

Atwood: It comes in three parts. One is ironic and individual, the first part. The middle part is political and social. The third part is mythological in the sense that a lot of the images are from films, fairy tales, pieces of mythology, plots of books, which have become normative. There is a Dracula poem in it, there's a King Kong poem, there's a Bluebeard's castle series of poems, and so on. The demon lover is in there from the folk song of the same name—Childs's collection. But the middle part is about Canada. It's about the relationship between large political power and small political non-power.

You see, I don't think that anything exists in isolation from anything else. I think that the problems that Canada is having at the moment are problems that are being had by the West Indies, you know, and by Afghanistan.

Phillips: When you were writing that book, did you have these poems you began to see forming connections so that you could put them into these three parts? Or did you have a sort of conceptual idea of what you were going to do, and you had these three parts and then sort of wrote the poems to respond to them?

Atwood: Well, let me see. I think both. I think I started, as I recall, with the weirder ones in the third section, as I often come to approach things. I can't really remember. That's hard for me to say. But I know that fairly early on, I knew that it was layers. It was like those black candies that you used to get in the drugstore that had a little seed at the middle and then they had layers, and it would be one layer and then another layer and another layer. As I see it, the first section is the smallest thing, and then there's one around like that, and then there's one that encloses the whole thing, which is the third section.

Question: Could you each name three poets?

Atwood: Yes, I'll name three. P.K. Page, Margaret Avison, and Anne Hébert. They're all Canadian.

Question: Margaret, are you choosing women poets or are these simply your favorite poets?

Atwood: They were poets that I read when I was between the ages of about twenty and twenty-three, who I thought were very good poets. They're Canadian and had an influence on me, and they *happened* to be women, although that was not my conscious interest in them at the time, especially Anne Hébert, who writes very Quebec sort of strange poetry.

Question: May I offer a somewhat different perspective? When you are talking about Canadian nationals ... I think there are a number of Americans who are quite aware of Canada and its problems. Perhaps this is because I grew up in Wisconsin, where everyone normally summers by going to Canada. But since I've been out here, there are plenty of people that I know in Virginia and Maryland who also do the same thing. I have friends who have houses up there, and they interact with Canadians. They're concerned with Canada's welfare.

Atwood: Could you name ten Canadian poets please.

Question: I can't. But ….

Atwood: I didn't think so.

Question: Would you do it for us? How about a few males that you like?

Atwood: Okay. Patrick Lane ... Michael Ondaatje. You can even buy that in the States because it's been published.

Brown: He does very odd prose work too. Wonderful.

Atwood: John Newlove. Al Purdy. How many is that? That'll keep you busy. On the West Coast, the first one you should probably go to is George Bowering .... What poets do you like, Rosellen?

Brown: There are so many, it's hard to think of them just like that. Well, I can't say Margaret because everybody's obviously already discovered her. She doesn't need to be recommended .... Louise Glück.

Atwood: Right.

Brown: Glück is a fantastic poet, I think, of extraordinary power.

Atwood: Could you name her most recent book and the publisher for those of us who are taking notes?

Brown: Okay, yes. *The House on Marshland*, it's called, and it's a book published by the Ecco Press, which is distributed by Viking. She had one first called *Firstborn*, which was published, I think, in '68. It took a long time to publish her second book. *The House on Marshland* came out two or three years ago, and I think it's a book of staggering control and power.

She's the only poet who has ever made me respond by bursting into tears at a reading and being inconsolable. She reads in an incredible incantatory fashion. She puts the book on her lap and just kind of sits, and the poems seem to come through her pores. They just emerge—you can barely see her mouth moving. She's staggering. She'd be mortified to hear herself described this way.

Charles Simic. I don't mind mentioning men. I think he's a wonderful poet. His last book is called *Charon's Cosmology*, and it's a Braziller book. It's lovely, lovely, lovely. It's small, personal myths. They're *domestic* in an interesting way. I don't know if anyone reading him would know if he was male or female. I don't know if the question would come up.

Atwood: What about John Haines?

Brown: John Haines. I think his best book was called *Winter News*. He lives in Alaska.

Atwood: It's very hard to feel your way through all the critical and reputational things in the States—because you find these poets that you think are really very good, and then you find out that nobody reviews them or they don't have any poet's reputation, and then you wonder why not. Why not? I think that's probably a whole other story about who controls what magazine and who reviews who and who knows who and who's the friend of whom. Haines seems to me to be somebody who has been quite overlooked. Is that so?

Brown: I assumed he was well respected, but I don't know.

Phillips: I wonder if any of you have read Marina Tsvetaeva? She's a Russian, and she's dead long ago. She hung herself, but she was a contemporary of Pasternak and Mayakofsky and Akhmatova. I think she is sort of looked on as their leader, or they revere her as being the mother of Russian poetry at that time. She's just unknown in the United States.

She had one book of collected works that was published by Penguin and is supposedly coming out again, and *Selected Poems* from maybe Norton. I don't know who is doing it. She's an incredible poet. Another woman I wanted to mention is Lorine Niedecker. I was wondering if you know her work? She's never really been published very much in the United States.

Brown: Truck Press did a wonderful little book of hers a few years ago.

Question: Does it have to be contemporary people?

Brown and Atwood: No.

Question: What about Wallace Stevens, William Butler Yeats?

Wilson: Emily Dickinson wasn't bad.

Question: Emily Dickinson.

Bellamy: Name some contemporaries, too.

Question: John Engels—whose new book, *Blood Mountain*, was just published by the University of Pittsburgh Press.

Brown: John Engels.

Question: Jon Silken, who writes out of England—these absolutely wonderful poems.

He has a whole book of poems about flowers, in which they are all described as though they were made of pipes and gears and fly rods.

Brown: He's got good eyes. He used to write very wonderful, very sentimental poetry. He was one of the first poets I ever loved because I could understand him. "The death of a son at age one in a mental institution"—you know, poems like that. It sounds, in a way, as if this is maybe more successful.

Phillips: I just wondered if you could comment a little bit on that form of writing from one's journals or diaries, which I think both of you do in some form—I mean, as in *The Journals of Susanna Moodie* and *Cora Fry*.

Joe David Bellamy with poet James Tate
at Saranac, 1976.

Atwood: No, not the same. I don't have journals and diaries, unfortunately.

Phillips: No, I don't mean that you keep them. I mean as you use the form in your books. They are about personalities.

Atwood: They're about—yes. This woman that I was writing *through* was a nineteenth century woman who came to Canada in 1832 as one of that wave of English immigrants who were all told that they could be gentlemen farmers, and they came to Canada and ended up in swamps and were totally incapable of dealing with it whatsoever. She had a sister who was more

competent than she, who wrote a sort of how-to guide, you know. "How to Make Your Floor," "How to …"

Phillips: There was really a Susanna Moodie?

Atwood: There was really a Susanna Moodie. She wrote two of the first full-length books that ever came out of Canada— that part of it. The first one was called *Roughing It in the Bush*, and it was about all the dreadful things that happened to her when she came to Canada.

The second was called *Life in the Clearing* …. By that time, she had made it

YOU FIND THESE POETS THAT YOU THINK ARE REALLY VERY GOOD, AND THEN YOU FIND OUT NOBODY REVIEWS THEM OR THEY DON'T HAVE ANY POET'S REPUTATION, AND THEN YOU WONDER WHY NOT.

to a town, and she does things like going to Toronto and saying how wonderful the new insane asylum is that they've just constructed, and you think it's funny; but in fact it *was* wonderful if you know what came before it. You know, before it, they put people in holes in the ground! And then how wonderful the new penitentiary was, and again, it sounds very silly to us. But, in fact, it was wonderful for them.

Anyway, she has a lot of anecdotes, but the main thing about her was that she *hated* Canada. She hated it when she first got there with a passion because she felt that it should be like Wordsworth having experiences with nature, and she could have Wordsworthian experiences with the parts of nature that were far enough away. She could have it with mountains and sunsets and waterfalls, but she could not handle the tree stumps, the mosquitoes, the swamps, and all the things that were impinging on her daily life. Anyway,

that was the person I was writing through. A lot of the incidents in the poems are from her actual books; like the poem called "Death of a Young Son by Drowning" comes from a section in her book.

She was very reticent about herself, very reticent about her *self*. She was describing the world, and she doesn't talk about her emotions very much. She has a section in her book in which she describes a strange child drowning, somebody she didn't know. She goes on for about three pages about this with all of the details about how he fell in a logjam and how they got him out. So at the very end of it, she says, "I also had a child who died in this way." That is the only thing she says about that.

So I was picking up on little hints. I wrote the poem about her child drowning, not about the one she had already described. So I felt that I was filling in the voice that was there in her to begin with but that she had suppressed because it was not proper for a gentlewoman to talk about those things.

Brown: If I could add something to that, the thing that *The Journals of Susanna Moodie* and *Cora Fry* have in common is that they come from observation of other people and the world, and they are *not* about ourselves except in the way in which everything you commit to paper is about yourself. *Cora Fry*, although it appears to be about a contemporary woman, is infinitely less about me and my menstrual periods and all the rest of it than it is about *things out there*. These come from being more interested in all of that than in this.

Phillips: Is it like a person being defined by their perceptions rather than by talking about …

Brown: Than by talking about their biography!

Atwood: Well, you're not trying to define yourself. You're trying to define somebody else.

Brown: Somebody else—yes—and not kidding, either, not saying, "I only appear to be trying to define somebody else—but really, I'm talking about myself."

Atwood: I had the material for *Susanna Moodie* because, in fact, I grew up in the North. But my relationship to it was the exact opposite of hers. She felt very alienated in the wilderness and unable to cope with it. She came from a civilized country. I grew up in the bush, and I felt unable to cope with cities. So, in a way, her feelings about that were the upside down of mine and backwards. Then people say to me, "Oh, I see you have all these bad feelings about trees!" [Laughter.] I say, "Well, those aren't my feelings. Those are somebody else's feelings, and I'll refer you to the page number."

GAIL GODWIN

Gail Godwin is the author of twelve novels, three of which—*The Odd Woman*, *Violet Clay*, and *A Mother and Two Daughters*—were National Book Award finalists. She has also written one nonfiction book, *Heart: A Personal Journey Through Its Myths and Meanings,* and two story collections. *Dream Children* won the St. Lawrence Award for Fiction for a first collection.

Her most recent books, both published in 2006, are the novel *Queen of the Underworld*, and *The Making of a Writer, Volume I,* edited by Rob Neufeld. She has also written ten librettos with the composer Robert Starer. Her other highly praised novels include *The Good Husband, Glass People, The Perfectionists, The Finishing School, Evensong,* and *Evenings at Five. A Southern Family* and *Father*

< Gail Godwin at Saranac, 1977.

Melancholy's Daughter were both *New York Times* bestsellers and Main Selections of the Book of the Month Club. She has been a Guggenheim Fellow and the recipient of the Award in Literature from the American Academy and Institute of Arts and Letters. She holds a doctorate in Modern Letters from the University of Iowa and has taught at the Iowa Writers' Workshop, Vassar College, and Columbia University.

This interview was conducted at Saranac in 1977.

Gail Godwin: Well, I have about three people who already have questions. I hope everyone will ask questions. Yesterday, in my workshop, somebody suggested that I prepare a list of answers and then have you guess the questions. I thought about that, and then I also thought about, oh, how one comes to places expecting certain things and they never turn out quite that way. I go to places like this, and I always expect to be asked certain questions, and sometimes I am asked and sometimes I'm not asked. Sometimes I wish I had been asked.

So I thought to warm things up, I would place three invisible questioners in the audience. They are quite distinct personalities. They are people I know very well and fear sometimes. They are not always in agreement and, naturally, since I'm placing them there, they might be said to be parts of myself. One of them is sitting next to Jim Perkins, who's in the red and black. One of them, a very thin person, is between Robie Macauley and Tess Gallagher, and then the other one is back in the corner.

I see one already has her hand up. Yes? ... Well, that's a very philosophical question. [Laughter.] I write, primarily, to discover things that I don't know—to discover things that I wish I did know—to uncover things, both in a scientific way and an FBI way, and to reveal things

that I think ought to be changed. To play games. To meet people, both real readers out there in the world and imaginary people that I wouldn't want to be or that I wish I could be. To experiment with different forms of life, better forms, worse forms, alternate forms. [Pauses, as if listening.] Is that so? Well, we can talk about it later. [Laughter.]

Yes? [Pauses to "listen."] That is a very practical question. Robie mentioned it yesterday. People do want to know how to go about it. It's a very practical thing. If you feel you need one, I would suggest— do this. First go to the *LMP—Literary Market Place*. It's a big fat kind of a handbook. You can find it in most libraries. There is a whole section of agents. One thing you might try: just cold-pick some names that you like and submit letters to them. Tell them who you are, what you have to offer, where you've been published, and wait for the replies. Then consider it sort of a shopping trip. You're interviewing them as much as they're going to accept or reject you.

Or you might ask your friends for the names of their agents and query them that way. Well, mine is John Hawkins at Paul R. Reynolds, and there are a lot of other good ones. There are new ones who want new clients. There are old ones who have gotten stuffy and complacent and feel that they can pick and choose.

You can also just submit without one. There is the famous example of Judith Guest, who wrote *Ordinary People* and simply sent her manuscript in and the remarkable happened.

Yes? ... Well, that's a workmanlike question, and it's something that I happen to have been thinking about a lot lately: How much detail to put in your work—the use of detail, the purpose of detail. It's a very tricky thing. I've noticed in a lot of my students' writing, as Theodore Weiss was saying yesterday, there's a sudden respect for and maybe even a worship of detail, sometimes just detail for detail's sake—names of cars, names of cameras. He focused his something, something on a something, something— names, brand names. I would say maybe a rule of thumb is how it *does* fit into the larger pattern. Is there a reason to use a brand name? If you're writing about a lawyer, and that lawyer is sitting in his office, how much detail should you put in a story to satisfy your readers' need for verisimilitude?

I was reading a story recently in *The New Yorker* by Cynthia Ozick. It was about a young woman lawyer who works in the offices of a legal firm. When you finished that story, when she went to get something out of a file, you knew which drawer it was in, if it was on the bottom—and what was in the file. You knew that after a year of doing this, the various cases she looked up, she lost—she even used the word for it—so much sight in each eye. She used the optometrist's term for it—diopters. Now that "diopters" impressed me. I don't know if it was really necessary, but it was impressive to have that little bit of inside knowledge. I think that what was in the legal files was very necessary to the story—the kinds of cases she had to look up.

If you're writing about a person with a specific job that he or she does, how much detail do you have to put in to convince the reader that you know this person and you know what this person does when he or she works? Now, Rochelle was telling me about her story about the cellist, and she'd written one draft and then she suddenly read an article about a real cellist and she found out that they had to humidify their rooms. They padded the walls and the floor. Once she knew these details, they actually influenced the plot. They gave her ideas for new things to do.

Does anyone else have a question? Oh, this one has another one. Very practical creature .... Three novels published and one book of short stories. About six unpublished ....

Question: Short stories or novels?

Godwin: Novels.

Question: Say some more about the unpublished ones.

Godwin: They're just things written at various times. One I wrote in college, which was a rewrite of a novel my mother had once written, and the plot appealed to me. It was about three college girls. They were all in the same sorority, and one was a former prostitute who had been adopted by a senator. One was a lesbian, and one was a nymphomaniac. It was more subtly done than it sounds. And I used her title, *The Otherwise Virgins.* She had sort of used it to develop her plotting skill, and I rewrote it and used it to develop my sense of just how to sustain my way through a novel.

Then I wrote another novel when I was living in England working for the American Embassy. It was very dull in the afternoon, and I wrote it at the desk. It was a good novel about a failed first marriage, and I sent it to several people in London and they didn't want it. So, I saw an ad in the paper and it said, "We're looking for fresh novels by unpublished writers with love interests." This is a true story now. It gave an address where to send this novel. So I sent it off. I didn't have but one copy of it. Nothing happened for a while. Then I tried to call, but there was no number in the phone book. I took a taxi to the address, and

it was just an empty building. So, I look for it from time to time, and that one was called *Gulf Key.* That was the name of the island where the unhappy wife lived in her very nice house with her very nice, but unsatisfactory, husband. Then there was a novel about a man who was an alcoholic who lived with his daughter ....

Question: What did you do when you discovered that empty building—shoot yourself?

Godwin: What? No.

Question: Has the novel appeared somewhere?

Godwin: I haven't seen it. But, you know, one day I will. I feel sure.

Question: It might have been published somewhere.

Godwin: It might, and that will be fun to see who wrote it. [Laughter.]

There was one about a father and, wait a minute, let's see. Then there was a novella, a gothic one I did last year, which is sort of sitting around. It's about a Dutch woman who is very mean, and actually I'll probably only use about a paragraph of it in the novel that I'm just finishing up now because there's a writer of gothic novels in that. It's just a paragraph from one of his books. So that's something that happens, too. You spend

$\mathcal{A}$ GOOD WRITER IS ON EVERY-BODY'S SIDE, EVEN THE VILLAIN.

a lot of time on something and realize you should have made a paragraph out of it or an anecdote. Does that account for six? I know there are six.

Question: What's the relationship between the one that got lost or stolen and the others?

Godwin: Well, to be quite brutally truthful, the first, the one that got lost, was based on my first marriage, and the first one that was published, *The Perfectionists*, was based on my second marriage. So, you know, the first one was about a young woman who lived on Key Biscayne, which was then not notorious, and how she walked to the lighthouse every day and she was a painter. I think I must have had Lilly Briscoe [from *To the Lighthouse*] in mind and was trying to get this lighthouse right. *The Perfectionists* was based somewhat on an English experience.

The themes were roughly the same. I think *The Perfectionists* had more to offer. It had some suspense. It had that interesting little boy. Whereas *Gulf Key* was just a young woman who got tired of sunning herself on the beach and wanted to be a painter but—ah me, the old days ....

Question: You were saying yesterday afternoon that you wished *Glass People* was no longer in print. I mean, do you really feel that way?

Godwin: Yes, I do. I do, and I'm terrified that *Dream Children* will go out of print, and I'm pleased that *The Odd Woman* is in its second printing. No. I really hate *Glass People*.

Question: Why?

Godwin: Well, because I don't think that I should have published it. But I wrote it and published it. I wrote it when I was studying for my comprehensives, my Ph.D. comprehensives. I was afraid that I would turn into an academic who could no longer write. So, you know, I sort of set myself that. The book that it was, I loved. It had a little bit of science fiction in it, and Francesca goes to New York and meets a woman who she knew years before who's now in the computer world, and they're experimenting with humanoids. Francesca simply has a humanoid made and sent home to her husband, and he never knows the difference. [Laughter.]

But my editor made me take that out. He said it would ruin my chances. So I had to kind of rewrite the book, and I had to do it because I wanted to publish my second novel to get that out of the way—because of, you know, the second novel syndrome. If people could just write their first novel and their third novel, it would be fine. But I flinch every time I see the book, especially in paperback, because it looks like some real cheap parody with that awful kind of blond thing on the front. Francesca has black hair.

Also, I feel that my attitude towards the characters in *Glass People* was superior. I considered them as characters all the way through. I felt that their destiny was mine to control. I could make fun of them if I wanted to. I secretly felt Francesca was kind of weak. I think I resented her being so beautiful and never having to develop her mind or her spirit, and I think it comes across.

Question: You weren't on their side, then.

Godwin: Yes. Who was that? Someone told me I said that last year.

Question: You said that last year.

Godwin: Did I say that? [Laughter.]

Question: You said a good writer is on everyone's side.

Godwin: A good writer *is* on everybody's side, you know, even the villain. If any of you are watching *The Pallisers*. You know,

even Lopes. Trollope makes you feel that when Lopes dies, you're even kind of sorry, and yet he was a villain. You suddenly realize what made him the way he was .... Yes, I was *not* on everybody's side in *Glass People*.

Question: I heard some mumblings this morning and a few last night, and I think I'd like to follow up on Joyce Carol Oates's statement about the writer's relationship to insanity.

Godwin: Can you give a more specific question—because this is difficult.

Question: I think perhaps your approach to it has a lot to do with "The Watcher at the Gate." Could you tell us about that?

Godwin: "The Watcher at the Gate." That came out of last year's conference, and then I wrote that essay about it for the Guest Word section of the *New York Times Book Review*. So I have to thank you for providing a stimulus for that. But you think that my way of dealing with potential insanity has something to do with "The Watcher at the Gate"?

Question: Possibly.

Godwin: I think you're right. I wonder how right you are. "The Watcher at the Gate" also came out of a sentence in Freud. "The watcher at the gate" is my phrase for someone in you who makes it difficult for you to write in a variety of ways. This inner person I believe in very much. It's a tricky thing. I think a lot of writers have them. I can't completely despise my Watcher because he does sometimes stand between me and that gate of insanity. Perhaps too much sometimes. I wish he would kind of get out of the way and let me …. No, I don't know if I should say that. [Laughter.] Insanity. That's such a nebulous word. Losing control might be another way of putting it.

What can you do about this? I sometimes put it into fiction. My first story in *Dream Children* came directly out of a bout of, well, something that can be embarrassing to talk about. When you start saying "out-of-body experiences," half the room gets turned off. She's one of those "O but for the wings of the dove" or something. But I was living in this old house at the time and for a period of months, every time I would start to fall asleep, I would start floating around the house. It got very annoying. I'd go down the stairs and look through the house, and there would always be some people sitting there. I never knew who they were going to be until I got there. I didn't know if they were going to be friendly or unfriendly.

The first time this happened I was utterly terrified, and then I began to wonder who they'd be next. Sometimes they were not friendly. Sometimes the house would change. It seemed like it was a house from another time, or the land outside would change. I won't go too much into these different people and what they might have been. But one night I went to sleep and went roaming around the room, and I went into my study and I found two children. I knew they were *my* children—and I have no children in real life—a little boy and a bigger boy. Then I floated downstairs, and there was a head at the table, and I realized it was my husband as he started to turn around. Then I woke up or whatever happened, and the light was on in the room and I realized I had been semi-asleep.

I was writing to Joyce Carol Oates and I told her about this dream, and then I said I'm writing a story about it. Then I felt guilty because that was a lie— because I knew, you know, if she'd had the dream *she* would have written a story about it. So, I thought, well, I should write this story. [Laughter.] So, I sat down that morning. But, I thought, how can I start it? I couldn't think of a way to start it. So, I thought, I'll pretend that I'm Joyce Carol Oates, and I'll just see how she would start it. I'm sure Joyce wouldn't have started it this way. But I just tried to have a kind of incantatory tone and just get into this story. *There was a woman and she did this and she did that and she*, you know, then I got into it, and then I realized that I could go on by myself.

Joyce Carol Oates: That sounds exactly like me. [Laughter.]

Godwin: Oh, thank you.

But, as I say, I really don't know what official insanity is. I do have times when I feel that the webbing or whatever it is, is mighty thin, and that if there were no mirror in the world (and by mirror, I mean other people, too), that if there was no mirror to reflect me, no one to give a response that I was actually existing, that I might not exist. This is both terrifying and comforting, but lately I'm finding it very comforting— that I might not exist, that it would be possible to just be invisible. So, that's … is that a beginning? But you had something else. What are these rumblings that you were hearing?

Question: I'm not sure I want to talk about this. I think my trouble is that I feel hopelessly sane.

Godwin: Hopelessly *sane*?

Russell Banks, Gail Godwin, and Stein & Day editor Mary Solberg at Saranac Lake, 1976.

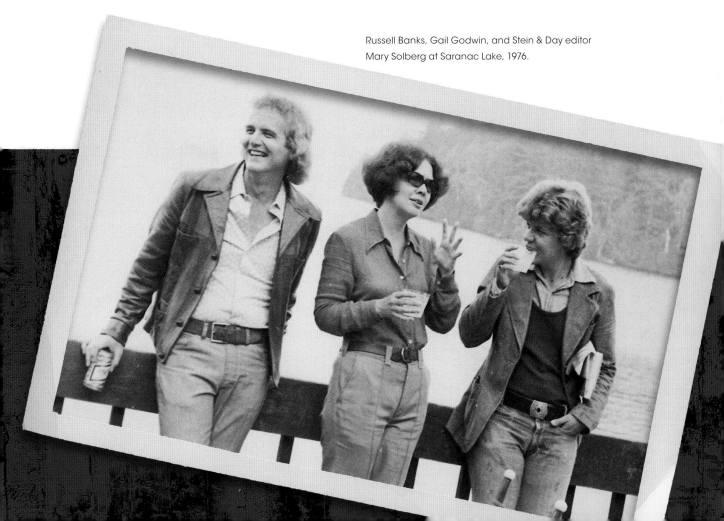

Question: Yes.

Godwin: One thing that may be your trouble—you're in too good physical condition. [Laughter.] It helps to kind of deteriorate. Sit around, eat a lot of white bread. Drink. Don't run. Don't exercise. Things will start to happen. [Laughter.]

Question: I was just going to ask you about—in *The Odd Woman*, you speak of a revolutionary psychiatrist, who doesn't think anyone is really mad. I was wondering if this is Thomas Szasz by any chance.

Godwin: Listen, I have some horrible confessions here. I'll probably never get through the day. Joyce, I'm sorry again. But, those passages were sort of reworked from a letter from Joyce.

Oates: Just some overtones.

Godwin: Yes. But, no. About boundaries.

Question: About the condition of madness ...

Godwin: Yes.

Question: Which is something that Szasz believes, too, and is trying to get changed into law. He thinks a great many people are put into asylums who should not be.

Godwin: Oh yes. Well, that's an idea that's in the air very much. It's Szasz and R.D.

Laing,[1] you know, and Doris Lessing, of course—her brilliant scenes on the two women in the basement—finding their boundary. But that's actually how those scenes came about—because I was fascinated with these passages in Joyce's letter, and because Jane Clifford in *The Odd Woman* is very earnest and questing and questioning and wants to have everything proved and visible, if possible; and these things aren't visible. So that's why she copied it all out to her notebook.

Joe David Bellamy: It seems to me that in *Dream Children,* especially, there are a number of places where phony forms of salvation are made fun of, and you seem to be making a statement about art as the ultimate salvation. I'm wondering if you noticed that you were doing that.

Godwin: No. Wait a minute. What, for instance?

Bellamy: Oh, the business about the V8 cans and the people who were going to be transformed ... It seems that you make a great deal of fun of most of the

---

1 Beginning with *The Divided Self* in 1960, R.D. Laing (1927–1989) was a popular psychotherapist who challenged conventional ideas about mental illness. Thomas Szasz (1920–), in *The Myth of Mental Illness* (1974) and many other works, has deconstructed psychiatry and argued against many of its fundamental premises.

psychoanalytic forms of salvation in this and other places.

Godwin: The V8 juice, yes. Of course, that is what scientologists use—because the V8 juice can is made out of a particular kind of alloy that works well on those psycho-galvanometers, which Jung helped develop. They're sort of a very sensitive lie detector. Has anyone ever done any scientology? It's a frightening thing, but it's very seductive for a time—because they promise you they have the answer to everything, and if you do what they say, you could become a super person. A super person—a power processee.

Question: Is that like Dianetics?

Godwin: Yes, that's the same man, Ron Hubbard.

Question: What does V8 juice have to do with it?

Godwin: Well, they have these very expensive machines with a meter to read your responses. He names them. There's everything from the "Theta bop," which means you're very upset, to the "rock slam," which means you've just gone over the edge, to the "free-floating needle," which means you're in a moment of pure grace. The auditor, the one who's reading the meter, sits on this side of the table and the auditee sits on that side, and this machine is hooked up to these V8 juice cans. [Tittering.] No, this is all scientific. The whole way the lie detector works is from the sweat in your palms, you know, how anxious you are; and the sweat in the palms seems to do best with the alloy in the V8 juice can, so that Ron Hubbard, who is also a scientist and a nuclear physicist, blah, blah, blah, uses V8 juice cans—stripped of their covers, of course.

Question: What do you do, hold on to them?

Godwin: You hold on. It's a ridiculous thing. You sit there and, you know, and they ask you, "What is the source in your life" or something. You hold on and say, "A tomato," and they say, "Thank you." "What is the source in your life?" And you say, "God." And they say, "That's enough, you're free. Your needle just floated in." Or else they say, "It's a rock slam; go to ethics and declare your suppressive person." This is all true—just one of the things in our world.

Question: How do you know about that?

Godwin: Oh, in England. There were a bunch of my friends who were doing it. So I did it, too. It's quite expensive.

Question: Did you find out anything?

Godwin: I found out one thing. It was, you know, quite costly. They said, "What is your source?" And I said, "The imagination," and I had my first free needle. So, and I felt good about that. Because I thought it was true.

Question: What story is that in?

Godwin: That's in "Some Side Effects of Time Travel" with a few alterations.

Question: Is that one of your favorite stories?

Godwin: No. That's one I'm beginning to outgrow. I get letters from young people who seem to identify with Gretchen, so now I understand why I'm not enjoying it—because I'm just getting older. I think Gretchen throws herself around so much. She's like a rock slam herself.

Bellamy: Even so, there is a humorous distance from Gretchen in the story. It seems to me that you really do take the scientology very lightly and make fun of it. I find the whole scene with the V8 can very comical, and the fact that she takes it so seriously is also funny. Then she gives up God, and when she gets home her mother says, "You go upstairs and write God a letter and tell him you're reconnected." [Laughter.]

Godwin: Right .... Sometimes when I, or maybe when other writers, make fun of something, it may be something that

we're scared of also, that we're afraid we might embrace. I mean, some of these answers are very seductive, the promises of certain religions and many of these pseudo-scientific practices that are out now. TM. EST.[2] They're all very seductive because they promise what we all really want, which is to live a perfect, ideal life, to be happy and to fulfill our full potential and, you know, they promise you that—if you pay your $200 and don't go to the bathroom for twenty-four hours. [Laughter.]

Theodore Weiss: You say we neglect or we shy away sometimes from things precisely because they attract us. Isn't the other true as well of any of these things that are going on now? We gravitate to them because we're leery of them. I mean, the other side seems to be also deserving of some acknowledgement.

Godwin: We're afraid we might be cheated if we don't try them?

---

2 TM is an abbreviation for Transcendental Meditation, a movement founded by the Maharishi Mahesh Yogi, an Indian mystic whose ideas were popular in the U.S. during the sixties and seventies. EST was a popular example of the human potential movement that spawned encounter groups in the sixties and seventies. Founded by Werner Erhard, EST is an abbreviation for Erhard Seminar Training, and Latin for "it is." Erhard's organization was loosely based on various examples from Eastern mysticism and the ideas of Alan Watts.

SOMETIMES WHEN I, OR OTHER WRITERS, MAKE FUN OF SOMETHING, IT MAY BE SOMETHING WE'RE SCARED OF ALSO, THAT WE'RE AFRAID WE MIGHT EMBRACE.

Weiss: No, if we *do* try them—cheated of ourselves, whatever that is. Cheated of our sense of reality.

Godwin: Yes. Cheated of the big rich package—because, I mean, there *is* no big rich package.

Weiss: That's exactly what I mean.

Godwin: Yes. I think you're right. I thought when you started your sentence, you were going to say: "Don't you find we're also attracted to them because they repel us in some way?"

Question: Well, getting back to the question, or train of thought, about insanity or lack of control or whatever, do you think you do your best writing at those moments when the web between sanity and insanity is the thinnest?

Godwin: I really have mixed feelings and strong feelings about this. No, I don't feel I do my best writing when the web is thin. I believe it's important to experi-ence that, but I find that when I'm writ-ing in that frame of mind, it has to be rewritten later. I'll give you an example: I was trying to get my novel finished be-cause I promised to get it in by January 8. I did get it in. But I wasn't satisfied with it. To do that, I had to cover a lot of space in a few months. So I decided I would get through it by the help of my friends. I call them Ernest and Julio Gallo. [Laughter.]

And, so I did. I would go out and buy big bottles of white chablis, Gallo Chablis, and in the morning I'd do my earlier revi-sions, and in the afternoon I would have lunch and start. I got through quite a few pages, and it was a very uninhibited kind of writing. A lot of things came out that were interesting—now that I have gone back and reworked them. But they just wouldn't stand up in the shape or the tone they were in because the tone was wrong.

You know, when you're under the influence of alcohol, your chemistry is different. It sort of plays on whatever mood or inflation you're in, and I found a great deal of the book was written in the style of one of my inner beings who ... I can't describe her, but her most prevalent gesture is this. [Laughter.] It just had to be. But I did get through it. So there is something to be said for that. But I do find I have to recollect in tranquility. That works best for me.

Bellamy: Isn't there a sense that we've all been short-circuited in our thinking about unconscious mental states by the early days of psychoanalysis? Because Freud always dealt with pathology, he gave us a whole vocabulary of pathology having to do with the unconscious, so that we can't even talk about the unconscious without bringing up insanity.

Godwin: I think that's true. That's what these new psychologists, Szasz and Laing, and Lessing and others, are getting us away from. These states of the unconscious don't have to be pathological.

Bellamy: I think there *is* such a thing as pathology—having worked in a mental hospital.

Godwin: Oh yes, there *is* insanity.

Weiss: That's the danger of Laing et al. They go too far. In redressing the balance, they throw everything out.

Godwin: Yes.

Question: Virginia Woolf did have periods of real insanity. But that's not when she wrote.

Godwin: That's right. There's no question about that. She didn't write; she went to bed.

Question: The writing was marvelously sane, and you always had the feeling of sanity and control, even in her notebooks.

Godwin: One of my students wrote a brilliant paper last term on her writing. It was based on the thesis that the writing was used to control the insanity, or to shape it, to order it, to keep her world in order. I'm trying to think. I don't know of any writer or any painter or any musician who has done anything—during madness—except maybe John Clare and that other English poet ... Christopher Smart .... I don't feel I'm qualified to talk really a lot about these unconscious states. I sort of wish I had more of them.

Weiss: Don't you find—at least I do ... I know it may be different for poetry. But my states of best well-being are when I'm writing well, and I'm writing well when my states of well-being are best.

Godwin: I find that.

Weiss: And to take what you said earlier .... When I write well, I don't exist in a sense, but I totally exist in a sense; and therefore I am more and more convinced that it is the health of my work and not the illness of it that matters.

Godwin: I would agree with you there. I mean, for myself. When I'm writing well, I also feel the healthiest. I also feel the least visible, in a nice way. I can remember recently, you know, really being in a lovely ferment of writing, really just in it, and I went to the bathroom and happened to look in the mirror, and I was shocked that there was a face there—because it really was terrifying to see. I also noticed, though, that the blood was up in the cheeks in a way that it isn't usually—so that I was healthy and visible when I felt most invisible.

Question: What about the poetry of Sylvia Plath? Isn't there a romantic notion that she …

Godwin: I cannot discuss poetry.

Question: Oh.

Godwin: But, what? [Laughter.]

Question: One of the romantic notions one picks up in graduate school is that she was insane at the end. It may be impossible to say, but some say that at the end, her last poems were written when she had disconnected herself from reality.

Godwin: I wonder about that. Because, you know, she really did her homework. She learned how to write. She did her sonnets ….

Question: The craft was learned when she was healthy.

Godwin: Yes. She had the craft, and it may have been what carried her. That's something I don't know about. You may get into such heightened healthy states and you push your energies to their very end and then go over. She may have done that. I just can't say—because I've heard so many things, too …. There's a real mystery with Sylvia Plath.

Question: I think great art, and even good art, is in contact with a great sadness or a desire to disappear or a feeling of oneness with the universe. Whether it's a very happy feeling or a very unhappy feeling, to fully experience that kind of clarity, some people might mistake it for insanity or might *label* it insanity.

Bellamy: I don't think that one can generalize about insanity in the arts. I think it comes down to individual cases. But as a nineteen-year-old working as a psychiatric aide in a mental hospital, I was very interested in seeing what sort of art the patients created in their art therapy room. This is taking into account the well-to-do patients at a place like the

one I worked in were generally well-educated people who were certifiably insane, but who were not necessarily artists or intellectuals.

But when I examined the kind of art they made in their therapy room, I was appalled—because what I found was the dullest, drabbest, most useless, lifeless art that you could ever imagine in your life. It was far less than mediocrity. It was just poor, just pathetic. There wasn't a grain of anything in that place, and I went back a couple of times to see if it had changed, and no one was doing

anything .... I found that gratifying, to a certain extent.

Godwin: Yes—so you know you don't have to go insane to write something.

Question: Most madness is dull as hell.

Bellamy: I agree.

Question: Mann thinks that the artist is really a borderline case. You know, he talks about this in *The Magic Mountain,* the idea that insanity is important and that writing is a kind of disease. If you can manage to have tuberculosis, your writing will be improved thereby. Don't quote me.

Godwin: No! That's not the book I read.

Question: I worked once with very disturbed juvenile delinquents, and there was this one boy, sixteen years old, who committed suicide while he was there. Just prior to his death, his senses seemed very heightened. I have a whole notebook of quotes from him during walks and other activities, and that anticipatory state he was going through did seem to produce a very heightened sense of awareness and consciousness.

Godwin: I've heard of that kind of thing, too.

Bellamy: That doesn't necessarily contradict what we've already said. Individual cases vary. I guess I want to come back to Jim Perkins's statement that he felt "hopelessly sane." Jim, I wouldn't worry about it. When I was nineteen and took that job in the mental hospital, I did so partly with the idea of asking: Does one have to be insane to be an artist, or is there an obvious connection? Then, if so, was I willing to make that leap, if it was required? I decided, for my own purposes, that, no, one does not have to be insane to be a writer. In fact, it is most likely an insurmountable impediment.

Godwin: Good news.

Bellamy: One has to find one's own answer to that question, I suppose. But I don't think it's helpful or good advice to romanticize insanity or to suggest to people that insanity might improve their abilities.

Godwin: Nobody would do that—I hope.

Question: The judgment about whether the art of an insane person or a disturbed person is art is always made by a sane person. You would never trust the judgment if an insane person said it was great.

Weiss: We receive poems by people who say, "I wrote this while I was on something or other"—as though that gives it some special ring or authority or something. All I write back is: "Since I'm not on it, I can't follow it." It's strange that I have to be on dope to appreciate the work. Hell, if that's true, then I don't need the art. I mean, I'll take the dope straight.

Question: I would like to ask you a question about the structure of a novel. I was really impressed by *The Odd Woman* in that, chronologically, it takes place over just a few days. I mean, she goes to her grandmother's funeral, she goes to New York and comes back, and yet a great deal happens. You *know* a great deal about her past and other people's pasts and maybe even her future within that framework. Did you make a kind of outline for that time frame, or did you write passages and kind of think out how to fit it all in? How do you organize material?

Godwin: Well, with that novel, the first draft was set in 1905. I started with the grandmother and her sister sitting in the window, and the sister ran off with the melodrama villain, and I got through their youth. I wrote that at Yaddo five years ago. It was two hundred pages wasted, wasted, wasted.

Then I realized I was really dying to get to the granddaughter. I had done the grandmother, now I had to do the mother, but I was really dying to get to the granddaughter. So then I recast it, and the minute I recast it, I knew I was in the right frame. I like to read novels that are chronological, like *Great Expectations,* where "I was born" and then at the end, you know, the narrator is some old, old person. But I don't find them satisfying to write, and I don't like to read modern novels that are like that.

We have thought so much about time, and I would like to write so that time exists where the mind is—without doing, as Kurt Vonnegut used to call them, "sandbagging flashbacks," which is the hard thing, to avoid having a flashback just, you know, come sailing through the air and just knock you right down. So that was the one thing that I had to worry about and go back and sand and smooth.

But with that kind of structure, I think if you're faithful to the movements of the minds of the characters, to a certain degree, you're safe. Just follow the movements of the mind. Sometimes they'll go off on tangents and say, "Oh, that reminds me of," and you may even write it out, and then it may have to go later. But the main structure of that book was simply following the movements of the mind, and I did set up finally the time span. She would get one week to have her say. But some people didn't like that. I remember *The New Yorker* said it was like being trapped for a week on a very long journey in a car with all the windows closed with a very chatty harem. So, you know, it wasn't everybody's cup of tea.

Question: You once described how you had reached a kind of impasse in your work and you turned to your journal to work out what to do next. Can you discuss the way you read your journal now and then to work out problems in a piece you're writing?

Godwin: My journal over the years has become more and more about my writing. It used to talk about how unhappy I was or boyfriends or something. For instance, if I go to the typewriter and just cannot imagine what is supposed to happen next, you just have that awful kind of engorged feeling. I will sometimes get the journal and sit down on my chaise lounge and put my pillows up and just write: "June 9, I'm having such trouble with this character. If only I could make her ..." And then the funny thing is, the minute I forget, "If only I could make her, if she could just be this, this, this and then I could have her do this and this," then it gets all right. I just leave it and go back. It's a way to outwit the Watcher or whatever you want to call it. Because I think sometimes we sit at the typewriter and we have this official notion of our writer with our writer's hat: "I'm now writing." As a result, you don't.

Question: I'm curious about your relationship with your real characters—since the main characters are always females.

Godwin: Oh, I don't know what to say about that. They're not all me. They're parts of me or they're the way I wish I could be or the way I have been at one time. I very much wish I could write a believable male character. Maybe I will one day. I admire people, like John Casey,[3] who can do that. In his new

---

3 John Casey (1939-) is the author of *An American Romance*; *Spartina*, for which he won the National Book Award; *Testimony and Demeanor*; and *The Half-Life of Happiness*.

novel, he's written about a woman. I believe that woman is as good a woman as D.H. Lawrence could have written. Well, I won't say that—that's too much. But I really admire people who can break that sex barrier. Yet there is too much phony breaking of it. You know, I remember a writer at Iowa—she's a woman. She was so sick of being a woman that she was going to write a novel about a man who was a forester. She'd never been in a forest in her life, but she was going to research it all, and you were so bored already just hearing about this forester. So there is a fake way to do it. But I think that crossing the border will have to come when you understand that men and women aren't so different after all. If there is a place where they are the same, then work out of that. It'll have to be that for me.

Question: Why should you cross it?

Godwin: Oh, I'm interested. I want to know what it's like to be man, to grow up like a man. I probably won't write a novel ever, a long novel in which the main character, the focal character, is a man. But I hope to get more and more into men. Is that an answer or a diversion? That should be, I think, enough—for now.

the pitfalls of first novels

E.L. DOCTOROW, CHARLES SIMMONS, MAXINE GROFFSKY & NANCY NICHOLAS

This panel discussion occurred at the Saranac Lake Conference Center of St. Lawrence University during the summer of 1979. The panelists were literary agent Maxine Groffsky, Knopf editor Nancy Nicholas, and novelists Charles Simmons and E.L. Doctorow. Other commentators were Houghton Mifflin editor Robie Macauley and conference director Joe David Bellamy.

Charles Simmons was, at the time of the conference, an editor for the *New York Times Book*

< Top: E.L. Doctorow, 1979.
< Charles Simmons.

Review, a position he held for more than two decades. He is the author of several novels, including *Powdered Eggs*, *An Old-Fashioned Darling*, *Wrinkles*, *Salt Water*, *The Venus Game*, and *The Belles Lettres Papers,* and a winner of the William Faulkner Award for Fiction.

E.L. Doctorow is the author of many widely read novels, including *The Book of Daniel*, *Ragtime*, which was a winner of the National Book Critics Circle Award, *Loon Lake*, *World's Fair*, which won the National Book Award, *Billy Bathgate*, which also won the National Book Critics Circle Award, *The Waterworks*, *City of God*, and *The March*, also a National Book Critics Circle Award winner. He has also written plays, screenplays, and essays on literature and politics.

It's not the first novel written that gets published. It's usually the second or the third that becomes the first publication.

Maxine Groffsky: Most of the fiction writers I work with have recently published or are writing first novels. Or, to be accurate, in my experience, it has not been the first novel *written* that gets published. It's usually the second or the third that becomes the first publication. I think that this is very important for you to know. I'm not telling you this to demoralize you but to give you some hope, to encourage you. I suppose it's encouraging or demoralizing, depending on which unpublished novel you're working on at the moment.

There have been many "first" first novels that have been published, and published successfully. I think, however, that most first novels remain unpublished—for a variety of reasons or pitfalls—and there's one that I would like to mention because it's one pitfall I come across most frequently. It's the matter of the writer's voice. The writer simply hasn't found his proper voice yet. It's uncertain, imitative, or a mixture of other people's voices, and that is *the* problem that I find. How do you get your voice? A lot of work, some talent—that's all I have to say about it right now.

Nancy Nicholas: What I have to say about "the pitfalls of the first novel" is essentially: "Everybody's pitfall is different." It's not always the first novel that is full of pitfalls.

Just as an example, how many people here know Lisa Alther's book *Kinflicks*? The book came in over the transom. I read two drafts. Here was a novel by a young woman living in Vermont that was obviously an autobiographical novel. She was a good writer. It was a serious book, well written, with some humor, some sex and violence—something for everyone. But it was boring. It was a book about a young woman who gets married and goes to live in Vermont and is unhappy in Vermont and bakes bread and tries to meet the people in the community.

Each time we wrote back to her and said, "You know, you have a lot of talent, but this doesn't seem to be the book." Suddenly, as she kept working on it, something happened. She rethought it, she lived a few more years—whatever—and she realized that she could be funny about it, that she didn't have to be self-serious. It was the same book, with the same story, only she was parodying; and the rest is history on that book. So, your first novel, as Maxine says, could be your third, fourth, or fifth novel, but it could be the same novel that you have just restructured. If that's your pitfall, I don't know what sort of advice we can give you on it.

Charles Simmons: My first novel was my sixty-fourth! Some of the earlier first novels I wrote in a night. Some I wrote in six months. I found I was desperate to write a novel, and I kept starting and I couldn't stay interested—that was my problem. Luckily, I didn't get to finish any of them. But I think the idea of finding your own voice is absolutely correct. I was writing somebody else's voice—all of those sixty-seven first novels were other people's novels.

If I may be specific, not to talk about myself, but just as an example of how a voice was found (something in me got quickly bored with those earlier pedestrian efforts, I'm glad to say). At the time, I was writing to a friend of mine out on the coast. He had moved away with his family—he was a very close friend. We had known one another intimately. I felt he understood everything I wrote to him. When I wrote letters to him, there was no exposition problem. There were no inhibitions. I would sit down when I was tired, lonely, late at night, kids were asleep, day was over, and I'd rap out these letters to him; and it was the writing that I enjoyed most. It was *my voice*. It was my talking voice. Then this idea occurred to me: "Don't write to Joe. I'll write to X." And I wrote an epistolary novel. It was exactly the same voice that I had been using with my friend. The guy didn't get a letter from me for two years!

Question: Was that novel published?

Simmons: That was the first novel that I published. But, as I was saying, it was the first novel I *finished*. I was lucky in that respect.

E.L. Doctorow: I think the key is to accept the accidents that happen to you when you're writing. Someone asked Thurber why he had never written a novel, and he said because he got bored with the characters after the first five thousand words. If *you* are bored, the reader will be bored. So the worst possible thing to do, I think, is to finish a book from a sense of obligation or simply because you've made an investment in time and energy—because then you're constricting the possibilities of accident and discovery. Charlie is very lucky to have realized that a book should come out of what is effortless for you to do. I think professional writers eventually find out that it's when something *yields*, when it *gives,* that you are in good shape. So that if you read the famous *Paris Review* interview with Samuel Clemens, you will discover that he said, "I never write a book that doesn't write itself." (George Plimpton is a lot older than you think he is.)[1] [Laughter.]

It may be that what frees you up for that run through the book is some kind of formal restriction on your own person—on the voice that you talk to yourself with and have talked to yourself with since you were born. What happened to me was that I was writing this tortured novel about a young man who goes away to college to find himself. At the time, I was working for a motion picture firm as a reader. There were two kinds of readers in those days: outside readers and inside readers. Outside readers were paid by piecework. They read a book and

---

1 George Plimpton (1927–2003), an American writer, journalist, and actor, was the long-time editor and driving force of the literary magazine *The Paris Review*. The magazine's tradition of interviewing living writers was one of his foremost legacies, but even Plimpton did not interview Samuel Clemens. Doctorow is making a joke.

synopsized it and wrote a comment—in effect an entire review. You got ten or twelve dollars, and for a while I made my living that way. I read and reviewed a book a day—$12 a day, seven days a week—and then I was offered a job as an inside reader, which was a chance to get essentially the same pay for far less work. So I took it. But the pitfall there was you had to read *Westerns*! Paperback Westerns, Western screenplays. So I did that for six months, and I began to get very ill.

Simmons: Saddlesore.

Doctorow: Saddlesore. I said to myself that I could lie a lot better than these guys were lying. So I sat down really pissed off and I wrote a story, and I showed it to somebody who said that maybe I ought to turn it into a novel. So I crossed off the title of the story and I wrote "Chapter One" on the story and then, just like they do in the movies, I put another sheet of paper in the typewriter and wrote "Chapter Two" and I picked up from there. Because it was this fellow talking, Blue, and I didn't have to worry about myself. The point of the story is that maybe the voice is the key to the first novel. The way to find it is to give it to somebody else rather than yourself—to find some restriction on your own language, your own diction that changes it, puts it through a prism, so that you're freed up through the book. The end.

Simmons: May I make a comment on what you said? I started working at the *Times* when I was very young, and I found out that copy boys and such could write editorials!—not on Red China, but on giving blood, on the weather, and things like that. You got fifteen bucks an editorial. *Well*, I was doing these things one–a–day. I would come in a half-hour early. I'd go through the paper and look for some little item they had and I'd store it. If it was raining out for three days in a row, I would write on how it was raining for three days in a row, and I could turn these things out quickly. They were almost always accepted. But with my "own writing" or my true voice, I was having a hell of a time. I was using the *Times*'s voice and it was great.

Doctorow: It was the voice of God!

Simmons: Well, it has a high Latinate content, you know, and you can *roll* along. And if you have a little joke, the joke goes over so well inside of all those big Latin words, you know. I remember people would say, "Oh, Charles, *was that your piece* today?"—because it had a joke in it. But it was easier because it was somebody else's voice.

Doctorow: It's the same principle as art students who go to a museum to copy paintings, to copy great paintings. It somehow frees them.

Simmons: You don't have a responsibility for it, in a sense. You are being a mimic.

Joe David Bellamy: Don't you think there are some writers who are less talented as mimics? Writers who may have a voice of their own they can't escape? I think of somebody like Vonnegut. I can't imagine Vonnegut writing a novel except in his own voice, and who gets so much out of that voice. Maybe he had to discover that. But I think he would have a hard time escaping from it.

Simmons: Did he have it in his first novel?

Nicholas: He *didn't* have it in his first novel, *Player Piano*.

Doctorow: It does seem to me it was a whole other thing he was working toward.

Groffsky: What about the fact that Salinger's voice is so distinctive that if you saw a page of his blowing across the desert and picked it up, you would know it was Salinger?

Doctorow: I think the point of the mimicry—if you want to call it that—is that there is a certain amount of self-deception. What you're really doing is permitting whatever it is *you have* to emerge. So you could say of the flute player: "He's

Clark Blaise conducting a workshop at
Saranac, 1975.

playing the flute, which other people play, but it's *his* playing, and the flute is *changed*, no matter what his illusion may be about what he's doing."

Simmons: When you are using somebody else's voice or a made-up voice, it *is* like a musical instrument. I can't play a tune on the recorder, but I've learned what it is to play a musical instrument. It's like talking. It's coming from your head but it's not coming out in "words." It's from you to the other person. If you use a special voice that you've tripped upon or stolen, you're not being false to yourself. It's just convenient for you at that time in your life. Isn't that it?

Robie Macauley: What about the next novels that come along? It's fine for the first novel, but then what? Hemingway used his own voice so much that—by the time he wrote *Across the River and Into the Trees*—he was parodying it, as everybody said. Everybody had gotten awfully tired of that individual voice of Hemingway's, and I think that's true of a lot of writers. Talk about the seventh novel or the fourth novel.

Doctorow: You can start with the second. You don't have to go any further. That's the *real* pitfall. The first novel is a cinch—because you don't know what you're doing.

Question: Could you talk about how you got into doing *Wrinkles* as opposed to some more traditional form?

Simmons: I finished this first novel—I turned out *Powdered Eggs*. But I wanted to write a proper novel. By that, I meant the kind of thing that I had written sixty-seven of and had failed. Obviously, something was in me to do that. But my marriage had broken up. I was living alone. It was a big change in my life. I couldn't get my act together enough to go to the bathroom, let alone write a novel. The most I could do was to write these little pieces.

Some people here may not have read this new novel of mine, *Wrinkles*. But it's made up of forty-four little chapters going through a man's life from past, present, to future in respect to one activity or feeling. That's the most I could do. I wrote twenty of those things in about a month, and I thought they were just exercises, something to get me out of the bathroom, so to speak. Then they dried up—I didn't do any more—and I put them away. I did write a *proper* novel—which was a flop—and after that, I pulled these out and worked two or three more years on them and made a novel out of them, which was how it worked. Finally, it was pure desperation. The novel has a desperate feeling to it.

Nicholas: I watched this process, and what happened was Charles decided it was time to write another novel. He started with so-called real novels, regular novels, and he would tell me, "I've got a great plot." Then there would be three or four days of typing and sort of laughing and sighing and admiring and then *dormant* for weeks. Obviously that had been judged by his fine, critical mind to be a false attempt. Those may be in a drawer, too, waiting to be revived. But I gathered that those were more straightforward plotted novels with a beginning, a middle, and an end. When he found he just couldn't do it that way, for whatever reason, they went into the trash pile.

Simmons: Those were my sixty-ninth, seventieth, and seventy-first "first" novels. I didn't run. But you sit around and you get terribly anxious if you're not writing. Time doesn't stop for you. You think, *My God*, and you'll do anything to start going again.

Doctorow: Desperation is the key to the whole thing.

Simmons: What makes you start?

Doctorow: What makes you start? I was up to my third novel, and I wrote about one hundred and fifty pages of it, a novel based on what happened to the Rosenbergs in the 1950s, which is rather sensational material. At the end of the one hundred and fifty pages, which represented about eight months of work, I was so appalled at how bad it was that I decided to give up writing. I was quite serious. I was close to suicide. Because I figured if I could take material like that and make it boring, then I had no right to write. So I threw the book away and sat down at the typewriter, having given up the idea of writing, and I started to write the book. What happened was I was so irresponsible and vicious and reckless and desperate that I found myself writing in the voice of Daniel—and that was the central discovery I had to make: that *I* shouldn't write the book, *he* should.

So that one hundred and fifty pages and those eight months were a kind of preparation, and they resisted me and I didn't heed the lesson. I kept fighting it and fighting it, and when I finally hit rock bottom and started to write the book, it just gave way before me. I had the voice and I had the first line and went right through.

Bellamy: Are there any generalizations you might make about the kind of typical first novel that might be written by a talented writer but that fails simply because of subject matter or a theme that is overworked? How outlandish does it have to be to be original? I think of an example like Updike's first novel, *The Poorhouse Fair*, which is about an old people's home. He was obviously a young man, writing about people far away from himself in age. It seems a clever choice. In his first novel, *A Long and Happy Life*, Reynolds Price was writing from the point of view of a woman. Do you think it's important for first novelists to get themselves far away from their own world and go out on a limb, so to speak? Writers are usually told to write about what they know. But sometimes what they really know isn't very interesting. They're twenty-two, they're just grown up, and they have similar problems to every other twenty-two-year-old.

Simmons: It's funny. If I were to say what I'm about to say now and you said, "How about Reynolds Price and how about John Updike?" I'd say, "Oh, I'm wrong." But I'll say it anyhow. It's a sort of a counterresponse to what you're saying, I think, perhaps an exception.

I don't read novels as a publishing editor would, but in thinking about it—if a person in his or her twenties writes a novel, what should it be about? Do they know enough about the world to interest me, to entertain me? Could they write a comedy of manners at this age? I don't think so, and I think a lot try. I think most first novels—we all know—most first

*I*F A WRITER HAS TALENT, THAT'S OBVIOUS IMMEDIATELY, WHAT-EVER IT IS THAT THEY'VE WRITTEN.

novels are autobiographical. But those do have a very strong chance of interesting me because they know what they are talking about and they are telling me about something I *don't* know. I think the other kind of first novels that are authentic are surreal novels—*Other Voices, Other Rooms*, for example. They can be absolutely authentic—as dreams and imaginings sometimes are. They know more about that than I do, and I'm going to listen to them. But Updike—that's a good novel.

Nicholas: I think the answer is, "Yes and no." I think Rosacoke Mustian [the heroine of *A Long and Happy Life*] is Reynolds Price in drag. It's his sensibility. It's obviously not his personal experience, but people are people—and he had chosen a rather clever way to frame it.

I read a lot of what I assume are first novels—unsolicited manuscripts—and there are genres that keep coming up over and over and over again. "English professors whose marriages have broken up" is a big one. This is not to say that there isn't a brilliant novel about an English professor whose marriage has broken up. But it depends upon who is writing it.

In my curriculum vitae and the conference brochure it says that I worked with a first novel called *Birdy*. Now, if somebody said to me would I want to buy a first novel narrated by a canary, I would be extremely dubious about it. In fact, the book is narrated by two different young men, and there are two different versions of the author himself. He has a macho side and a fantastic side. But he figured out a unique way to do it. This is his tenth, twelfth, fifteenth novel—it's his first one published—and I think he had tried all of the other ways about writing about his experience. Then he figured out that what he needed was to split things up. On the face of it, if you were describing it, you would say it is a novel all about a boy growing up in Philadelphia during the Depression. Well, God knows there have been hundreds of those. But he found another way to say it.

Question: How did the book come to you?

Nicholas: Well, in a shopping bag. He lives in Paris. He had a friend who had a friend who had a friend who lived here. It was sort of handed like a mailbag across the Atlantic until it got to someone who was in publishing who knew I was interested in fiction and brought it to me.

Doctorow: My answer to that question would have to touch on the dangers of writers' conferences and writing courses, where so much of the advice given by instructors has to do with just this question: "Write about what you know."

I've always been really angry about that idea because part of the assumption of that advice is that you can only know what you've actually lived, or seen, or experienced. If the idea of knowing were enlarged to include intuitive knowing—that is, knowing somehow what you haven't lived and experienced—then I would accept that advice. But I think the reason so many novels come in about English professors whose marriages are breaking up is that somehow they think that in fiction, your subject can only be your own experience.

I subscribe to that idea clarified by Henry James in one of his essays on fiction, which everyone ought to read. He says that if a young woman is the example, and she had lived a very sheltered life, and she walked past an Army barracks and heard coming from the window a fragment of soldiers' conversation, she could (if she were a novelist) go home and write a novel about the Army—and

it would be very true. That, I think, is the key thing: The game is to get into other people's skins and to talk through their voice boxes. There is no reason why "what you know" must be restricted to your own experience.

The Hemingway example seems to defy all this, but all I can think of is he began as a parodist. His first work was parody. But he found a really valuable voice through that parody, and a lot of novelists begin as parodists, which is a kind of mimicry. Jane Austen and Henry Fielding were parodists in their first books. So, when Hemingway ended up parodying himself, maybe he was getting ready to go on to the next stage. If he hadn't killed himself, he might have found it.

Simmons: I think that's right. You know that first suppressed chapter of *The Sun Also Rises* was recently published, and it was *amazingly* bad. I mean, it wouldn't have ruined this great novel, but you just could not believe it. It was self-deprecating. It was deprecating of novel writing. It was down on the whole thing, and that explains it—it was a parody—and he had the sense to take that out and, of course, you're left with that startling work.

Nicholas: But another thing possibly is when he wrote his first novel, it was in a certain time and place. History moved on. Everybody began copying. He invented a voice, and everybody began copying it. So by the time he was using it again, it was something you heard a million times from a million different people. It wasn't him alone anymore.

Simmons: I claim not. Because he *did* get the voice right in this rotten book—it was a morally rotten book, but it was a gorgeously written book—*A Moveable Feast*. You start reading that thing and you're just swelled with delight because you're back in that Hemingway ambience, and he had those sentences down, and the movements. You know, how he would describe places and so on and so on. But it was a terribly rotten book—despite that.

Macauley: Ford Madox Ford had a theory that Hemingway didn't have any voice. He was just an ordinary journalist until he read some Maupassant. Ford said he gave him the Maupassant to read, and he said this is an example of it: Hemingway starts out one story "All the company was drunk," which is a direct translation of Maupassant's story. He said just getting that key, a couple of key phrases out, Hemingway got "a tone" from Maupassant that started him off, and it was partly imitation, and then it became very Hemingwayesque.

Simmons: It was like Laforgue and Eliot. You read Laforgue and it sounds like Eliot. You are thinking he's copying Eliot, but Laforgue just gave him that tone. You used that word—that "tone."

Groffsky: I don't think it makes that much difference whether you write about something you actually lived, or not—as long as you can fool me or convince me, and that it seems real. It just doesn't make any difference.

Simmons: Absolutely.

Question: Actually, Hemingway had already found his voice before he published his first novel. It's in his short stories. I wonder if *that's* the place to start your first novel.

Simmons: I think most writers start there—sure. Everybody writes short stories in the beginning.

Question: I'm interested in Mr. Doctorow's taking a story and making it a first chapter. It seems to me that some of us have written stories and perhaps journalism, and then we might decide to try a novel. It seems a very grown-up thing to do, but such a responsibility. But every time I try to make that transition, I think, "Oh, my God, the forms!"—Jane Austen, Dickens. I mean, I don't *know* the forms. How does one get through that, that sense of intimidation, from the shorter piece to a novel?

Groffsky: Chutzpah .... A lot of *time*.

Question: How do you do that? How do you say: "I'm going to write a novel, and I know I want to go on with this material. I know there is more to say about it." But the form is just so difficult.

Groffsky: I don't think it's a matter of being grown-up enough. I do think it's a matter of very practical issues—of having the time and the energy to sustain it. It's a lot of work! It takes a long time to write a novel—and to keep going at it. As far as the structure of your novel, use someone else's if you're uncertain about it.

Nicholas: Did you read the interview with Harry Crews in the *Book Review* when his autobiography came out? Somebody asked him how he had learned to write a novel. I mean, if you read his autobiography, you know he came from a place where they don't write novels.

Anyway, Crews said he got fixated on *The End of the Affair*, the Graham Greene book; and he just kept reading it over and over again and then he copied it. He figured out how many characters appear in the first chapter, and he put that many characters in; and then when there was a plot turn, and then he put the plot turn in there; how many pages there were in section one, and when a new character was introduced, etc. And he said it was terrible and threw it away, but it taught him how to write a novel.

I'm not recommending this—I'm just putting it forward.

Question: I know the key is to create our own forms. We don't have to write a form like Charles Dickens. How does one find that structure? The voice is one thing, but finding one's own structure, that's the problem.

Doctorow: Why don't you twist things around a little to make yourself feel good? My sincere opinion is the story is much harder to write than a novel. If only you can make yourself do a novel, you're deferring judgment. But I think, formally speaking, if you are going to do something that takes one-hundred-thousand words, obviously the value of each word and the rise or fall of your self-esteem is a lot less than if you're trying to accomplish something in two-thousand words, where the value of each word is really high. I don't publish stories, usually. Sometimes I write them and put them away. But I think they are far more difficult, and I often wonder why aspiring writers start with the hardest thing of all, which is a story, when they can jump right into a novel.

Question: Would you address again the story on *Kinflicks*? Did you know the author? Was your first rejection encouraging? How did you feel when you saw the same book come back to you again and then again? Did you look at it and say, "I rejected this last year"?

Nicholas: No. This was someone who obviously was talented. It just wasn't right as a first novel. It wasn't right as *any* novel at first. It was not very interesting—it was a story that we had all read a million times, an unhappy wife living in the country. But she was a good writer. She had good things to say. There were parts of it that were very memorable, and I wrote her an encouraging letter. Then she reworked it and sent it back, and it was not noticeably different. She'd tightened it; she'd taken some things out; she had added things. It was still the same book, just changed, and what was wrong with it was the essential "whatever was wrong with it."

Then I think two years went by, and suddenly this entirely transformed book came in. In fact, I'm not sure I would have even known it was the same author, except that we keep a file. But she had transformed it. No, if a writer has talent, I do think that that's obvious immediately, whatever it is that they've written. It's worth being encouraging about that because somehow when they find whatever this thing is that we are groping around to describe, then they may produce something of merit.

Photo courtesy of Mike Simmons.

Question: I think we all hear the stories of the book that goes to twelve publishers before it's accepted, so how do you decide? Shall I work on it and send it back to the same person who sort of liked it, or should I send it along to somebody else?

Nicholas: Well, I happen to know about *Kinflicks*. I don't know what happened to the two earlier versions, but I think she must have sent one to another publisher at least and gotten an encouraging letter, because *Kinflicks*, before it came back to us, went to another publisher who said, "Yes, I like it, but you've got to take all the mother stuff out," and had various suggestions, so Lisa thought she'd get another opinion before she made the changes.

Groffsky: It isn't an unusual situation to send a novel to a publisher, editor, or agent and have an enthusiastic response with a suggestion to change something and let us see it again. I often work with people that way, in an editorial capacity, and finally get a novel that's ready to be published.

Question: Do you make specific suggestions?

Groffsky: Sometimes.

Doctorow: If the publisher sends you a letter of encouragement, you want to try to get a little money with it. [Laughter.]

Groffsky: Let me say: Be very careful about those letters of encouragement. Because

it's usually a form letter because publishers don't want people to be mad at them. Maybe I'm letting the cat out of the bag.

Nicholas: There's a large population you *want* mad at us. [Laughter.]

Groffsky: Sometimes I receive a manuscript from someone saying, "X publisher has said," and I can just read right through the lines. It's a nice rejection—it's their "A" rejection—it doesn't really mean anything. So I wouldn't, unless you get a very specific letter from someone asking you to do something, I wouldn't send the manuscript back.

Question: Is it all right to send copies of the same manuscript to different publishers at the same time?

Groffsky: If you let them know.

Nicholas: Let them know because often a publisher says, "I like it, but I'm not going to be bidding for this book."

Question: So, if you got a manuscript from me that said this, would your reaction be "Well, I'm going to take my time" or "I'm going to rush to read it"? Does it speed it up, in other words?

Nicholas: It doesn't do anything *except* that if I read it and liked it and wanted to publish it, it would make me think about it in a slightly different way, because I would think, "Do I really like this enough so that I want to bid against Harper & Row for it?"

Doctorow: It will take six months anyway.

Nicholas: Not true!

Question: Beginning writers usually get a lot of advice from lots of different people, and you have your own opinions about what you think the problems are and what you think the strengths are. Very often the advice will conflict with your own sense of it, but because you are so committed to the materials, it's very difficult to separate what is good about it and what's bad about it. Sometimes the advice you get is very good and sometimes it's, you know, totally not.

Simmons: Follow the good advice and not the bad advice. [Laughter.]

Question: How do you tell what is good and what is bad? It is very confusing.

Groffsky: You have to trust your own judgment.

Question: I don't think a beginning writer really can handle that.

Simmons: Well, I have a story. I was trying to write what used to be called "slick stories." They were going in a lot of magazines like *Saturday Evening Post* and so on. I didn't have any talent for it, but I

went on. I literally rewrote a story at the direction of various editors *thirteen times* and did not sell that one. At the end of it, I didn't know *what* was going on! I didn't have the slightest notion. I remember the last guy was Knox Berger, who is now an agent. He had the kindness to let me write the story over four times, and he'd say, "Give me a little of this or that ...."

Nicholas: That's why I was interested in what Maxine said about specific advice. My rule on this is I don't give any specific advice unless I've bought the book.

Groffsky: Oh, I don't give specific advice unless I'm working with the writer and I have made a commitment to the writer. I think it's unfair.

Nicholas: Don't listen unless they've given you money.

Groffsky: If you do, you're rewriting for someone who has not made a commitment to you or your work. I'm sorry if that was unclear.

Question: Have you ever seen material, which, because the beginning writer isn't certain of his or her own intentions, the writer became confused by conflicting advice and ended up ruining the material?

Nicholas: Well, that's why we don't give specific advice. Because, for instance, suppose Lisa Alther had listened to the other publisher who had not given her a contract. They said take out the mother stuff and then said we really don't want to publish it and she sent it to us. It wouldn't have been the same book if she had followed their advice, and I don't know if we would have wanted to publish it or not.

Simmons: If I were an editor, I would look for things that I thought the author could improve. It would have nothing to do with the possibilities of the English language or the form. I would say, "Does this person have in him or her *this thing*?" You know.

In a workshop, we were reading a story the other day, and it was a terrific story. I thought it had a little something …. it wasn't much as far as what was on the page. But it seemed to me to be attached to something fragile, or perhaps the opposite, something rigid in the author. I didn't say, "You have to change that." I suggested, "Look at yourself." I do think that's often the case. Hasn't everybody written a story and thought, "Something's wrong here"? You know it yourself. You can't fix it, and you will do everything you can and possibly ruin the story.

I think if that happens and you find that the story is resisting you, put it away. I think sometimes a *change in you* is what is necessary. It's almost like a psychoanalytical thing. The doctor can't say to a patient, "Calm down."

Question: "Grow up?"

Nicholas: Well the other thing, of course, is that it's your name that's on it. So no matter how much advice you're given, you're the one who is going to be responsible.

Doctorow: I don't know if this is apocryphal or not, but someone was telling me recently that, as an exercise, this fellow typed up one of Jerzy Kosinski's novels …

Nicholas: *Steps* [a novel which won the National Book Award in 1968].

Doctorow: … and sent it around and it was rejected!

Nicholas: Right.

Doctorow: By how many companies?

Groffsky: Many.

Nicholas: Twenty-three, I think.

When manuscripts come in unsolicited at Knopf, they go into a room; and several times a week, because I like to do this, I go through it. I have been at Knopf for twelve years—I'm not a first reader. I was a grown-up when I came to Knopf, and I think that one of the few things that twelve years at Knopf and various other experiences have taught me is: I may not know what's good, but I know what's unpublishable. I go through and assign what should be read, and anything that has a glimmer gets assigned to somebody.

Then there are two other levels of rejection of books. There's just a form letter when something is hopeless, and then there's an encouraging polite letter when something has promise. But then there's also something that goes to academics who are hopeless—because for some reason Mr. Knopf wants us to be nice to academics—which is a polite, hand-typed form letter. And then I have invented another one, which is "reject gingerly," which means the person is crazy, and you don't send him a form rejection letter. You treat this person carefully because they're going to come back at you with a machete or something. (We had somebody come in with a gun. It was a poet.)

This man who retyped the Kosinski retyped part of the novel and sent it in under an assumed name, and we don't keep a record of the stuff that just gets rejected out of hand. We don't keep a copy of their correspondence. All we keep is the fact that it came in and that it went out—just so that we know. What was written on that one was "reject gingerly." I don't know what the covering letter was, but there was something about that that made me think that this was a nut and that he should be rejected, but rejected very gently. But it was two years ago and I don't remember it very well. You just open the book in the middle sometimes.

I think that something made me a little suspicious, but ordinarily I would go back to the beginning of the book because there's obviously talent there. I think I thought it was nut talent.

Simmons: Jerzy Kosinski is a little scary.

Macauley: We got the worst criticism on that because we're Kosinski's publishers and we rejected it. [Laughter.] But there's a pretty good defense for that.

In the first place, we never buy a novel on thirty pages. He'd retyped it, but he got tired after thirty pages. We never buy thirty-page novels, and the second thing that never got into print is that Daphne Abeel, who was the editor, read it and said, she had never read *Steps*, but she said, "This reminds me very much of Jerzy Kosinski, and I think this is a very derivative novel. So it's an imitation so, therefore, we shouldn't accept it." But this guy got *a lot* of publicity out of it, and he was trying to make publishers look bad and at the same time attract attention to himself so that somebody would buy his novel.

Nicholas: The other thing is, I looked him up in our file after this hit the press to see if we'd turned it down and what happened. He has *four unpublished novels* that came through—at least at Knopf. This is, you know, his idea of revenge.

Groffsky: I was a first reader with my first job in publishing. I was the only first reader at Random House, and I read thousands of books each year. I was fresh out of college and very interested in literary novels and serious novels, and a terrible thing almost happened. A novel by one of the big commercial best-selling writers ended up—by mistake—in my office with the other five hundred novels of that week, and I rejected it! Except I wasn't allowed to send novels back right away—I could get them in and out very quickly. I had to hold the manuscripts for three weeks just to let people think I spent a lot of time on them.

Fortunately, it was one of Bennett Cerf's books. He went through the house and searched and found it finally on my shelf. I hadn't sent it back. So there I was looking for serious work, and look what almost happened. However, one does find serious work in the unsolicited pile, and it's often new people who are reading it. Since it's the younger people in publishing who are reading unsolicited manuscripts, it's really quite unfair to expect that they will have read all of Kosinski or know every writer who is publishing.

Nicholas: Well, doesn't that seem to be the moral of the story—that *nobody's* read Kosinski?

Simmons: May I tell a story about how I was accepted twice? I published a story when I was a kid in *Esquire*, and a now-dead agent wrote to me and said, could he be my agent? I said, "You bet." He sold another story for me and it was published, and I got another letter from him and he said, "Can I be your agent? [Laughter.] I read your story in so and so …." I withdrew myself from him.

Question: I've heard a lot about selling the first novel by writing the first chapter and then submitting an outline. It seems to me that if you subscribe to the unconscious process whereby the writer discovers where he is going along the way, that can't be done.

Doctorow: I think you're talking about my remarks. I should clarify this—we were talking about the sort of sub-rational process at the beginning of it. But that is succeeded by the editorial process, which is quite cerebral. You write to find the book, and then you begin to pick and choose among your material and start to build. Of course, at a certain point, you've committed yourself and have to find what is presumed by what you already have. In other words, at a certain point in a book, the rest is inevitable, and you can't deviate from it. At that point, you are not writing from the unconscious. You are writing from what the book is forcing you to write.

Theodore Weiss.

The Fiction International/St. Lawrence University Writers' Conference, consisting of a splendid staff, all able, serious, and congenial, was, I think, as good as a conference could be. Mr. Bellamy is especially to be commended, not only for collecting such a happy staff but for developing a program that exercised that staff and the students to the richest extent. His quiet, firm commandeering of the week ensured a steady, exciting course.

—Ted Weiss (and Renee)

Authenticity, exploration, honesty, intellect, and an avoidance of posing and literary hustling—a very high level of teaching and a nice feel to the morning discussions. The setting generates a marvelous feeling of informality and intimacy. The conference was uniformly excellent.

—Rochelle D., Highland Park, IL

fiction international

St. Lawrence University

Writers' Conference

June 4 – 11, 1975

On Saranac Lake in the Adirondacks

General Information

The St. Lawrence University Writers' Conference is designed for aspiring writing students and those seriously interested in writing as a career — for students of literature interested in how writers practice their art — and for free-lance writers seeking to sharpen their skills and gain insights about the current publishing situation. Instruction will include professional training in the art and craft of writing as well as practical attention to editorial needs of fiction, poetry, and nonfiction markets, and guidance toward producing marketable manuscripts.

The conference will include these features:

* Daily workshops in the novel, the short story, poetry, and the magazine article.

* Lectures and panel discussions of: The Prose Poem; Writing a First Novel; Magazines: Big and Small, Popular and Literary; The New Fiction; and other topics.

* Eminently qualified staff of widely published writers and editors.

* Close personal contact between students and staff in an informal setting.

* Individual manuscript conferences.

* Unusual range of recreational opportunities.

* Lovely natural lake-and-forest site and relaxed atmosphere.

The Saranac Conference Center of St. Lawrence University — originally owned, contiguous family camps of the Bentleys, Rockefellers, and deBruns — offers spacious living quarters for 70 guests on the northern and western shores of Upper Saranac Lake. Facing the sunrise over high peaks, buildings at the Center include a central lodge with enormous stone fireplaces; a teahouse; a boathouse; a reading lounge and library; a recreation hall; well-equipped meeting rooms; and numerous comfortable residential cottages — many combining architectural features of the Swiss chalet and the Adirondack log cabin. Meals are served in Loysen Hall, a modern, air-conditioned facility.

For leisure hours, there are two excellent, crescent-shaped swimming beaches of firm sand. A variety of watercraft is available: motorboats, both inboard and outboard; sailboats; rowboats; a paddle wheel; and canoes. A nature trail winds through several acres of wild forest south of the main lodge. There is a tennis court on the tract, and the 18-hole Saranac Inn Golf Course is within a five-minute drive.

Upper Saranac Lake itself is eight miles long, about two miles wide at either end, and reaches depths of 100 feet or more. It is an excellent lake for sailing and one of the best Adirondack waters for lake trout. Accessible islands offer opportunity for picnicking, exploration, or solitude.

The Adirondack Park is the largest of all state or national parks in the Continental United States. This enormous patchwork of mountains, wild forest, and lakes is the most authentic wilderness left east of the Mississippi.

Registration: Individuals wishing to attend the St. Lawrence University Writers' Conference should complete the Registration Form (or a facsimile) and return it with a $50 deposit to: **fiction international**, St. Lawrence University, Canton, New York 13617. The deposit will be applied to the tuition cost. Balance of tuition and fees will be collected at registration.

Register early. Conference size is limited. Students will be notified of acceptance on receipt of application and deposit. Deposit will be returned in full if enrollment is closed.

Fees: Tuition: $150 non-credit
$235 credit

Room & Board: $130

ROBIE MACAULEY is Fiction Editor of **Playboy** and formerly editor of the distinguished literary quarterly, **The Kenyon Review**. He is the author of **The Disguises of Love**, a novel, and **The End of Pity**, a collection of short stories, as well as **Technique in Fiction**, a study of the craft of fiction widely used for college writing courses. His stories have frequently appeared in the **Best American Short Stories** and **O. Henry Prize Stories** anthologies and in magazines such as **Esquire**, **Playboy**, and **Cosmopolitan**; and his reviews and articles, in **Vogue**, **Saturday Review**, **The New Republic**, and **The New York Times Book Review**. He has been a fiction judge for the National Book Awards and a recipient of Fulbright, Rockefeller, and Guggenheim fellowships.

ASA BABER'S novel **The Land of a Million Elephants** was serialized in three issues of **Playboy** in 1970-71. Kurt Vonnegut called it: "An enchanting and wicked and poetical toy." Later published in hardcover by William Morrow and in paperback by Belmont Books, it became a Book-of-the-Month Club selection. His stories have appeared in **Transatlantic Review**, **Iowa Review**, **The Falcon**, and **Playboy** and have received mention in Martha Foley's **Best American Short Stories**. A graduate of Princeton and the Iowa Writer's Workshop, he has been teaching for the last several years at the University of Hawaii. Currently on leave from Hawaii, he has been living in Illinois and managing his own farmland in addition to writing.

MICHAEL BENEDIKT is the author of three books of poems published by Wesleyan University Press, **Mole Notes**, **Sky**, and **The Body**. His poems have been anthologized in some 15 anthologies of recent and 20th century British and American poetry, and he is the editor and part-translator of **The Poetry of Surrealism** (Little-Brown) and of the forthcoming **The Prose Poem** (Dell). He has published writings on art, film, and rock music, and has edited four books on modern drama. An Editorial Associate on the staff of **Art News**, he is now Poetry Editor of **The Paris Review** and was a judge for the 1974 National Book Awards in the area of "Translation." He has taught at Bennington, Sarah Lawrence, and Hampshire Colleges.

DIANE WAKOSKI is "one of the most accomplished and exciting young poets in the country," says Sheila Weller reviewing **The Motorcycle Betrayal Poems** in Rolling Stone. Her twenty volumes of poems also include **Inside the Blood Factory**, **The Magellanic Clouds**, **Greed**, and **Trilogy** (recently from Doubleday). She has held Poet-in-Residence positions at the University of Virginia, University of California at Irvine, and Michigan State, among others, and has received grants from the Cassandra and Guggenheim foundations and from the National Endowment for the Arts. A featured columnist for the **American Poetry Review**, her poetry has been published in anthologies and magazines ranging from **The Young American Poets** to **Poetry** and **The New Yorker**.

CLARK BLAISE is the recipient of the St. Lawrence Award for Fiction for 1974 for his story collection, **Tribal Justice**, published by Doubleday. Of Blaise's **A North American Education** John Hawkes commented: "Clark Blaise . . . . . turns personal perception into the rarest kind of fiction." Blaise's stories have been published in some thirty-five magazines and anthologies in the U.S. and Canada: **New American Review**, **Journal of Canadian Fiction**, **TriQuarterly**, **Shenandoah**, **Tamarack Review**, **Minnesota Review**, **New Canadian Writing**, and elsewhere. He was a Canada Council Arts Fellow in 1973-74 and a recent winner of the Great Lakes College Association Prize for Fiction. He has taught at the University of Wisconsin, McGill, and Concordia University in Montreal, where he is currently Associate Professor of English.

BHARATI MUKHERJEE is Director of Graduate Studies in English at McGill University and a novelist of growing reputation. Her first novel, **The Tiger's Daughter**, was published by Houghton-Mifflin in 1972; the British edition was published by Chatto & Windus in 1973; and the novel was reprinted in Hamalian and Volpe's **The International Short Novel** in 1974. Her second novel, **Wife**, is to appear in May, 1975, also from Houghton-Mifflin. Born in Calcutta, she came to the United States to attend the University of Iowa, where she received her M.F.A. and Ph.D. A frequent reviewer for the **Washington Post**, she has also contributed to the **Massachusetts Review**; and she is currently at work on a nonfiction book about India (co-authored with Clark Blaise) scheduled for publication by Doubleday in 1976.

JOE DAVID BELLAMY is author of **The New Fiction** and editor of **Droll and Murderous Visions: American Fiction in Our Time**, forthcoming from Random House. His interviews have appeared widely in such magazines as The Atlantic, New American Review, Chicago Review, and Writer's Digest. His fiction, poetry, and criticism have been published in Paris Review, Iowa Review, Partisan Review, Novel, Quartet, The Vonnegut Statement, and elsewhere. His writing textbook, **Apocalypse**, emphasizes material using fictional techniques for nonfiction writing. Publisher and editor of **fiction international**, Mr. Bellamy teaches writing and literature at St. Lawrence University and is Director of the Conference.

For me, it was an extraordinary experience to spend a week with outstanding writers. The spirit and the enthusiasm for writing was contagious and inspiring. In fact, the conference was like a week-long banquet with a limitless supply of talent and wit. It was intense, inspiring, exhausting, and fun! I feel I made a number of new friends and eagerly look forward to more contact with them through their stories, novels, and poems in print, as well as personal notes.

—Hanna F., Princeton, NJ

If it weren't for the conference, I would never have dreamed that I could write a short story, and I have a book of them coming out in November. Students there always comment on the fact that the faculty is willing to spend so much time with them on their work. They are amazed. Pleased and amazed.

—James P., New Wilmington, PA

Coffee on the sun deck.

DANIEL HALPERN, G.E. MURRAY, JAYNE ANNE PHILLIPS & ANNABEL LEVITT

This panel discussion was held in June 1979 at Saranac Lake. The panelists were Daniel Halpern, G.E. Murray, Jayne Anne Phillips, and Annabel Levitt, with moderator Joe David Bellamy. Respondents from the audience included Carolyn Forché and Robie Macauley. Biographical information on the panelists is included in the opening remarks.

The small press movement was more of a fledgling enterprise and more of a novelty in the seventies

< Annabel Levitt, Jayne Anne Phillips, Daniel Halpern, and G.E. Murray at Saranac, 1979.

than it is now. This discussion shows the kind of thinking, generally, that was going on then that led to
the relatively more well-established organizations we
see today. But the cultural conditions that fostered
a need for the small press have not changed.

How can John Crowe Ransom and Louise Bogan and Marianne Moore go out of print in this country? It's amazing.

Joe David Bellamy: Due to the revolution in low-cost printing technologies in the last twenty years and the development of the National Endowment for the Arts [NEA] in the last decade primarily, and other sorts of funnel organizations that now provide grant money to little magazines and small presses, the small press movement in this country has grown to mammoth proportions and has come to be an alternate to trade sources of publication for writers. Our idea for holding this panel was to try to introduce you to that phenomenon, to explain its ins and outs, and to allow you to ask questions of our panelists that may be pertinent to your own concerns.

We have two members of the panel who have published with small presses: that is Jayne Anne Phillips and poet Gerry Murray, author of *Gasoline Dreams* and *Repairs*. We have Annabel Levitt, who is the publisher of Vehicle Editions in New York, which published Jayne Anne's prize-winning collection called *Counting.* We have Dan Halpern, who is a one-man publishing conglomerate—editor, of course, of *Antaeus* magazine and the Ecco Press.

As is usual with panel presentations, we'll ask for a word or two from each member in an effort to define a very large entity and then we'll open up for questions.

G.E. Murray: I've had my books published by small presses, and I've probably been publishing in little magazines for about fourteen, fifteen, sixteen years. Consequently, I am very much in support of them. I think they work. As someone once told me, there's a rather broad range of small press work. It goes from excellent to abysmal—and everything in between—and that's true. I think what's happened to date, especially with small press books, is that in many ways (and the Ecco Press is certainly an example of it) their work is as good as or better than some of the commercial houses, particularly when it comes to poetry and fiction; and I'm talking about both the quality of the work and quality of the production.

You pick up some of these books, a Joe Bellamy book, for example. It is as good or better than a lot of the so-called big commercial houses are doing.

Daniel Halpern: Without going into a history of how the Ecco Press or *Antaeus* got started, a "conglomerate" presupposes a large salary. So I would argue that point with you, Joe. But the Ecco Press[1] actually got started socially, which is the way certain ventures get started.

My publisher was a friend of Tom Guinzburg, who is the president of Viking, and they made an arrangement so that Viking would warehouse and distribute and bill for us, which would allow us to do all the editorial work on our books—and we could get our own designers. So we worked out an arrangement where we could publish three or four books of poetry a year, a couple of books of fiction, if we could find them, and some neglected books—to reprint. We'd shoot from old copies, which would be less expensive, and those books have done very well for us. We've done books like *The Collected Works of Jane Bowles*, *A Legacy* by Sybil Bedford. We've done *The Diary of Helena Morley* translated by

Elizabeth Bishop. We have a Boland book coming out.

People want to read. Everything goes out of print. Books go into the bookstores for three months, and then they are returned to the publishers. Then they go out of print. It's amazing what's out of print. For example, Marianne Moore is out of print. It's staggering.

Question: Are you going to do Moore?

Halpern: We tried. But Viking has the rights. They ought to do it. That was two years ago. So there's no Marianne Moore[2] in print. Boland has just been picked up by Avon. Avon, as you know, has been redoing these novels. So she's in print and very accessible.

Question: You did *The Blue Estuaries*, too, didn't you?

Halpern: *The Blue Estuaries* by Louise Bogan—yes. How can John Crowe Ransom and Louise Bogan and Marianne Moore go out of print in this country? It's amazing. You're talking about, maybe, $4,000 to keep these books in print. I think that speaks for something you want to consider when you think about publishing and what it's doing—what its concerns are and what its interests are. You

---

1 Dan Halpern is still running Ecco Press and still doing fine work. But Ecco is no longer a small press. It is now under the auspices of HarperCollins, where Halpern is a vice president.

2 *The Poems of Marianne Moore*, edited by Grace Schulman, was published by Viking Penguin in 2003.

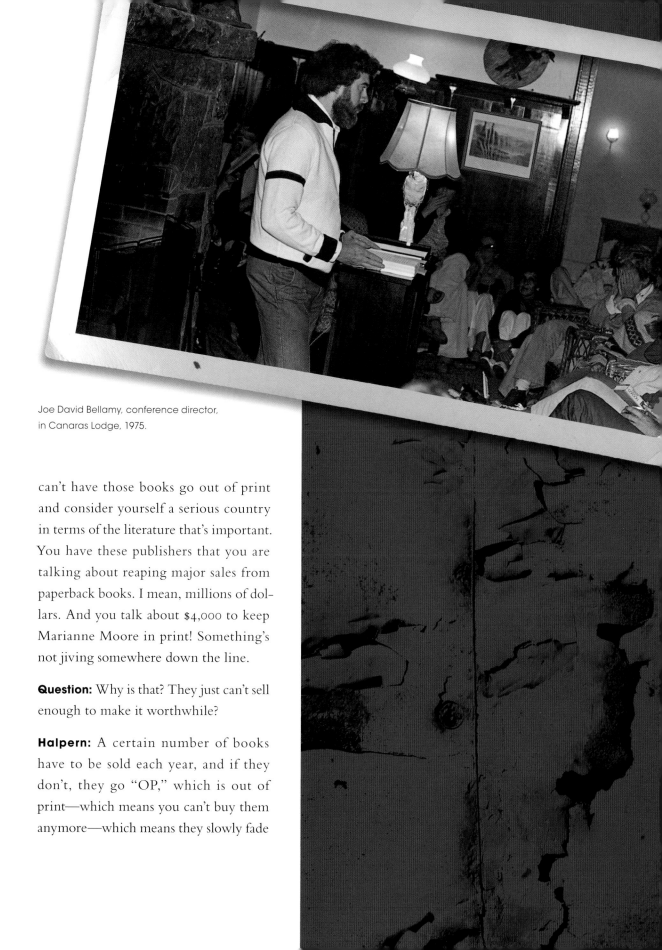

Joe David Bellamy, conference director, in Canaras Lodge, 1975.

can't have those books go out of print and consider yourself a serious country in terms of the literature that's important. You have these publishers that you are talking about reaping major sales from paperback books. I mean, millions of dollars. And you talk about $4,000 to keep Marianne Moore in print! Something's not jiving somewhere down the line.

Question: Why is that? They just can't sell enough to make it worthwhile?

Halpern: A certain number of books have to be sold each year, and if they don't, they go "OP," which is out of print—which means you can't buy them anymore—which means they slowly fade

SMALL PRESSES BLOOMED IN THE PAST FEW YEARS BECAUSE THE COMMERCIAL PRESSES BECAME INCREASINGLY NON-RESPONSIVE TO LITERATURE.

from your consciousness. It's the library or nothing. You can't own them.

Jayne Anne Phillips: Well, it raises the basic issue, which is why small presses bloomed, so to speak, in the past few years, and one reason is because the commercial presses became increasingly non-responsive to literature. I mean, most of those large commercial houses regard poetry especially, and fiction, too—that is, literary fiction as opposed to commercial fiction—as almost like write-offs. They don't even expect to make any money from them, and they only keep publishing a certain amount in order to be able to say, "Well, we are involved in literature. We aren't just involved in money." Or at least that's the way it appears to me.

There's also the fact that the government started subsidizing small press publishing, partially because there was probably a feeling that unless that happened, *what would happen* to literature in this country? I mean, already you've got

the whole organization number about television and *Jaws I*, *Jaws II*, *Jaws V*, and *Jaws VI*. It's a general lack of imagination in the media, a tendency to co-opt anything that comes along and reduce it into the Watergate soap opera, which we all probably noticed last winter. (I noticed it while it was raining for seven months in California and it was Watergate on television.) So in terms of a general presentation, we can address that area of it.

This is something we talked about last year at the conference, about the fact that there are very few magazines to publish in, and this is especially true with fiction even more than with poetry. Poetry has a very small audience, but there are a lot of magazines to publish poetry in, even though maybe five hundred people see each of those magazines, or something like that. But for fiction, there are actually now very few small magazines that publish fiction; and, of course, there are only three or four large commercial magazines that are publishing fiction on a regular basis. So it makes fiction almost something that a very small in-group is aware of, and the small presses are, I think, a response to that. In some ways, I think it's very healthy in terms of writers taking a certain amount of control over their own kind of expression, their own kind of work.

On a personal level, I can talk about my own experience with small press publishing and the advantages I felt it had for me. My first experience with small press publishing was just in a few magazines. I happened to publish when I was about eighteen in this magazine called *Truck*,[3] which came out of North Carolina at that time. I put together a collection and just sent it to the editor, David Wilk, sort of out of the blue. I said, you know, "I'm sort of thinking about publishing this." He was the first person I had sent it to, and he wrote back months later and said, "Well, we decided to do this." And by the time the book actually came out, the manuscript had actually changed quite a bit and grown up quite a bit. It was about a year in between there.

---

3 *Truck* was a literary magazine started in 1970 by a group of Yale undergraduates that included David Wilk. With issue #8 of the magazine, Wilk took over sole responsibility and went on to found Truck Press and Truck Distribution. His success at these enterprises led to his eventual appointment as director of the literature program of the National Endowment for the Arts.

The nice thing about publishing with them was that he does very nice books, and also that I had a good deal of control over what the book looked like, and what went into the book. I went down there and helped to work it out. There was a very good book designer down there named David Southern who had a press and who was doing freelance design.

I should have brought a copy of the first edition. Well, anyway, the first edition was larger than this. It was probably this tall and it was bigger, basically, and it was published on a grant from NEA, a publishers grant. The designer did this whole business with the curve. They used brown ink. They used very nice papers, and they used this photograph of my parents on the cover. Actually, I finally came up with the idea of maybe using this because (a) we didn't have a cover, and (b) the first piece in the book was a little poem called "Wedding Picture," which I had written maybe two or three years before with no idea that the actual picture the poem was written from would ever be on the cover of a book.

So, without asking my parents, who are divorced and who would *not* have said yes, I put the picture on the cover. I didn't think anyone would ever see the book, and my father to this day has never seen the book. But anyway.

The frontispiece was from a 1948 postcard of my hometown, and it was actually just a little postcard. I took it down to David Southern, and they did this very nice offprint blue representation of that photograph. They did it in two colors originally, with a blue line around each piece, and that was sort of how the book came to be. They printed only five hundred copies of the book. Very few people actually saw the book, but I got to give it to my friends; and it did actually indirectly give me some money because it won a Fels Award, which was $500 for me, and $500 for David Wilk. Then there were three pieces from it selected for the Pushcart Prize, which was also very nice.

Then when I was in my second year at Iowa, I wanted to get it reprinted because I didn't have a book in print at the time. I figured if I didn't have a book in print, I would have to be a waitress again. (The book had gone out of print within about a year and a half, which for small presses was sort of unusual.) So, when I got an individual NEA grant, I took $500 of the money and bribed David to print the book again. I said, "I'll give you $500 bucks, and surely you can come up with the rest." So he finally agreed. He came up with about $300. Then they did another edition of the book, but they reduced the whole thing to this size, which makes the print on the inside rather small. So

our arrangement was that I had bought two hundred copies of the book for this $500, and the other copies are in limbo somewhere. I don't know where the other copies are, or if any of them are even available anywhere because David Wilk became the director of the literature program of the National Endowment for the Arts and had to dissolve any connection to Truck Press. So about the time the book came out again, he was gone, and it's still not very clear to me who is doing his books now. I don't think anyone is doing them. I don't know where they are. Maybe they're in a garage somewhere. So that is the story of this particular book.

Annabel Levitt: The kind of publishing that I'm doing is really basically a one-person operation. On the East Coast, running a publishing company this way is an exception to the rule. For example, Dan explained how his press had some connection with Viking, and so his distribution occurs through a much bigger outlet. With the kind of publishing I'm doing, most of my distribution is handled right out of my apartment; all of my warehousing is done in my apartment. I do a lot of the printing myself, typesetting myself. So it's all very one-to-one. When there are people who do the work for me, it's really very direct. Also, as Dan said about his company, it does have a social origin in the way that this publishing came about—except that for me it just had to do with knowing writers, being a part of that world of writers where readings are happening, small magazines are happening; small magazines are being put out for poetry and are being put out by writers.

Anyway, as I said, what I'm doing on the East Coast is somewhat unusual. On the West Coast, particularly in the San Francisco area, there are a lot more people who are running operations that are similar to mine. Those people have actual presses in their houses. I don't own that kind of equipment, but that has a lot to do with the kind of overhead I have living in New York. It's a lot cheaper to have the kind of space you need to have as a publisher if you are living in the San Francisco area, and there, it's fairly common. There are hundreds of presses within a fifty-mile radius of San Francisco, where people are putting out books on a fairly regular basis and filling that gap that major publishers are not facing at all.

This kind of publishing—that has to do with one person having an interest in books and having an interest in the process by which the books are made and being interested in working on the books technically and manually in that way—it goes way back. A very good example of it historically, and a way to approach finding out about it, is through the work of Virginia Woolf with the Hogarth Press. Woolf was filling a similar kind of need during her time, and she also was in a position where she was a writer. She was coming out of the community of writers. She knew what the work was, she knew it wasn't available to the public, and she took it upon herself to get the press and to figure out how it worked and to get the work out.

I think what we're all talking about has to do with the sense of responsibility. At this point in the history of publishing, the responsibility for getting short fiction, in particular, and poetry to the public really rests on the writers because the commercial publishing world is not now directed that way. The big publishers are owned by other companies—oil companies and communications companies—who, to a very large extent, have interests in a much bigger money world than the world of publishing. Publishing has never been a business where people get tremendously rich.

Question: How did you get started? Do you rent space because you don't have the equipment?

Levitt: I rent time on the equipment.

Question: Does it take a lot of money to begin?

Levitt: No. Not at all. Briefly, what my background had been was that I had worked in printing shops, commercially, and worked in trade publishing, commercially. So I had exposure from those sides. And when letterpress equipment became available to me, and I had learned something of book binding, relatively briefly, from a craft point of view, I started. I'm not an expert at it, but I just began producing very slowly, bit by bit. The first three books that I did weren't on grants. It was just on my own, book by book, saving my money to do that. The place that I live in is pretty much given over to my business, and whatever money I'm making from whatever source is pretty much going to my priority, which is into the books.

Question: Mr. Halpern, how did you get started?

Halpern: I started in Tangier in Morocco. Paul Bowles backed the first issue. He put up the money for it. We printed through Villiers printers in London, who used to print City Lights books. It was the blind leading the blind at that point.

Question: When was that?

Carolyn Forché and Daniel Halpern at Saranac, 1979.

Halpern: It was in 1969. That was the first issue. It was a one-shot deal, really. Then I was lucky. I got a publisher after that.

Question: Could you talk a little about unsolicited manuscripts and what you do with them?

Halpern: I'd like to say one thing about that. I'm sure all of the editors in this group would agree. The thrill in publishing a magazine or working in a publishing house is not to publish Robert Lowell, but to find somebody who has never published before.

Question: I'm not on the level of Robert Lowell.

Halpern: Nor am I. You know, if you get a poem by Robert Lowell that you love, and you want to publish it, that's great. But I think it's true for Howard Moss and *The New Yorker*, or even *Esquire* and *Playboy*—it's much more fun to find somebody who's never published before and present them in your magazine than it is to do Robert Lowell or Bishop. For me, that's the joy of publishing a literary magazine. It's an important point. Even though some magazines are getting two or three thousand poems a month, you shouldn't think that because you're not known, you're not being read by the editors of the magazine.

Murray: Let me say something about that from my experience—from the non-editorial side of that question, i.e., a person submitting an unsolicited manuscript. I'm fairly convinced that in almost all places someone reads them—which is not to say they'll like them. But is that what your question is sort of leading to? Do unsolicited manuscripts ever get looked at? I think they do. My evidence is that people who are publishing me obviously never heard of me. When I was seventeen years old, *Malahat Review* in Victoria, British Columbia, published me, a kid out of western New York. Obviously they read the poem, they liked the poem.

Question: I wasn't thinking about whether or not they were looked at, so much as *how*. I was just trying to get a feel for it because I didn't have a feel for it from other sources.

Phillips: Well, I think there's a big distinction between the way small press magazine editors work and the way commercial magazine editors work. Of course, I'm not an editor for a commercial magazine, so I can't really speak from a position of great authority. But from what I've heard in talking to editors of magazines, if you are submitting to *Redbook*, or even *Harper's*, I think they put it in what is known as the slush pile. If you submit without knowing someone who works at the magazine, without having an agent, it cuts down the chances of the manuscript being read really slowly and carefully. But on the other hand, if some junior editor reads the first page of the story and thinks, "Wow, this is really incredible," then they would show it to a senior editor in their department. I mean, the book *Ordinary People* was a slush pile book. It became a bestseller. There are those stories, you know.

Levitt: Often, those aren't even junior editors who are recommending the book up to the higher ranks. They are hired readers, who are reading like about ten books or more a day, going through them fast.

Halpern: I really want to say something to this question because it's a good question on all counts. The conversations that I've had with editors, from small magazines to large magazines, more or less, come down to the same thing: There is no thrill to publish somebody who is well-known. I'm thinking of some conversations I've had with slick magazine editors, and they've all said something like this, and I think Robie [Macauley] would agree with this, too: "Guess what I found! I found this amazing short story by somebody nobody has ever heard of!" That is what I think people are looking for.

Question: I worked on a small magazine, and I used to like to discover people, too. But you still like to sprinkle in a few names of writers known at least within small press circles so that people would pick up the book and buy it maybe because of the names, but then would turn to the people that I felt like I had discovered. So that way, it kind of increased the distribution. Do you ever feel that?

Halpern: Yeah—it's called balance of nature. [Laughter.]

Question: When you're not related to Viking, how do you handle distribution?

Halpern: We're always related to Viking. We never leave the fold.

Question: But for those small magazines that are not?

Halpern: Distribution is a big problem.

Levitt: There are distributors across the country now, some of whom are getting state arts council and government funding, some of whom are just kind of squeezing by handling small presses. At this point, it's not something that's very well organized. A lot of the responsibility falls back on the individual publisher. As I said, most of the distribution that I do, I'm handling directly myself, and it has to do with individual orders from individual bookstores. That's how most of my distribution happens, although I now have active distribution by four national distributors. There are also a few in Europe.

It's a very complicated question because the problem of distribution has a lot to do with the fact that there are only a limited number of bookstores that are handling poetry, or just new authors in general. So that becomes something you are constantly running up against, even when you are able to get very organized distribution. Also, a number of those distributors who are handling small presses across the country are being very exclusive about who they want, and they're acting almost like small presses themselves, where they're making a list that they think looks good, and they will not always handle the whole list of a publisher. So a lot of it really falls back on the publisher.

Phillips: Another difference, too, is that we're talking about books that are published in editions of five hundred copies. We're also talking about the fact that most small presses don't have any sort of advertising budget; and even if they did, they would still have only five hundred copies of these books to sell. So, in a way, you're talking about publishing as an art. You're talking about making books—as a craft, as an art—and that is part of what people are doing.

Bellamy: I agree with that. Publishing is an art. But to place it in a somewhat broader context, the fact that the Ford Foundation gave a grant of $400,000 three years ago to aid small press distribution is a sign that some of the cultural commissars realize the importance of the small press world and the importance of developing a distribution network.

It's important for potential readers of small press publications to realize now, however, that you will have to go after what you want. In most cases, the books or magazines are handled from the publisher's house, or at least from a fairly modest establishment, and most of the business is done by mail order. So you have to take the initiative to get it. You won't find it in your local bookstore, in most cases. The grant from the Ford Foundation was given to CCLM, the Coordinating Council of Literary Magazines, which also funnels various grant funds from government and state sources to small magazine editors to help them publish magazines. My reading of the impact of that grant, a realistic reading, a kind of frank and not especially optimistic reading of the success of the Ford money, is that I'm not sure it's made much of a dent, unfortunately, in the problem.

Levitt: It's a huge problem.

Bellamy: I don't know how much money it would take to solve the problem. I think part of the problem is on the other end. It's in finding readers who want to buy small press books and who are willing to pay for them.

Levitt: Or who will go into the bookstores and ask for titles and ask that they stock the books.

Halpern: It's not enough to get books into Doubleday. There was a little project to get literary magazines into Doubleday and Brentano's, and we did do that. They sat there for three months and then they came back. That grant was a joke because most of that money was spent on travel expenses. So it's not really a matter of money. It's a matter of thinking it out. How do you go about distributing books to people who basically don't want to buy a small press book? The people who want to buy it, buy it. They don't need to go into Doubleday. In fact, they don't.

Bellamy: I think there are some who might want to buy it, but they just don't know about it or don't know what they have to do to get it. They don't even know about the small press world at all.

There was one highlight of the Ford grant. What happened was that several people who had some connection to the small presses were given seed grants of, what was it, Dan, $10,000 or so …

Halpern: Uh-huh.

Bellamy: … to start distribution networks for small presses in different regions of the country. David Wilk, the man who published Jayne Anne's first book and who had done Truck Press, received one of these grants. He had moved by that time into the Minnesota/northern Midwestern region, and Wilk, who went to Yale and had some chutzpah, really did a job on that region and turned over something like $75,000 worth of small press books in a year.

His innovations were not that unusual. He did careful invoicing. He kept track of everything. He published good lists of the books that he had available— he had a big list—and he did a lot of traveling. *He kept track of things.* Partially, and I think primarily, because of the success of Truck Distributors, David Wilk was given the job of director of the literature program at the National Endowment for the Arts. Unfortunately, that took him out of Truck Distribution, so now they may not be as good as they were when David was there.

Halpern: Typical.

Bellamy: But that gives me hope that maybe—with the right people—there is a way. The job is really something like being a traveling salesman. You get out there with your station wagon and you hit the bookstores. You hit the road. Some-

body has to make the contacts, and David Wilk did that. If the right people could be found and they could be financed a certain amount of the time at the start, maybe they could get to a point where they could actually make a profit, or at least enough to live on—and continue to do that kind of work.

Halpern: These are very professional questions. I think there are also some other kinds of pragmatic questions that we could be speaking to …. One's been raised in the far corner.

Carolyn Forché: I didn't know whether anybody else was thinking about this. But if you're somebody who has written a book of poems or a book of short stories, what are the sources you can turn to to find out about where this book could be sent? How do you approach a small press publisher? I'm someone with a book to be printed, and I want to go to a small press as a possibility. How do I go about that?

Phillips: The way that I advise students to go about it is this. In the first place, maybe buy this book, which is an encyclopedia basically of all of the small presses and small magazines happening: *The International Directory of Little Magazines & Small Presses.* It will be up front, and you can get a look at it. This book contains a list of all the magazines and presses that are known about in the small press world.

Murray: You should read this book carefully, though. There's much craziness in it and places that you probably don't want to be involved with. So there is a lot to pick and choose from. It's a very large asylum.

Phillips: The way that I do it myself, and the way I tell my students to do it, is that, first, you have a good piece of work. Then what you do is this. Of course you'd like to get paid for it if you possibly could because then you could write more good work. So first of all, you send it to the paying magazines. Chances are the paying magazines won't take it, especially if you're doing something a little different. Or if you're just starting out, they probably won't take it because you've got a lot to learn. But still—maybe, maybe if you're very lucky, you'll get a letter back that will point out what is wrong with the story, that will give you some kind of encouragement. Maybe you just get a slip back. You just keep sending it out.

You have to sort of detach your ego from the piece of work—because once it's done, it really has its own life. It's not a matter of "you're supposed to be crushed" if it's sent back fifteen times. You just keep sending it out. After you go through the commercial magazines, there is a battery of better distributed small press magazines, like *Antaeus* and *Ploughshares* and the *Iowa Review* and *Fiction International,* and a few others. (I'm talking more about fiction now.) After you have gone through those, you sort of increase your chances because those editors are probably a little more approachable, and you're more likely to get a letter from them and they're more likely to say, "Send us something else."

Then, if you haven't gotten any bites and you still really want to put the piece in print, there are other places. This book is full of places to publish. It's always better if you've seen the magazine before you send your work there so that you know what kind of stuff they publish and you know what form they present it in. But there are reasons to publish that are almost business reasons, considerations that are a level below the actual work. That has to do with the fact that you do have to publish two or three times to be considered for an NEA grant, and that kind of money is very, very important. It gives you money to live on while you try to write, and people have to have that.

In terms of publishing books, especially with short collections, you find out about presses through some of these magazines. At least that's how I found out about them. I mean, I was very lucky to have run into David Wilk. He was actually the first person to ever publish me in a magazine. Then he was the first person to publish something in book form, and he was a very good person to have ended up with. It was just fate or something. But there are a number of small press publishers who are doing beautiful work.

Question: How do you *find* them?

Murray: I was just going to say: I've been fortunate in that two of the books that I've published have been published by people who do a magazine as well. They ran my poems and eventually said, "Would you be interested in having us do a collection?" So that has at least happened twice to me. That's one way.

Levitt: As a poet, I have a slightly different kind of approach to that whole realm of getting these books out. As a poet and a publisher, I encourage people to become publishers themselves. It's not that much of an investment to get out a reasonable-sized book. If you look in bookstores and get a sense of what books are there, especially in the bookstores that are carrying poetry and less available fiction, they're really very inexpensively produced books that are there and available. It works—as far as getting the work out—just starting down that road. It's also, from my experience, a very satisfying kind of activity—to be producing books. Who knows what it can lead to once you've produced

a book of your own? But if you do produce a book of your own, then you also have a book that you're sending around to various people, which puts you a number of steps ahead as far as other publishers looking at your work. To some degree, it hardly matters that you've produced that book yourself. It just seems like an important way to get your work out there.

It's very important to be getting some response from other writers. These are often writers who are doing a lot of the small press books anyway, so to expose your work to that community is crucial, whether in the form of readings or in the form of getting it into smaller magazines. It's really a wrong idea if you think that by putting your work into a small magazine it's not going very far, that it's going to mean a dead-end for that work. It's not at all. It's really a first step. It's the way a lot of editors are seeing work anyway—through magazines. So that whole process of sending to the places that are paying is less critical for poetry. There's hardly any question of finding money for poetry—very few people are getting paid any kind of money for having their poetry published.

Bellamy: It really depends on the kind of work. Some self-publishing is vanity publishing, and vanity publishing has a bad name. But self-publishing of a certain kind has become more respectable lately.

Again, it depends on what kind of book it is. There are even examples of self-published books that have become bestsellers. This is a terrible example, but one is a recent book, which is not more than thirty or forty pages long, called *How to Flatten Your Stomach*.

Phillips: My mother just bought that! [Laughter.]

Bellamy: If you have written a novel, first of all, you send it to Knopf and Farrar, Straus and Houghton Mifflin, and the good literary houses, and you work your way down through the list of well-known houses. What you want, first of all, if you're a writer, *you want your book*—and preferably you want a beautiful book. You want an expensively produced book, if you can get it. Then you want the book to be distributed as widely as it can possibly be distributed and paid attention to—and you'd like people to buy it, too. You'd like to make money.

I think, in reverse order of priority, those are increasingly less likely to happen, and in shopping for a small press for your book, at least you would like to have: competent distribution, a handsome book, a publisher who's going to stay around for a while, and a book that's going to stay in print for as long as possible. If you get those things, you can consider yourself very fortunate. There

is a range of prestige value in the names of the small presses, too, just as there is in the world of commercial presses. As you get to know the small press world, you begin to know which presses would be more desirable among the many choices. The way to find out is simply to ask people—and examine the books yourself. You snoop around the bookstores that have small press works. You examine the paper. You sniff the spine and you get a sense of what the books are like, and just whether they turn you on or not.

Forché: I think that the only way that you can really discover what magazines to send your work to is to know the magazines. It's very important to write to those magazines and ask them if they have sample copies for a certain amount, like a dollar for a sample copy. It's very important to subscribe to the magazines that you submit to—so that you know what they're publishing and what they're interested in. It's very important to buy the books from the small presses that you're considering submitting manuscripts to—not only so that you support them and that they can stay alive but also so that you would know whether or not they might be interested in something like what you have written.

I think we've all discussed from time to time the terrible fact that there are often three and four times more submissions to competitions that award prizes than there are sales of the book that wins the prize. Year after year, people submit their manuscripts for this or that prize, and they don't seem to think it's important to read what the judges selected over what they submitted, for whatever reasons it was. It seems to me that if we are going to continue as writers, we have to support these enterprises financially to the extent possible for us. I really think this is important.

Robie Macauley: I think that is a very important speech, and I just want to add one thing. You see a lot of letters saying, "I'm considering submitting to your magazine, please send me a sample copy." Well, half of that idea was right. The writer wanted to see the magazine but wanted to get a free copy. I think that's an insult.

Forché: You should pay for it.

Macauley: You should buy the magazine. You should subscribe to it, and you should read three or four issues to get an idea of what you're submitting to. The writers are often oblivious about what the magazine actually publishes. Everything that Carolyn says is exactly right on.

Levitt: Or go to your local bookstore and ask them to order it for you.

Halpern: How many of you subscribe to literary magazines? At least one. That's it?

Murray: About a third.

Halpern: Great.

Murray: How many submit to literary magazines? All the rest! You don't need to raise your hands.

Forche: Buy from independent bookstores, that's the other thing. Buy from independent bookstores! Not Walden's.

Murray: Brentano's will not miss you that much.

Phillips: I was just going to say, if I were you, I wouldn't buy from Walden's *at all*—because they do not stock first novels!

Bellamy: Is that right?

Phillips: Never. Unless the novel is a bestseller, they do not even stock them. That's what I was told.

Macauley: They won't order books for you, either.

Phillips: That's right. I don't even do business with those people, and I think writers should avoid them. I mean, it's a political act not to walk in there. There are other places to buy books that are much more actively engaged in the process of literature, and I think we should support those places.

JAYNE ANNE PHILLIPS

Jayne Anne Phillips was born in West Virginia in 1952. She is the author of three novels, *MotherKind*, *Shelter*, and *Machine Dreams*, and two collections of widely anthologized stories, *Fast Lanes* and *Black Tickets*. She is the recipient of a Guggenheim Fellowship, two National Endowment for the Arts fellowships, and a Bunting Fellowship. She has been a recipient of the St. Lawrence Award for Fiction (1979), the Sue Kaufman Prize for First Fiction (1980), and an Academy Award in Literature (1997) by the American Academy of Arts and Letters. Her work has appeared most recently in *Granta, DoubleTake,* and *The Norton Anthology of Contemporary Fiction*. This interview was conducted at Saranac in 1979.

< Jayne Anne Phillips.

Question: Do you think of yourself as a writer of "women's fiction"?

Jayne Anne Phillips: I don't really think there *is* such a thing as "women's fiction." It seems to imply something in the spirit of "IT&T fiction," or "leper's fiction." However, "women *in* fiction" is something totally different, and I've taught courses on "women in fiction" that have been very interesting to both men *and* women. In the final analysis, writing is a human act, and I resist a little bit the implication that what women are writing, especially the best of what women are writing, should be applicable or interesting only to women; and I think that's what that title, "women's fiction," implies.

Question: Do you think "women's fiction" is strictly synonymous with feminist fiction today? Is there any other kind of women's fiction? When you hear discussions or lectures on women's fiction, it always turns out to be feminist in some way.

Phillips: Are you talking about things like *Good Housekeeping*?

Question: No. I'm talking about books that are listed in the book review sections under "women's fiction." They're either the new independent, "liberated," women, or it's the Marabel Morgan school. I'm wondering if there is any other kind of "women's fiction" because there *are* other kinds of women.

Phillips: Well, I can only say, again, that I don't think there is any such thing as "women's fiction." I mean, there is good fiction, there is timeless fiction, and there is bad fiction. I think it's fine that there is an isolationist aspect of it because sometimes people need to go through that phase on the way to something else. There's nothing wrong with there being feminist magazines or magazines for black writers or Chicano magazines or whatever. But I think in the final analysis, what you are doing as a writer is breaking down those sorts of barriers; and if you write something that is real, it is going to affect everyone—because it is finally working through that male-female separation and breaking out into something that is much larger.

I think it is probably true that some books have been repressed or some books haven't been paid attention to maybe because of subject matter. That happens to both men and women—maybe more often to women, especially in the past. But those books now are being read again, partly through some very dedicated work by scholars. But it still proves that if something is good, if something is timeless, it's going to continue to exist. It's really because people are so desperate for something that can give them some sort of connection.

Question: Isn't some fiction by women now about the importance of female

WRITING IS A HUMAN ACT, AND I RESIST THE IMPLICATION THAT WHAT WOMEN ARE WRITING SHOULD BE APPLICABLE OR INTERESTING ONLY TO WOMEN.

bonding? And about the politics of female bonding?

Phillips: Bonding itself is a political act in any relationship, and right now one of the most interesting things that people are working through has to do with bonding between men, bonding between women. The end result, hopefully, is that there's a healthier bonding between men and women.

Question: How did you get started as a writer?

Phillips: One thing I am always interested in talking about, which has to do with female bonding in my particular case, is how people start writing—what a person's initiation into writing is and how that later affects their writing. It's the idea of emotional programming or conditioning at age two months or what happens to you when you are in the womb. So I'm just going to tell a little story about how I started writing—and how this tainted me forever. [Laughter.]

When I was ten years old, I was in the Girl Scouts, and we had a troop of about thirty Girl Scouts who were managed by two of the mothers of the Girls Scouts, two very beleaguered women who later quit on the verge of nervous breakdowns. Anyway, we met in a church, and there was a Central Methodist Church, the First Methodist Church, and the New Methodist Church, all in the same block in my hometown. We met in the Central Methodist Church in this huge room with a polished blond floor that was behind the sanctuary, and it was a room in which there was a large open space and then there were these cubicles that were made of mahogany. They were maybe ten feet deep, about as deep as from this table back to the fireplace, and there were five of them in a row. There were these heavy burgundy velvet curtains on brass rods that closed off these little cubicles, and what they did with us was they sent us in groups into these cubicles while they sat out there on the blond floor and counted merit badge slips or something.

Front foreground: E.L. Doctorow. Other writers pictured, from left: Dianne Benedict, William Kittredge (with glasses), Jayne Anne Phillips (center), Daniel Halpern, and Elizabeth Inness-Brown (far right). Scene is from the *Fiction International*/St. Lawrence University Writers' Conference, 1979.

The way I first started writing when I was ten years old was I was writing a serialized novel, which used all the names of my friends. It began in the hometown of the heroine of the novel, who was me, of course, who very shortly moved to New York City and fell in love with a gang leader, and it was a fantastic thing. There was this whole business about carrying out gang wars in the night in the sewers of New York City, and I would go secretly from one cubicle to the next at the meetings reading the latest installment. I don't know what ever happened to that book. I've looked everywhere for it. But my writing career was cut short when the leaders quit and I no longer had this opportunity to read my serialized novel.

I didn't start writing again until I was sixteen, and I entered a poetry contest (in which there was no prize) and that got me started writing again. But all my Dickensian inclinations were sort of brought up short by the fact that the Girl Scout leaders quit, and after that, I was old enough that my life had become much more fragmented. I think I started writing about my childhood when I was pretty much out of it—one hopes—when I was about eighteen, nineteen, or twenty, and life had become a series of Mack trucks, eateries, backpacks, and pretty towns.

So I started writing about my childhood, and I think there is a tendency to maybe remember the far past in terms of isolated incidents that in some way convey a spirit or feeling as a whole. Memory plays some role in that, but not that large a role because we really don't remember things word for word or gesture for gesture. Memory itself, I think, effective memory, is not really something that is cerebral. It is more like your skin remembers things, or what you're trying to convey is the air, the air of the place or the time, a smell or a movement that someone made or something very specific that connects with the reader really in a sensual, associative way.

What I am going to do now is read some of these short pieces to more or less illustrate how this worked in my own writing. The reason that I gave you that Girl Scout story is because I think that maybe that strange beginning—the curtains and the organ and the secrecy of these girls in these little cubicles—started something for me in terms of writing about women together and how they are together, and also a fascination with ritual and secrecy and how writing in some way remains for me a secretive act.

One good thing about writing short forms is that reading to people is painless, that is, painless for them, because these things are over almost before they start. This is a piece called "Cheers," and we can talk later about what is real in fiction and what isn't, that is, how things start out and what is the seed in a piece of work, what moved the writer to try to capture something.

"Cheers"

The sewing woman lived across the tracks, down past Arey's Feed Store. Row of skinny houses on a mud alley. Her rooms smelled of salted grease and old newspaper. Behind the ironing board she was thin, scooping up papers that shuffled open in her hands.

Her eyebrows were arched sharp and painted on.

She made cheerleading suits for ten-year-olds. Threading the machine, she clicked her red nails on the needle and pulled my shirt over my head. In the other room the kids watched *Queen for a Day*. She bent over me. I saw each eyelash painted black and hard and separate. Honey, she said, Turn around this way. And on the wall there was a postcard of orange trees in Florida. A man in a straw hat reached up with his hand all curled. Beautiful Bounty said the card in wavy red letters.

I got part of it made up, she said, fitting the red vest. You girls are bout the same size as mine. All you girls are bout the same. She pursed her red lips and pinched the cloth together. Tell me somethin Honey. How'd I manage all these kids an no man? On television there was loud applause for the queen, whose roses were sharp and real. Her machine buzzed like an animal beside the round clock. She frowned as she pressed the button with her foot, then furled the red cloth out and pulled me to her. Her pointed white face was smudged around the eyes. I watched the pale strand of scalp in her hair. There, she said.

When I left she tucked the money in her sweater. She had pins between her teeth and lipstick gone grainy in the cracks of her mouth. I had a red swing skirt and a bumpy "A" on my chest. Lord, she said. You do look pretty.

This is another piece called "Sweethearts." I find that, especially in this first book, a lot of it had to do with young, adolescent girls or even younger than adolescent children discovering things together—not in any conscious way, but sort of being together at the moment that something happens that will later organize their minds, or their feelings about loving.

"Sweethearts"

We went to the movies every Friday and Sunday. On Friday nights the Colonial filled with an oily fragrance of teen-agers while we hid in the back row of the balcony. An aura of light from the projection booth curved across our shoulders, round under cotton sweaters. Sacred grunts rose in black corners. The screen was far away and spilling color—big men sweating on their horses and women with powdered breasts floating under satin. Near the end the film smelled hot and twisted as boys shuddered and girls sank down in their seats. We ran to the lobby before the lights came up to stand by the big ash can and watch them walk slowly downstairs. Mouths swollen and ripe, they drifted down like a sigh of steam. The boys held their arms tense and shuffled from one foot to the other while the girls sniffed and combed their hair in the big mirror. Outside the neon lights on Main Street flashed stripes across asphalt in the rain. They tossed their heads and shivered like ponies.

On Sunday afternoons the theater was deserted, a church that smelled of something frying. Mrs. Causton stood at the door to tear tickets with her fat buttered fingers. During the movie she stood watching the traffic light change in the empty street, pushing her glasses up over her nose and squeezing a damp Kleenex. Mr. Penny was her skinny yellow father. He stood by the office door with his big push broom, smoking cigarettes and coughing.

Walking down the slanted floor to our seats we heard the swish of her thighs behind the candy counter and our shoes sliding on the worn carpet. The heavy velvet curtain moved its folds. We waited, and a cavernous dark pressed close around us, its breath pulling at our faces.

After the last blast of sound it was Sunday afternoon, and Mr. Penny stood jingling his keys by the office door while we asked to use the phone. Before he turned the key he bent over and pulled us close with his bony arms. Stained fingers kneading our chests, he wrapped us in old tobacco and called us his little girls. I felt his wrinkled heart wheeze like a dog on a leash. Sweethearts, he whispered.

And then one more, sort of an initiation piece—it's called "Blind Girls." It's sort of the blind leading the blind leading the blind. This is about a ritual as ingrained in the lives of American girls as is anorexia nervosa—the slumber party.

"Blind Girls"

She knew it was only boys in the field come to watch them drunk on first wine. A radio in the little shack poured out promises of black love and lips. Jesse watched Sally paint her hair with grenadine, dotting the sticky syrup on her arms. The party was in a shack down the hill from her house, beside a field of tall grass where black snakes lay like flat belts. The Ripple bottles were empty and Jesse told pornographic stories about various adults while everyone laughed; about Miss Hicks the home-ec teacher whose hands were dimpled and moist and always touching them. It got darker and the stories got scarier. Finally she told their favorite, the one about the girl and her boyfriend parked on a country road. On a night like this with the wind blowing and then rain, the whole sky sobbing potato juice. Please, let's leave, pleads girlie. It sounds like something scratching at the car. For God's sake, grumbles boyfriend, and takes off squealing. At home they find the hook of a crazed amputee caught in the door. Jesse described his yellow face, putrid, and his blotchy stump. She described him panting in the grass, crying and looking for something. She could feel him smelling of raw vegetables, a rejected bleeding cowboy with wheat hair, and she was unfocused. Moaning in the dark and falsetto voices. Don't don't please don't. Nervous laughter. Sally looked out the window of the shack. The grass is moving, she said. Something's crawling in it. No, it's nothing. Yes, there's something coming, and her voice went up at the end. It's just boys trying to scare us. But Sally whined and flailed her arms. On her knees she hugged Jesse's legs and mumbled into her thighs. It's all right, I'll take you up to the house. Sally was stiff, her nails digging the skin. She wouldn't move. Jesse tied a scarf around her eyes and led her like a horse through fire up the hill to the house, one poison light soft in a window. Boys ran out of the field squawling.

I think the main reason people write, or at least when you pick up a book and you open it and you feel compelled enough by what you read to continue reading it—you feel immediately that something is at stake for the writer, and this has nothing to do with publication. It has more to do, I think, with survival—this idea that you are dealing with something that's no less than your life and the lives of the people you love, that in some way you are holding on to those lives and keeping them from wasting. I mean, it's not really life itself—it's your consciousness of it and your perception of it. I think there is a real desire to keep things from wasting, to keep them from simply drifting by. There's, I think, the need to preserve what is somehow lovely to you and hold on to it—or to celebrate it—and there is also the desire and the absolute need to transform what is frightening and what is life threatening. You may not understand the sadness of a life, or you don't understand the grievance for that sadness or how people continue in that sadness; but when you write something about it, you are basically admitting that you are powerless to change the events that contributed to that sadness because you are documenting the fact that a life continues; and maybe in that act, you discover something that contributes to your own survival.

I didn't plan it this way, but I seem to have several pieces about fathers. So I'm going to read this little piece called "Stars."

All winter in Florida he poked his cane at calcified dog turds and swore. In summers he sat on the porch in West Virginia, yelling for the fly swatter and shooting at groundhogs in his fields across the road; so proud of the girl he fathered at sixty. Jit! he yelled. Jitterbugger! Bring the swatter out here!

That summer she was nine. We read *Star Parade* in a tiny back bedroom strung with ribbons from horse shows in the forties. I was a little older but she was taller, her eyes were cerulean and her legs were freckled. When he dies we won't come back here anymore, she said, and her mother, a heavy woman in her fifties with shoulder-length white hair and those same pure eyes, spent afternoons in town. Jit had to sweep the linoleum floors with a broom. He spat in a bucket and she emptied it. We went behind the house to pick mint for his pitchers of ice water; she cracked the ice trays in the sink and cursed him in even tones. He was deaf and couldn't hear unless she yelled. Lazy Jitterbug? he shouted. Where's my water? His sparse white hairs on his concave chest were damp and he wiped his armpits with a towel. Here, you old buzzard, she said. What's that? he asked, and watched her lips. Sir, she said. Yes sir.

Finally he went to sleep in the room with the double bed. We walked up to the snake pit on the winding cow paths and threw pebbles at copperheads coiled on the rocks. Cows gathered farther down at the trough, licking the salt block to a bulging oval. Sometimes she walked slow motion into their midst, then turned up her head and screamed. They jerked, stumbling away, and rolled their broad eyes like palsied girls.

When the heat was worst we slipped through the double doors of the old garage. The mossy walls were covered with license plates of dead Mercurys and photos of their ghostly two-tone fins. Burlap bags of feed, torn lawn furniture, hoses and pieces of cars; a radio that played Top Ten at three in the afternoon. We lay on a cot pretending we were Troy Donahue and Sandra Dee, touching each other's stomachs and never pulling our pants down. The Lettermen did billowing movie themes. There's a summer place, they sang. Where our hearts. Will know. All our hopes. She put her face on my chest. You be the boy now, she whispered. Insects got caught in the warm putty of the windows and horseflies drifted up and down the panes. They were furry and weighted, blunt, and their heads were blue.

In winter she sent me her picture and wrote letters. Just because you're a year older than me, her last one said, is no reason not to answer.

This is a short piece called "Solo Dance."

She hadn't been home in a long time. Her father had a cancer operation; she went home. She went to the hospital every other day, sitting for hours beside his bed. She could see him flickering. He was very thin and the skin on his legs was soft and pure like fine paper. She remembered him saying, 'I give up,' when he was angry or exasperated. Sometimes he said it as a joke. 'Jesus Christ, I give up.' She kept hearing his voice in the words now even though he wasn't saying them. She read his get-well cards aloud to him. One was from her mother's relatives. Well, he said, I don't think they had anything to do with it. He was speaking of his divorce two years before.

She put lather in a hospital cup and he got up to shave in the mirror. He had to lean on the sink. She combed the back of his head with water and her fingers. His hair was long after six weeks in the hospital, a gray-silver full of shadow and smudge. She helped him get slowly into bed and he lay against the pillows breathing heavily. She sat down again. I can't wait till I get some weight on me, he said, So I can knock down that son-of-a-bitch lawyer right in front of the courthouse.

She sat watching her father. His robe was patterned with tiny horses, sorrels in arabesques. When she was very young, she had started ballet lessons. At the first class her teacher raised her leg until her foot was flat against the wall beside her head. He held it there and looked at her. She looked back at him, thinking to herself it didn't hurt and willing her eyes dry.

Her father was twisting his hands. How's your mother? She must be half crazy by now. She wanted to be by herself and brother that's what she got.

I think if you're working with material that is in some way autobiographical and in some way totally fiction, that maybe you are able to exert some control on your past, and that what is probably an illusion of control is one thing that makes writing worth it. We were talking too in some of the sessions earlier about changing your voice, or using voice itself as an entry into something you could not possibly be without it. So I wanted to read a couple of pieces in which there is a total projection of consciousness into something that is a total fabrication. Those pieces, basically, were written purely according to voice, according to "practice being something that you aren't."

This is a short piece called "Accidents" that is about some strange, attracted, intense energy that people put out when they are falling apart—that in some way other people are drawn to them because they are taking risks that someone else may not be brave enough to take, or foolish enough to take, or desperate enough to take ... and that sometimes in relationships you are practicing what may later happen to you or what you are avoiding, what you manage to avoid.

"Accidents"

I'm not sure anymore when the first accident happened. Or if it was an accident. Now when I tell you about my accidents you are sympathetic and some of you fall in love with me. Men whose childhoods were slow and smooth want my straitjacket stories. My sugar is a panic that melts on your tongue and leaves a tiny hole in what you taste. Taste me Sugar, I'm fried around the edges. Mom used to say I was born with my eyes crossed. That was a joke she quit telling when I was old enough and wrapped up tight. You feel me spinning and the music's on too loud. You remember all the little dangers in your past. My body that long sleek car someone spun on curves. Hey, you wanna drag? Yeah, I'll do ya, and it degenerates. Six girls giggly drunk jumping out to run circles around an old Chevy at a red light. Hey wait a minute Honey, you dropped somethin. I keep dropping how things went, which story goes where. This week and next week and next week. Somewhere out there there's a winner but I'm losing track. I try to stay home and turn the pages in my books. But the words are a dark crusted black that cracks. Black as wine or water. I keep wading out and the deep part is over my head. I wanna dance I wanna just wrap my legs around you like those rings are round the moon. Lemme press my mouth against you like the rain against the glass it's see-through. I can see clear out there to the end and I'm alone I'm burning like a fire fuel. I'm hot. I'm hot I'm a streak across the sky. You watch me, now bring me down hard and hold on. It doesn't matter if I tell one truth or another. I wanna feel a hand on my waist. He and I are through, why don't you come over? See, I hurt my head again. I hit it on the bed.

Similarly, this next one is another voice the only basis for which, in fact, is an observation. I had a friend once who was a mime artist who was dancing in topless clubs in Denver for money to get the bread to go to San Francisco and dance in the streets in white face. She was about thirty-two and had been actually a kindergarten teacher before she wised up. But she was dancing against this young girl who was about seventeen or eighteen and who wanted to be a professional stripper, and they were basically having a dance-off. They had both been dancing in this club for about two weeks and they'd come down to a contest between them. The contest was done according to applause, and she talked me into going with her the night of the big contest. I wrote this piece from that young girl's voice, so that's what it's about. It's called "Stripper."

> When I was fifteen back in Charleston, my cousin Phoebe taught me to strip. She was older than my mother but she had some body. When I watched her she'd laugh, say, That's all right, honey, sex is sex. It don't matter if you do it with monkeys. Yeah, she said, You're white an dewy an tickin like a time bomb an now's the time to learn. With that long blond hair you can't lose. An don't you paint your face till you have to, every daddy wants his daughter. That's what she said. The older dancers wear makeup an love the floor, touchin themselves. The men get scared an cluster around, smokin like paper on a slow fire. Once in Laramie I was in one of those spotted motels after a show an a man's shadow fell across the

window. I could smell him past the shade, hopeless an cracklin like a whip. He scared me, like I had a brother who wasn't right found a bullwhip in the shed. He used to take it out in the woods some days and come back with such a look on his face. I don't wanna know what they know. I went into the bathroom an stood in the fluorescent light. Those toilets have a white strip across em that you have to rip off. I left it on and sat down. I brushed my hair an counted. Counted till he walked away kickin gravel in the parkin lot. Now I'm feelin his shadow fall across stages in Denver and Cheyenne. I close my eyes an dance faster, like I used to dance blind an happy in Pop's closet. His suits hangin faceless on the racks with their big wooly arms empty. I play five clubs a week, $150 first place. I dance three sets each against five other girls. We pick jukebox songs while the owner does his gig on the mike. Now Marlene's gonna slip ya into a little darkness. Let's get her up there with a big hand. The big hands clap an I walk the bar all shaven an smooth, rhinestoned velvet on my crotch. Don't ever show em a curly hair Phoebe told me, Angels don't have no curly hair. That's what she said. Beggin, they're starin up my white legs. That jukebox is cookin an they feel their fingers in me. Honey

you know it ain't fair what you do Oh tell me why love is a lie jus like a ball an chain. Yeah I'm a white leather dream in a cowboy hat, a ranger with fringed breasts. Baby stick em up Baby don't touch Baby I'm a star an you are dyin. Better find a soft blond god to take you down. I got you Baby I got you Let go.

I don't mean this to be morbid or anything. But I think there are several opportunities in life to practice for death. (Ooh, that does sound awfully morbid.) But those things are the great pleasures, too. Anything that allows you to leave this small identity that you have is a real blessing, and that can be any sort of passion. I mean, it can be skiing or taking cars apart, or it can be writing. I think that if you are allowed entrance into some sort of passion, you are extremely lucky because there are people who don't have that passion. That really is the point, and that's about all I have to say. I'm going to read this teeny weenie tiny goodbye. This is my goodbye to Saranac Lake. It's dedicated to Frank Sinatra. It's called "Strangers in the Night."

"Strangers in the Night"

Like everyone else, she thought a lot about eating and sleeping. When she was sleeping, she felt like death floating free, a white seed over the water. Eating, she thought about sex and chewed pears as though they were conscious. When she was making love, she felt she was dancing in a churning water, floating, but attached to something else. Once she almost died and went so far she saw how free the planet floated, how it is only a shadow, and was frightened back to herself. Later, when she explained this to him, he put his arms around her. She thought she had come home and they were in a shadow, dancing.

The end. [Applause.] So, are there any questions?

Question: Eating pears as though they were conscious? [Laughter.]

Phillips: That's right. The next time you eat a pear, think about it. [Laughter.]

Question: What do you mean by rehearsing? I don't understand your methods.

Phillips: I didn't say rehearsing—practicing. I should never have said that.

Question: It's too late.

Phillips: It seems to me that everyone has a real desire to get outside themselves, to combine with something else. And that's

Jayne Anne Phillips.

why people eat. I mean, basically no one has to eat three times a day. I mean, no one needs that much food. But there is this desire about three times a day or four times a day if you are awake past 1 A.M. to put something in your mouth and chew it up and swallow it—because it's a grounding thing. I mean, this is not meant to sound Platonic, but you are taking something into yourself, and you're sort of extending yourself at the same time. I think, you know, sexuality has a lot to do with the same thing, and any act where you are creating something that you in some way put yourself into but you also are able to escape by doing it.

I think at the same time that there is this desire to move out of yourself, there is an incredible fear once you get to a certain point. There is always the tendency to back up and not quite go, not quite do it because, of course, once you have left yourself, you have no idea. You have nothing. You have no idea what there is besides yourself because it's all you've ever experienced. Of course, when you die, your only hints or clues about how to experience that have come in these kinds of experiences. Well, there is *The Book of the Dead*, which is an interesting book that gives step-by-step guidelines as to what's going to happen and what it is going to be like. I think there is a feeling there that maybe you create—that you create whatever is going to happen—like the Indians going to a happy hunting ground or Dick Nixon going to a mock up of San Clemente or any kind of extension of that.

But I think people who write are, in some strange, perverse way, very lucky because they are using something that is almost not there. They are using language. People who play instruments, or people who paint, or people who make sculptures out of 7-Up bottles, or people who stuff fish are actually working with something tangible. So their illusion that "I am alive" or their illusion that "I have some control over something" is more fully supported. People who write never have that illusion because they are working with something that's utterly intangible and that is utterly created with air almost—so that you, in some way, practice, maybe being air or traveling in air. I hope that that is some kind of preparation.

Question: You practice being somebody else, which is an escape from yourself?

Phillips: You practice being somebody else. But I think really the crux of it is you practice not being anybody.

Question: Can you explain about writing as transformation?

Phillips: When I was talking about the movie this morning of the woman in Montana, and it ends up that all the kids leave and the house is deserted and the house is on someone else's ranch and blah, blah, blah .... I mean it's all horrible in a way, but also it's beside the point because, I mean, you don't write for the end. You do it to see what happens on the way there. The process of establishing that homestead is what the story is, and the process of writing a book is why you do it. I mean, that is the reason for the whole thing. It really has nothing to do with publication or making the movie or anything else. The publication business is really just a testimonial or a statement of faith on the part of someone else to the process that has already occurred. It in some way contributes to the process that has to go on inside anybody, whether it has ever been written down or not. It is just that for some particular people the act of writing it down is the entrance.

Question: You have spoken of this concept of transformation, and I haven't quite grasped it yet. Would you elaborate on that?

Phillips: The process of transformation?

Question: Yes. I just don't quite understand it.

Phillips: You mean in books.

Question: Yes. You said sometimes the act of writing comes out of the need to transform ....

Phillips: Well, it's like you're sitting there in the hospital room, and this event occurs.

Then it stays in your mind in amber. I mean, the mind has a selective process going on all the time. Supposedly, you remember *everything*, according to the electrical experiments with brains. Everything is up there. There are some things that are more or less frozen, almost like photographs, except you press a button and it goes on for about six frames and stops again—or whatever. If that has happened to you, that something has gotten frozen inside you, at some point you are going to have the need to write about it or to do something with it—to make it move again. Also, there is a great mystery about it—that you can never know why, or have any conscious thought why, you have remembered certain things and not others. Or why you are afraid of certain things and not others. You know you can sometimes write things down that scare you, that frighten you in some way. I think that's usually very good. And what I meant by the basic idea of transforming your material is just that if you don't transform it, it can be hurtful to you. It's like the only way to face something that could hurt you is to go right into the center of it.

Question: It's "transform" that I'm having trouble with. Transform means to create another form with it as opposed to the compliant or the releasing. You take something that is inside and turn it into a different piece?

Phillips: It's a sort of alchemy. But also you may transform your own feelings. That is, you may write something and …

Question: "Transcend." I have it mixed up with "transcend."

Phillips: No, I don't mean "transcend." "Transcend" would mean that you are moving away from your own closure, somehow getting outside your own feelings. I mean that you have your own feelings about any particular thing, whether it's your father or something else, and by writing about it, you discover something in those feelings that you did not know was there; and you also may discover something gorgeous, something lovely, that in some way enlarges your whole understanding of relationships, not only of the person that you happen to be writing about, but of the relationship itself and how a relationship continues.

It's interesting, too, that it has something to do with the collective, a collective spirit or a collective consciousness that when you are reading someone else's writing …. I always think of the image in James Agee where he's talking about fathers with their shy necks watering the lawns at night. When you read that, even though you didn't grow up in 1930, even if you never had a father that you remember, you are *there* as if it happened to you,

as if it is stored in your mind. I think that collective spirituality or that collective memory, that collective *future*, really, is what you are addressing when you're writing. It's extremely mysterious.

I have a friend who—this is a strange story, but I just happened to think of it—I have a friend who was sitting in class at Iowa one day, and they were looking at a poem called "We Are Many" by Pablo Neruda. She said, "That poem sounds so familiar. That's very strange." She went home and she looked through her old poems and found a scrap of paper on which she had *composed* "We Are Many," and she showed it to me, and she had actually written the first section of the poem and the last section only with the middle two parts left out. She had actually crossed out some lines that were not exactly it and written them over again, and some of the lines are slightly different but they mean the same thing. You know, that kind of thing happens. I mean, she may have read that poem once five years before that and it somehow floated up. Or she may not have read it at all, although that would be a little farfetched. But it's just a fact that people have these kinds of connections. It is something that is continually proven in the act of writing, in the act of reading ….

That's all I have to say. [Applause.]

RUSSELL BANKS

Russell Banks is the author of fourteen works of fiction, including *Continental Drift*, *Rule of the Bone*, *The New World*, *Cloudsplitter*, and *The Angel on the Roof*, as well as *The Sweet Hereafter* and *Affliction*, both of which were made into major films. He has received numerous prizes and awards for his work, including the O. Henry and Best American Short Story awards, the John Dos Passos Prize, the Literature Award from the American Academy of Arts and Letters, and the St. Lawrence Award for Fiction for his first collection of stories, *Searching for Survivors* (1975).

Russell Banks was a visitor at the *Fiction International*/St. Lawrence University Writers' Conference in 1975 and a faculty member in 1976. For many years following, he was a member of the writing

< Russell Banks.

faculty at Princeton. He is a native of New Hampshire and now lives in upstate New York. Sections of this interview were conducted on the campus of St. Lawrence University during the fall of 1983, continuing conversations begun many years earlier at the conference.

Joe David Bellamy: Around 1965, it seemed that the American short story changed and formal experimentation ran rampant. One of the terms used to describe that change was "superfiction." Then about ten years later, perhaps in reaction to what the superfictionists were doing, another critical camp came forward under the banner of "moral fiction," based on a book by John Gardner called *On Moral Fiction*. Gardner said, essentially: "Wait a minute. This new fiction may be formally innovative, but it's basically just game-playing. This is not what art is supposed to be about."

I've always thought that Russell Banks could be considered both a superfictionist and a moral fictionist, whether he knew it or not. What I'd like to know, first of all, is whether or not he thinks he *is* in this superfiction, or moral fiction, or whatever-comes-next category, and then the larger question—just to toss you an easy one, Russ—simply what *ought* art be about?

Russell Banks: An easy one, yes! Well, what you're describing is, I think, accurate so far as it goes. It's a way of describing some trends in fiction writing over a period of about twenty years, seeing these trends and categorizing them from the outside. But the way a writer experiences what may later become a trend is very different from the way it appears to a critic or a reader. As a writer, you're not aware that you're part of a trend or a school or anything of the sort at the time. You're doing what you're doing largely out of a personal need for usually quite eccentric and idiosyncratic reasons. You don't even know at the time why you're doing what you're doing. I'm beginning to see now, as I look back fifteen or twenty years, why I was writing stories that to a reader might seem formally experimental or strictly designed to test certain kinds of formal concepts about fiction. At the time, I wasn't that conscious of it.

I had a couple of stories in *The New World* that were direct address stories, for example. "You Are Simon Bolivar" [retitled "The Rise of the Middle Class"] is one such story. It's about the historical figure Simon Bolivar, and the reader is made to become Simon Bolivar. Another one is "You Are Edgar Allan Poe" [retitled "The Caul"]. Another one is "Hogarth's Wife" [retitled "Indisposed"]. All of these have a second-person narrator instead of first or third, and it's a direct address. At the time, I thought what I was doing was trying to find the English equivalent of the impersonal pronoun, which is common enough in Romance languages and in Latin, where "one does something." Then "one does something else." You can't very well do that in English without achieving a very formal and

I WRITE OUT OF THAT DESIRE TO BE AS SIMPLE AND CLEAR AS I CAN BE, AND AS HONEST AS I CAN BE.

somewhat literary tone. I wanted a more colloquial voice, but I also wanted an impersonal pronoun. The only near equivalent I could find was the "you." "You are this" or "you are that" and "you do this" and "you do that."

Well, as time has gone on, I found out more or less that what I was looking for in that experiment was not simply an impersonal pronoun. I was looking for a relationship with a reader that was intimate, colloquial—where I, the narrator or author, felt in cahoots in a way with the reader, where I felt a member of the same community. It seemed that there wasn't really a kind of narrative voice around that permitted that. The first person I, I, I, I, more or less makes the narrator talk about himself. The third person, which is a kind of impersonal narrator, more or less detaches the author/narrator from participating in the actions being described or participating in the community with the readers. I was looking for the equivalent, I guess, of a voice that works the way we talk to each other. We say, "You know." You know, "You know what I mean?" We use "you" a lot this way. We say, "Well,

you've got your Rockefellers, you've got your Duponts, you've got your, etc." We use that word "you" to embrace each other in a way—to share a common knowledge and understandings and experience.

I really wanted to achieve that over the years with readers. I wanted to have a sense of being the same as they were. Not different. So that little experiment came about, which looked rather radical perhaps from the outside, but, for me, was not at all. It was a necessary struggling to find a voice that would allow me to have a kind of relationship with the reader that I trusted and felt comfortable with, which would allow me then to talk to the reader as a member of the community about things that were outside the community—to bring to my own community things I had discovered out there somewhere.

There are other stories that I fooled around with, like "The Perfect Couple," where it was just basically told from the point of view of "we"—the town itself. "We thought *this* about these people. We thought *that* about these people." So it's a kind of community voice talking. It wasn't until really about my middle thirties or so when I began to understand and feel clear that I had worked out techniques, strategies, significant mastery of my craft, so that I could indeed talk directly to my reader—and be forced by the craft to be honest in that talking about something that was outside, that was over there. This is the only way, I think—this kind of desire on the part of a writer—that probably links me with the moral fictionists in a sense, a desire to be in direct relation or communication with the reader.

I do not want my word taken as some kind of found object that you might pick up, like a shell, and if it looks prettier this way, we'll look at it this way and say that's the way it is. There is a way I want my work to be read. I want it understood in a particular way, and I may be wrong. Maybe that's not the right way to see it. But I still have that desire, nonetheless. I write out of that desire to be as simple and clear as I can be, and as honest as I can be. So, in that sense, I think it probably does align me with what Gardner called "moral fiction" and the writers that he celebrated for that. Gardner was really talking about a desired relationship to the reader, I think.

Bellamy: Well, it certainly seems true that the superfictionists were people who sort of dared you to keep up with them.

I mean, they weren't going to cut any corners to make it easy for you, or even try to be entertaining.

Banks: I think what they saw, quite rightfully, from Robbe-Grillet on up, the theorists and practitioners of contemporary fiction, both French and American, was that the old conventions of telling a story no longer really provided that kind of intimacy with the reader. That, in fact, had broken down. Perhaps it was the modernists' fault in a way. Perhaps it was the result of *Dubliners* and Hemingway. Making such a virtue of impersonality made it almost impossible for the writer to communicate directly. What I know I'm after is almost a "gentle reader" form of address. You know how Fielding (and much eighteenth-century fiction) has that convention where he says, "Well, you're not going to believe this, gentle reader."

Bellamy: Or "dear reader."

Banks: Or "dear reader." But there is this kind of *communication* going on. You sense it. You sense a human voice talking to you politely, nicely, and honestly. You can tell by the voice when they lie, just as you can when dealing with each other. You pick up a phone and you're talking to somebody, and if the person starts to lie, you can tell. You don't have to see it. The same thing is true with reading.

We have lost that, I think, and I think the superfictionists were trying to find ways of returning to that kind of a basic relationship with the reader, looking for strategies that would permit it. I don't think very many have done it. I think that what most of them have done instead is to become amused and bemused by—and defensive about—the problem-solving for its own sake, and the art simply as an object, a beautiful object to be observed from twenty-eight sides (or however many sides you want to observe it from), rather than as a speech, an act of communication from one person to another. In the end, that's all I ever wanted was the ear of a listener.

Bellamy: What did you want to say to them?

Banks: What I saw over here. Yes, what I saw over here, what I thought they didn't perceive and what I thought I saw. Not that that makes me in any sense superior. You see, the reason I want to get myself in a place where I'm on the same plane as the reader is because I don't think what I see makes me unique or different from the reader. I think if the reader will just stop a second and listen, the reader will see it, too. It might be something inside; it might be something outside. It's as much one as the other for me, in terms of what I think I've seen. I mean, I'm a person

who has the luxury—if you want to look at it that way—of spending my life looking at the world and telling other people what I see. Most people don't have the luxury of that. Sometimes it's just looking at my dreams, and sometimes it's looking at how people really live. Sometimes it's just looking for an anthropology of contemporary life, looking to see what rituals and patterns are evolving. How do we deal with youth now and people growing into adults? What are the kinship systems in families where there are eight sets of parents? When nobody knows what to call anybody else? I think it's an extraordinary phenomenon of our time.

When you go to a foreign culture or society, it's commonplace that the best way to identify the kinship systems—which is to say, the best way to identify the patterns of responsibility and loyalty between human beings—is to ask the children what they call various adults. Because the children know where the power flows, the way the power flows. People without power always understand it better than people with power. So the children always know exactly where the power comes from.

If you go today to most middle-class American communities and watch the difficulty, let's say on Parents' Day at a college, as the children try to introduce the father's girlfriend's child from a previous marriage, or try to figure out what to call the mother's new husband, you sense they don't understand the kinship patterns. We don't know what they are yet. I bring this all out by way of saying I have the luxury of thinking about that and trying to observe it to see what those patterns are, and then coming back and trying to talk to people who don't have that luxury. This is a terribly simple way of describing what I think I'm doing ....

Bellamy: It's what Dickens thought he was doing, I think. It sounds almost sociological and historical.

Banks: Yes, there is that aspect. That's just one slice of it, you know. One can go in any number of directions. You're free to look at whatever you want to look at. That just happens to be fascinating to me at the moment, only because I teach and I have adolescent children, and I myself am the product of a divorced family. My children are. Most of my students are. And we all have very confused understandings about that—what that creates in society in terms of our lives, those puzzles, those questions, and the suffering that those questions cause. I think this is the proper field for a writer to work in, as well as the inner life. They're not separable to me. I can't divide economics and sociology and psychology and philosophy and history and so forth. To me, it's all collapsed into

what it's like to be a human being today in this world. I don't know if that's even touched your question.

Bellamy: It does. It seems to me that one way to define a writer is somebody who, like a heat-seeking missile, goes for where the emotion is in a particular cultural problem. That seems to be what you've just described.

When we were talking about moral fiction, I started wondering if there is a way that fiction could function as an art form, and yet that the writer might hold out hope that it might cause people to behave in a way he would prefer. It seems to me that the idea of moral fiction is that, as a writer, you allow, or try to cause, art to have an ethical dimension without resorting to propaganda. I'm wondering if you think that should be a goal or not. I was thinking about your story "The Lie." But that's a story that seems to me to take a complex moral position. It seems as if you're examining the facts of the matter and concluding that the reason this boy commits the murder in the parking lot is that there is a generational breakdown of responsibility that extends back to his grandfather.

Banks: Right, right. Yes, it's a three-generational story, as I recall it, and it is a long time since I've read that story and even longer since I wrote it, so I've lost the details. I remember the set-up, though. I don't believe a writer is interested in making people behave differently, in any explicit sense. I do think, however, that ... I trust my fellow human beings and myself enough so that if I can, for instance, show how cruel human beings are to each other, then if they see that, then they won't be so cruel to each other. I mean, I believe that's true. I might be very wrong about that. But I think that's the nature of the beast. We're so frightened and confused and ambitious and so forth, that we don't really see the consequences of our acts. If it's made vivid enough to us and clear enough to us so that we actually do see it, then we might not treat each other quite as badly as we would otherwise.

I just talked in an earlier workshop; a student had written a story about killing a deer. It was basically a story in which a character, a young woman, is repelled sufficiently by the killing of the deer so that she decides to not go hunting anymore. But to do that means she's got to have this big conflict with her family—because deer-hunting is a part of the family value system and way of life. One of the problems with the story was that she didn't make the killing of the deer vivid enough, clear enough, horrifying enough, for us to be particularly moved by the character's decision, or to feel that she has actually had a horrifying

experience in any way. So I told the writer, "Well, you've really got to make us feel this awful thing and to make us see it. You've got to stare it in the face, too." And she said, "Well, I don't want to." I said, "Of course not. You don't want to. You don't want to have to describe the gutting of the animal and its eyes and the tongue lolling out of its mouth and the wound and everything like that. The way it falls and crumples—you don't want to see it." You know, I don't want to see this stuff, either.

But writers—we do that all the time in our daily lives. I don't want to see the two little boys who were on the front page of the *Times*—carried on a stretcher out of Beirut—these little tiny kids. And the horrible caption said: "Boy on left later died." I thought that was one of the most awful lines: "Boy on left later died." They were little tiny guys like that. You know, I just want to flip over and get away from that stuff right away. But if we do look at it and see it, and go through the horror of it, perhaps it won't be quite as awful next time ... because it won't happen. The writer has to look at it—whether it's how men treat women, how adults treat children, how whites treat blacks, how blacks treat whites, how children treat parents. It's all unpleasant.

Bellamy: So the writer is not quite like Diogenes, who holds a lantern up to your

face to try to find an honest man, but rather, he's walking around and grabbing you by the back of the neck and holding your eyelids open, saying: "Look at this!"

Banks: Or, it's the old wedding guest analogy. It's Coleridge's ancient mariner stopping the wedding guest in his hurry to get to the church and to the wedding. He says, "Hold it a minute," you know. "I'm going to tell you something really horrible—the consequences of an act." The wedding guest doesn't want to stop, but he does. Yes, the writer is always in that position of halting the reader in a rush to be somewhere else.

Bellamy: It's also a good answer to students who sometimes complain to me that the stories I choose to teach them are so depressing. Why should we read these? What good is it to read these depressing stories? We want to be happy. This doesn't make us happy! I usually try to talk about the definition of tragedy and catharsis.

Banks: There's a nice bit that John Irving says in that interview you have in *Fiction International*. I just read it this morning. He describes humor as being *consolation*. I think that's terrific. We all have nothing but sad stories to tell, so

I THINK ONE MATURES AS AN ARTIST TO THE SAME DEGREE AND IN MANY OF THE VERY SAME WAYS ONE MATURES AS A HUMAN BEING.

you give an overview for consolation, to console you a little in the face of this horror. It is a way of letting you see it at the same time without making you die from the experience.

Question: One thing you said earlier is that you, as a writer, feel you have something to show the reader and that you want to make the reader experience what you've seen. I would think of it more as a case of the writer trying to justify his own cruelty as part of humanity, not just the cruelty he sees. You are almost showing someone else that you're romanticizing the bad and good aspects of yourself—and wanting people to look at those.

Banks: You think that's what goes on? That's what a writer does?

Question: I would think that would be the essential motivation of a writer. As opposed to "I see something and I want to show it to you," it's more like: "This is happening to me. I want you to see it because it's almost, like, therapeutic."

Banks: I see what you're saying, I think, up to the last clause there. I think I agree with you. Much of what I see when I point over here, I'm really meaning to say: "I look in here and see it in here, and I'm like you. I am one of you." That's why it's very important for me to keep in my own mind that constant "I am *like*, I am not different, from anyone else. I am like everyone else. Everyone else is like me." If I look into myself and see this thing, then I am telling you something about yourself as well. It's not necessarily therapeutic, I don't think. It may work as a kind of exorcism, which I like better than "therapy." I mean, you can exorcise, you can get rid of certain demons that way and free yourself from bondage to them. But therapy is too closely tied for me to psychoanalytic study, and I don't feel comfortable thinking about what I do that way.

Bellamy: If that's all it is, then the reader doesn't get much out of it, it seems to me. There's a good chance that your therapy won't speak to the reader's problems or interests.

Banks: Yes, my therapy isn't necessarily going to be your therapy. What's good for me isn't necessarily going to be good for you.

Question: I was seeing that more as a motivational factor, in deciding whether or not a subject is worthwhile. I'm not saying that the purpose of the labor is to cleanse the writer.

Banks: Well, one of the reasons I feel entitled to say that a subject is worthwhile is based on my assumption that if it interests me, it must interest other people—because I am *like* other people. I'm not weird. I mean, I may be real wrong about all this, you know, but it's my operating principle. It's what I take with me to the typewriter: If this interests me, it must interest somebody else—because I'm not that far out. I'm not that neurotic and crazed and obsessive and weird. And even if I am, that must mean everybody else is, too. I might be dead wrong about it, but I don't think I am. I think that what concerns me concerns other people. If I fail to reach a wide audience, then most people don't seem to think that's true, or it may very well be the fault of my technique. It might be the fault of my immaturity. It might be the fault of my neuroticism, my defensiveness that is manifest in the work itself. All these things might keep people away rather than invite them in. I think one matures as an artist to the same degree and in many of the very same ways one matures as a human being. If you don't mature, no matter how brilliant you are, or how talented (whatever that is), your work isn't going to mature either. You're going to stay there. If you're defensive as a human being, frightened, blocked up, you will remain that way as an artist.

Bellamy: So to be a great writer, you need to be a great human being first?

Banks: At least in front of the typewriter you need to be—that moment in your life. Obviously Pound was not a great human being. Hemingway was not, apparently, a very great human being. Frost. All of them are great writers. In front of the typewriter, they were great human beings, too. During that moment of clarity, everything cohered. When you step away from the typewriter, you have to deal with another human being.

Bellamy: I guess you can always excuse Pound and Hemingway because you can say they went mad at the end.

Banks: Whatever that means, you know. Pound was mad for most of his life. But he was not mad most of the time when he was in front of the typewriter. He was a person whose life was out of control in every aspect but one, and in that aspect he was absolutely lucid and clear and fine.

Bellamy: It doesn't happen very often.

Banks: Well, it's where a writer certainly feels obligated to bring his or her best attention. What should be inculcated from the beginning is that this is where *I can't lie.* I can lie, you know, in my relationship with my wife, let's say. Or I can lie with my boss. Or I can lie with my friends. I'm going to suffer for all that, of course. But I can't continue to be a writer and lie at the typewriter. That may be the last one to go sometimes.

Question: How do you deal with some of the more embarrassing moments in your stories?

Banks: By "embarrassing," I'm not sure what you mean. Sex?

Question: Yes.

Banks: Bodily functions?

Question: Yes.

Banks: Violence? None of these embarrass me particularly. So that makes it easier to start with. But I think that all three—bodily functions, sex, and violence—are hard to write about without embarrassing other people.

Question: It has to be.

Banks: My basic attitude toward writing about all three of those things has been to deal with them as literally and straightforwardly as possible; understanding, of course, at the same time that sex and bodily functions are ridiculous, and people usually get into ridiculous positions to do both. Violence is also abhorrent as well as ridiculous. So if you focus on that, that makes it rather easy. I can't write about sex with violins and so forth—lyrically—because it's too ridiculous. Too lovely and too ridiculous. And I can't avert my gaze with regard to human bodily functions, because it's too ordinary.

I don't know if I'm answering your question. I don't particularly find it a problem. You can't describe a human being going through a life from any age, really, without writing about those three things. If you blank them out, it's sort of like censoring history, doing what the Russians do. It didn't take place. You did *not* go to the bathroom. You did *not* think about sex. Or violence.

Question: Do you ever vicariously live the lives of the heroes in your stories?

Banks: As you get older, you really give up the alternate lives syndrome. Now, I don't think there's much left of me except elder statesman, or something like that. It's about the only alternate life left after the professional athlete's going. Rock singer—that was long gone. That's an interesting question. I wonder how much you do it? I don't know how much I do it. I think I lead, I live with, I play with, alternate lives in some respect—like what if I had *not* done this at this point in my life, but had done that.

I just finished a novel about a man who is a smuggler of Haitian refugees into south Florida. He starts out in New Hampshire, which is where I'm from and where he spent most of his life, until recently, as an oil burner repairman in New Hampshire—which is a class of people that I grew up with. My father was a plumber, and I was a plumber, and my grandfather was a plumber. And he starts out in New Hampshire as an oil burner repairman who goes to the Sunbelt .... First he works in a liquor store, and eventually he gets involved as a deep sea fisherman. He ends up owing a whole lot of money to the bank and then slides gradually into smuggling just to keep the kids fed and to keep the mortgage paid on the boat and to keep the men paid in the trailer. So he's a man under great pressure—economic pressure. He ends up doing something rather questionable, morally.

That story came from an article I read in a newspaper three years ago. I was going to write a book about Nathaniel Hawthorne and Franklin Pierce, who had a lifelong friendship. It's really about male bonding. I was very interested in, and much of my life—my energy and thought and emotions—has been taken up with male friendships, and it's something that I don't understand real well. So I was going to write about Franklin Pierce, the man of action, the president, the most ordinary president I can think of, the most forgettable president of American history, except maybe Millard Fillmore—and Nathaniel Hawthorne, the inner man, the writer, the artist, and so forth, who happened to have been college roommates. Hawthorne died in Pierce's arms in a hotel in New Hampshire. I was all set to pull this thing together, years of research, and I was in the library leafing through the *Times*, and there was an article on an event right off Palm Beach in Florida, an area I know very well. (I know southern Florida quite well, and I've lived there off and on at different times.)

A captain of a boat was smuggling a bunch of Haitians over, and he was suddenly approached by a Coast Guard cutter. He was a hundred and fifty yards off the beach, so he fired his gun into the air to scare the Haitians off the boat. The Haitians all drowned, and their bodies washed up on the shore. The people coming along the beach the next morning found their bodies floating in. In that second or so while I read that article, I knew that captain. I knew how he got there. He got there from being an oil burner repairman—I saw his whole life

in a flash up to this horrible moment. He was an ordinary guy who was trying to make a living, you know, just trying to get by, to keep hanging on and not be pushed down. And he ended up doing this horrible thing. I mean, I immediately appropriated him and understood him—and then wrote the novel.

But to get back to your question, I knew about him because I knew I could have ended up there myself—very easily. Without any trouble, I could have ended up there. Yes, I think it's terrible to smuggle and all that and to break the law. But put the squeeze on me, and I'll break the law in order to feed my kids or to make my payments—to keep going. I could just see the steps, how that could happen. So in writing the book, it's been very satisfying in that same sense that you've raised—that I've been able to live an alternate life in a way with him and to have the pleasure of

Tess Gallagher.

being a fisherman, which I always wanted to be, a charter fisherman. This guy always wanted to be a charter fisherman, too, and he ends up traveling around in the Caribbean and smuggling.

Bellamy: But mostly it was a life you would rather not have had.

Banks: I'd be very glad *not* to have had his life, too. I'm glad that it worked out the way it did.

Question: If it's successful, the reader will also become the fisherman, become the character.

Banks: Right. When I've told people about this book, most of them immediately think I'm writing about the Haitians. But I'm not. I'm writing about the smugglers. I mean, I know the Haitians are victims, of course. The Haitians are very much in the story, very much a part of the story. But most of us read about events like these, and we say, "Those bastards, those smugglers—what rotten guys they are!" We think of them as some kind of shark, feeding off these desperate people, when, in fact, it's obviously much more complicated than that. So, what I hope is that people will see that, and they may even realize their own desperate straits and say, "If they put the squeeze on me, I might do it, too." And, "If I did it, would I end up doing this horrible thing, too?

Would I be capable of such a horrible act?" I say, "I couldn't kill anybody." It's the easiest thing in the world to *say*. I mean, we all say it all the time. But given certain circumstances, could you? If the Coast Guard cutter is bearing in on you, and you're in the boat and you've got three kids and a wife at home in the trailer and you've got sixteen terrified Haitians on your boat and you're a hundred fifty yards off West Palm Beach, wouldn't you fire your gun in the air and scare them off and tell them, "You can make it. Swim, swim!" Of course, they can't swim because most poor farmers in the Caribbean don't know how to swim. There's no way for them to learn how to swim.

Bellamy: That's what happened? He just told them to swim and they couldn't do it?

Banks: Most poor people in the world can't swim. Middle-class people from Ohio can swim. People who've never seen a lake or an ocean can't swim. Oddly too, people who live on islands tend not to be able to swim. There is a certain amount of pride, too. I've heard it's true also of Nova Scotia fishermen—that they don't know how to swim.

Bellamy: That would be a real occupational hazard.

Banks: Well, what good does it do you if you are ten miles out at sea in a storm?

You're not going to get back anyway. You know, why bother to learn?

Question: So if your greatest advantage in being a writer is having the ability to share your experiences with people, or having the advantage of experiencing many different lives, which is the most beneficial for you?

Banks: Beneficial to me? That's really an interesting question because it's almost impossible for me to separate the two. It's hard for me to think about them separately. In a way, I'm not free to live alternate lives. It's not an accurate expression because it implies that there's a lot of fantasizing going on. But I'm not free to engage myself in the life of an imaginary human being without feeling obligated by an audience, a sense of an audience.

There's an abstract sense of audience out there that you can identify socio-economically, if you want. I mean, I know certain things about them, but only in abstract ways. I know that my audience probably reads English, is probably American, is probably white, is probably reasonably well educated, reasonably intelligent, and is more or less in the same world that I am in. I know that about my audience out there. But that's very impersonal and abstract.

Then, on the other hand, I have a sense of audience that is very intimate and personal. Equally imagined, however, but still very intimate and personal. When I'm working, I'm thinking of my audience as being *the person with whom I am in love*. Maybe one or two or three or four people in the world. Each of us has these kinds of living lie detectors that we internalize, I think. With me, it's always been the person with whom I am in love, which has varied somewhat over the years because I've been fortunate enough to be in love over the years, serially, with three different women, and with two friends, life-long friends, in my adult life. I can hear them just click their tongues when I avoid a problem. So I say, "Okay, I'll do it right. I'll do it."

But you know that experience, those of you who've been in love, when you're freshly in love, you carry around inside yourself this image of this person, and it gives you a kind of heightened, frightening self-consciousness. You hear your own thoughts as if from the point of view of this other person. You almost wish they could be inside your head all the time, especially when you're having brilliant thoughts. It's that kind of heightened self-consciousness, a sense of being observed by someone who could tell you everything, someone who's smarter about you than you are.

There's a great pleasure in writing. This works more for novels than stories, in that in the writing of a novel, I find the quality of my attention is much better than it is most of the time. It's like taking a consciousness-expanding drug. I pay more close attention to the world, to the ways people speak, to the ways they look, the way light falls, the way things smell. There's a heightened sensual alertness that I find extremely satisfying, genuinely thrilling. When I'm not writing, I feel like I've moved from a Technicolor world to a black-and-white world, or from stereo to monaural.

Question: Do you always have a concrete idea when you're composing a new story or a novel? Do you always know what the conflict is going to be or what the resolution is going to be?

Banks: No. It really varies a lot. Sometimes you have just a concept, an idea, a formal problem you want to see if you can tell a story this way, or that way. Backwards or something like that. Sometimes you have a character. Sometimes you just have an image. Sometimes you have a tone of voice you want to get. You just want to get somewhere—the tone you can hear in the back of your ears somewhere. What you hope is that by lurching in that direction, the lurch will evoke all the rest of it. I don't do it consciously and deliberately. I don't work that way. I agree with Nelson Algren, who said that if a writer knows what he's

doing, he doesn't know very much. While I'm working, I don't know very much. I don't know what I'm doing. I do trust the process, and I think I'm a reasonably alert and intelligent person and reasonably well educated. So I can see the various solutions to problems as they arise.

However, I don't know the ending of my stories until I get there. When I get there, that's the ending. If I know the ending, why should I write it? It seems like a boring kind of thing to do. The writing of the story becomes a performance rather than an actual voyage of discovery. I hate to use those kinds of terms, but sometimes they're apt. Much of what I'm telling you is peculiar to me, I know. It's my own private sense of myself and what I do. Some of it, however, is pretty general, and I think it's generally true that if a writer doesn't learn something with each succeeding word, the writer is going to start repeating himself or herself and is not going to grow as a human being and as a writer. If you don't grow, you die. It's the nature of the activity. You either grow or die. So if I know what's going on in the story before I write it, I can't really grow from having written that story. The only way I can grow from having written a story or a novel is *not* to know what's going on.

Now, I'm pretty smart and I'm pretty able to anticipate what's going on, so that means I've got to really work hard to keep myself from knowing what's going on. I've got to keep two possibilities alive at all times that are both viable, both equally viable. He lives or he dies. Each one is virtually possible. I have to keep them really believably possible all the way to the end. She leaves him—she doesn't leave him. *I don't know* until the very end. You turn the page—she left him.

This last book—I didn't know what was going to happen. I mean, I knew sort of in this rough sense, but I didn't know if the guy was going to die or live. I knew I was going to come down to a point where that was the only alternative, either one or the other. I knew approximately the circumstances that would make that possible, that kind of absolute choice. But I didn't know it until I got about three or four pages from the end. Absolutely. I knew I was going to get it pretty soon. I could feel it.

Bellamy: This book is seven hundred pages long, right?

Banks: Yes. When I knew I was getting down there, the last month or so was such a great rush of energy. I was staying up late, getting up early the next morning and just kept pouring it out. It's the equivalent of what you get near the end of a book you really love when you're reading, and you really start reading fast

at the end. You can hardly wait to get to the end. When I was writing it, I could hardly wait to get to the end. I was racing through the last seventy-five pages or so. It was just a real heat, and then when I got to the end, that kind of melancholy.

Question: Why do you write? Is it just simply something that you love to do? Is it a hope to be remembered? Is it the money or the prestige?

Banks: Well, it's obviously not the money, and it's probably not the prestige, either. It's not that prestigious. I was at a luncheon this week with a bunch of people who were almost all executives of large corporations—most of them, people my own age. On the guest list, I was the "novelist," and whenever I was introduced to one of these people, they would always say, "I *thought* you were the novelist." There was a slight edge to that. You know, "You look a little weird." You know, "You don't look like one of us." It was, "You look like an incendiary personality. You're the type, all right." So the prestige is not really there either.

Bellamy: Well, what do they know?

Banks: The prestige is really very narrow. But to be very specific about the question: I've often wondered about it myself because it never seemed that easy for me to do. I was never a person who found it

IF I KNOW WHAT'S GOING ON IN THE STORY BEFORE I WRITE IT, I CAN'T REALLY GROW FROM HAVING WRITTEN THAT STORY.

easy to just crank out the work without lots of false starts. There have been lots of false starts and blocked periods and so forth. Not long, but nevertheless painful. At one point, in my late twenties, I did try not to write, I did try to stop writing and simply say, "Okay, I give up. The hell with this. I'm not going to do this anymore …. This is a silly thing for a grown person to be doing, making up stories about people." I decided I was going to become a graphic artist instead—something very useful and grown-up like that. But very quickly, I found myself once again, you know, staying up late at night, doodling and idling away in words, perhaps the way someone who is a painter would end up sketching while talking at lunch. If you ever have lunch with a painter, they're drawing all over their napkins. Instead, I would make little rhymes and characters and start arranging different text. I might read something and want to cut it up and fool around with it a little bit and see how it looked from a different angle.

So it became evident to me after about a year of this that I was locked and caught by some kind of compulsion.

I'm not trying to avoid your question, but it's just … I think the reason I write is because there doesn't seem to be any other driving compulsion that I have in life. It does come out of this strict compulsion. Not to do it would be really to shut off a great deal of my mind and my responses to the world.

Question: Which part of it attracts you— the force to communicate, or the force to create?

Banks: I think that the desire to communicate and the desire to create something come in after you've recognized and given yourself over to the compulsion. You want to then make it useful and objectify it. So you desire to create something as a way of turning this otherwise slightly neurotic compulsion into something that's useful and that's visible and observable and admirable—and also social, something that is a connection to other human beings. The idea of communication from one person to another is important, but it might be somewhat misleading insofar as it implies that you have a message instead of just information to give.

Question: If you don't have a message, where's the usefulness?

Banks: Frank O'Connor says we *like* our storytellers. He explores the idea of what the function of old-time storytellers really was, and they often had several functions. But they'd be allowed in out of the cold to sit down at the fire—if they could tell the person who owned the fire who his ancestors were. Or if he could tell how far his kingdom extended, what it was like at the very edges of his geography, way out there. O'Connor says we like our storytellers to come from far places. But those far places can be inside us as well. They can be psychological places and spiritual places as well as geographical markers. That's a sort of metaphorical way, I guess, of answering your question.

I feel very conscious of that role, that relation to a reader. Once the obsession or compulsion is a given, then I can't fight it. Then you try to make it socially useful so you aren't a crazy, isolated person who is just compulsively doodling across the page. Then you do think, "Okay, what am I going to communicate?" I do have

to trust the information I bring back as reliable. I do know where the borders lie. I do know what the beasts out there are shaped like, and what their habits are. And I do know the ancestry of the people I'm speaking to, which is an aspect we're all too eager to forget in this country. We're very happy to forget our ancestors. As we enter the middle class, we ought not to forget the horse thief and the washer woman back there. Oftentimes the author is simply reminding us that where we came from is who we are. So much of American writing is really tied up with simply that—just trying to remind us that where we came from is who we are. Updike is doing it, and black writers and female writers are doing it.

Bellamy: I think that writers often get in the habit of talking about their role in a quasi-pathological sense—because of Freud—to see what they do, or to try to explain what they do, as some evidence of fighting off the demons of insanity or neurosis. It's difficult to grow up in this culture and to sort through all the confusion of adolescence and to discover one's calling as a writer. It's difficult to do, and so one grasps for all of the explanations that are available, and a lot of them come from psychology. But psychology developed historically as a way of explaining pathological conditions. Freud believes that the artist in general, not just the writer, is a neurotic; and I resist that. I resist that interpretation for myself. Artists are no more neurotic than psychologists or businessmen. I think that the role of the writer in society is a time-honored one.

Banks: The process I'm describing is no different than the process that makes a person into an architect—someone who found himself making little model houses, working with elaborate ideas for structures or something like that. The obvious way to make that into something socially useful is to become an architect, if it is indeed a compulsion. It's recognizing your own compulsions in life.

Bellamy: But I think that what the artist does, whether he's a writer or some other kind of artist, is much more important than what your average businessman does, and I think it's important to say that. I don't know if anybody else believes it, but I believe it. I don't think that selling sugar water to half a million people a day and then driving home in your Cadillac is a very socially useful activity. But I'm sure the president of Coke thinks it is very socially useful. At least, he makes his life doing it.

One way to cure yourself of the sense of absurdity about what you're doing as a writer is to think about the absurdity of all the other jobs in the world—ninety

percent of which are foolish, wasteful, or meaningless.

Banks: Yes, but that doesn't help me at all, because then I think about the ten percent of jobs which are wonderful and which I envy. I mean, I have a couple of friends that I admire so much, and envy so much, that I feel really stupid in their company sometimes. Not stupid, exactly—I just feel sloppy, lazy, self-indulgent, decadent, you know. I'm sure we all have friends like this.

I have a friend, a pal of mine, who's a Jesuit priest who worked for seven years in Jamaica organizing cane workers, and then he worked for another three years down in Florida organizing migrant workers. I mean, this is a very dedicated man, and he's helping the poor in a very clear, pointed way. Then I look at myself, running around Manhattan and writing all of these books, and I feel like such a jerk and such a useless person in the face of lives like that; and there are *thousands* of lives like that. It's awesome to me. It's in the face of lives like those that I get real writer's block. It makes writing seem insignificant. It's something every writer has to deal with in one way or another.

Question: What do you do when you get writer's block?

Banks: I haven't got any organized pattern. It just depends really on what I'm working on at the time. If it's a story, I can always drop it—come back to it later and try something else. If it's a novel, it's a bit of a problem. I can jump ahead and work on a later part and come back to the problem after a while. When it gets serious, then I've found I could just start doodling and trying to write nonsense. Pretty soon, I find myself trying to make sense of what was nonsense. Also, sometimes it's something simple enough that just reading will break it for me. If I just go and read fiction or poetry, something that's close to what I am interested in and want to do, that helps. It will make me want to get up and do my own again. Have you ever done that?

Bellamy: That's a wonderful suggestion. Reading can definitely reassure you and bring you back to a sense of desire and enthusiasm that you need to have.

Banks: Sometimes there's a sheer simple-minded macho competitiveness, too. You say, "I can do this better than that." And you go back and do it. There's that way, too. Writer's block is simply a failure of nerve. You're thinking, "This is either a preposterous thing to be doing, or a preposterous thing *for me* to be doing." That's really the bottom. It's a kind of failure of belief in your own worth, the worth of your activity.

Question: A lot of people say that writing is a really antisocial type of occupation. Even if you know the social justification for its usefulness, as a vocation, it does tend to be a little bit antisocial, doesn't it?

Banks: Yes, as a vocation, it is. You work alone most of the time with the phone off. Definitely, it's antisocial.

Bellamy: Or at least it's un-social part of the time.

Banks: Yes, yes. It's *un*-social.

Bellamy: You have to like solitude. You have to be comfortable with solitude.

Banks: Which is why I'm glad I didn't move to New York until my habits were deeply set—because I would have been terribly distracted if I had moved down there at twenty-five or thirty without having deep set writing habits. When I get up in the morning, I work; and I just do it in a kind of automatic way. It's absolutely essential that I don't see anybody until two or three in the afternoon, or I just won't get the work done.

Once your life with your mate and your kids and your relation to the economy is set up, it doesn't have to continue to be a struggle to do it. But for me, it seemed to take an unconscionably long time. It took me about ten or fifteen years to work it out.

Question: Where do you get your ideas for your stories? How do they develop?

Banks: Well, it's a different process than for a novel. With a novel, you're committing yourself to living with a bunch of people for a long period of time. With a story, the commitment is brief, so in that sense, it's a lot easier to write stories. They come from various sources: from dreams, from other stories, from stories people tell me, from actual events in my own life. I don't detect any particular pattern—they come from all over—it's when I can recognize the world in a moving way, a way that moves me. It may be just a dream that moves me—I wake up and I jot down something about the dream, or something that happened in my own life that I finally get clear enough of emotionally to see in a compassionate, integrated way. Then maybe I am moved by it. Just this spring, I started writing some stories about events that happened to me about twenty-five years ago, my own late adolescence, which I could never write about before. I have never really written about a young, late-adolescent male—American male, white—which I was. I've never been able to do that, and it was a period in my own life where I was very conflicted and tied up with guilt and family struggles. I was a deeply neurotic kid, and it took me until now before I could look back on that kid that I was and see him as a slightly comical, pathetic, but dignified kid. Maybe I had to have kids of my own that age before I could use that and see that experience clearly and be moved by it without feeling it was narcissistic.

Question: When you start a story, do you have a conclusion in mind, or do you just start writing?

Banks: I make a practice of keeping myself open as long as possible and writing until I know what the ending is, and then I stop. Just as with novels, I never want to know what the end of the story is until I write the end of the story, until the story tells me its ending. Then I stop because there's no point in going on. That's the end. A great deal of the pleasure of writing is the pleasure of reading, and one of the reasons I write the stories that I write is to enjoy the reading. I write the stories that I want to read.

One of the greatest problems in contemporary story writing is in the endings. If most writers fail at story writing—in which America is a place to excel—I think the reason they do is they don't end them well. They don't end them. They cop out instead. They leave the story with a kind of metaphorical gesture or symbol. They don't really see it through to the end.

Bellamy: What should they be trying to accomplish in writing endings?

Banks: They should be trying to push the action to the point where no other action is possible. Many, many stories that are remarkably well written and crafted, and highly intelligent in many ways, seem to me to have in the end no action. Nothing happened. They're just gestures. They end with a slightly hushed tone or a little upturn. There is no difference from page one to page ten—nothing happened! The character didn't have any deeper insight into his situation. He's not a different person at the end than he was at the beginning.

If you're going to select one moment in the stream of time, out of all the moments possible in the life of this one person—and you say this is the day you're writing the story about—then this guy comes home from work, walks in the door, has dinner, has a conversation with his wife, watches television, and goes to bed—that's not going to do it. He does that every day! There's no meaning to it. I think at the heart of stories is that "once upon a time." In all the moments of time, you took this one moment out because it casts light forward and backward in time. It clarifies time. So if something doesn't happen in that moment, you may as well have selected any other moment in the stream. I always feel cheated reading those kinds of stories.

Bellamy: Galway Kinnell says—about poetry—that it isn't just writing nice lines, but rather, it's coming to understand something.

Banks: I feel the same way. I feel very much the same way. I like to feel that every time I spend an hour or two hours of my time and energy and thought and open myself as a reader to a story, that somehow that experience is going to change me. I'm going to mature somehow, just an ounce or a millimeter. I'm going to be a slightly different person for having read that story. The process by which I am engaged in the story is identification with the narrator or the character, the emotional center of the story. But if there's no movement there, then how can there be any movement for me, either? You're getting Exhibit A—something interesting. "Yes, this is interesting—people in Tanzania have these problems." But

that doesn't change me any more than reading an article in the dentist's office in *National Geographic.* That's just information, but it's not information about that far place that is so hard to get to in my personal life, the emotional center of my life—that's the place that you need to reach as a storyteller. I do feel that the ending is where that happens in a story.

The ending is the most difficult, and yet the most pleasurable, part of the story for me to write. I can feel a literal, physical bearing down when I get to the end of the story. I almost feel as if my skull shrinks a little bit and the pressure increases, and I get a form of tunnel vision. I don't know who is in the room or anything like that. It's this real bearing down concentration for me. It's at that point, I think, that a lot of storywriters give up. They make a kind of aesthetic statement, and it is handsome sometimes. But it's just an intellectual solution. There isn't any personal risk.